A Reader on
Race & Ethnic
RELATIONS
Harmonizing Indigenous and Immigrant Voices

EDITORS

Michael T. Fagin
Kebba Darboe
Wayne E. Allen

Kendall Hunt
publishing company

Kendall Hunt
publishing company

www.kendallhunt.com
Send all inquiries to:
4050 Westmark Drive
Dubuque, IA 52004-1840

ISBN 978-1-4652-0912-2

Printed in the United States of America
10 9 8 7 6 5 4 3 2 1

Contents

SECTION FOUR

INDIGENOUS STRUGGLES   117

SECTION FIVE

APPLYING ETHNIC STUDIES IN NEW WAYS: COUNTERCULTURE IDENTITY AND CULTURAL EXCHANGE   169

Foreword

This reader is a unique academic undertaking in that it is not the standard academic reader that relies solely on so-called academic "experts." And while it does include contributors with expertise in their fields, it is also an attempt to include the voices of a diverse population of scholars—professors, junior faculty, and students—who all have a stake in the project of studying the plethora of issues surrounding the topics of race and ethnicity in the larger world.

The articles in this work are intended to challenge and stimulate students to ask questions, both of themselves and of each other, but also of our society, our nation, and our world. Can we learn from the mistakes of our past? And can we move forward in a constructive manner that brings redress to the mistakes that have been institutionalized and repeated over generations in our multiethnic, multicultural world? As a dear friend, colleague, and teacher of ours says—one who has dedicated her life to promoting diversity and equal opportunity for students and people of color, Professor Hanh Huy Phan—"In diversity studies we often have to focus on America the ugly, but in so doing we should never lose sight of America the beautiful."

That is our goal, all of us who work and study and teach issues related to diversity in our respective fields, to clean up past and present mistakes so that we can move forward on a positive footing that provides equal access, equal opportunity, and equal justice for all. And this is not just empty platitudes and promises, for all the people who have contributed to this volume, students and faculty alike, have been working diligently and fighting the good fight over the years. And we have all seen and experienced real-world results where lives and institutions have all been changed for the better. Occasionally there are setbacks but there is no gain without a struggle, and we hope the students and colleagues who take up this work and read it will also then join us in taking up the struggle and fighting the good fight of promoting equal rights for all.

Introduction

Dr. Michael T. Fagin

In the 1968–1969 academic year at Mankato State College (MSC) the Black Student Union, consisting of approximately thirty students out of a total population of sixty-eight black students, petitioned President Dr. James Nickerson to address the needs of all minority students attending MSC and to develop strategies to increase the minority student population and faculty. This petition was titled the "Black Student Union Task Force Report" (BSUTFR). The president of the Black Student Union who presented the report to President Dr. James Nickerson was William Flenney, who would later become the first Black Chief of Police in St. Paul, Minnesota. The Black Student Union Task Force Report was a very comprehensive document that had been edited by two Black faculty advisors, Dr. Robert Cobb and Dr. George Ayers. The BSUTFR not only addressed current needs and concerns of minority students attending a predominantly White institution (PWI) of higher education, but the report had a vision that laid down a solid pathway to guide MSC, now Minnesota State University, Mankato (MSUM), in transforming its academic curriculum and student services to meet the needs of minority students in the twenty-first century. The BSUTFR of 1968–1969 demanded that the institution hire a Director of Minority Affairs and that the director would be charged with the responsibilities of hiring a staff to work with the growing student of color population. The report also demanded that the institution develop and implement plans to increase the number of minority faculty and staff and to establish courses in what was then called Minority Studies. The BSUTFR insisted that the University begin to address the sociocultural needs of Black students and other students of color so that the activities at the institution would be of interest to all students.

It should be noted that the growth and development of a department and curriculum of Ethnic Studies at Minnesota State University was spearheaded by Black students, and it was designed to help all minority groups advance their concerns, issues, and causes. This coincided with the rise of the Civil Rights Movement of the 1960s and was led by Blacks on this campus who were attempting to help all underrepresented groups find their footing and their voice in campus community life. Growing out of the initial diversity initiatives contained in the BSUTFR, the Division of Institutional Diversity was established, led by a vice president who reported directly to the president and served as a member of the president's cabinet. The history of diversity education at today's Minnesota State University followed the nationwide movement for the inclusion of Ethnic Studies and Diversity in higher education that developed across the United States starting in the late 1960s and moving through the 1970s.

In the summer of 1970, Dr. James Nickerson, President of MSC, accepted the BSUTFR and after a national search hired Dr. Michael T. Fagin, who was charged with the responsibility of establishing an academic and student service program to address the rapidly changing racial demographics at the institution and to begin meeting the needs of a diverse student population. The model put in place by Dr. Fagin hired four faculty members who had expertise in teaching African, Asian, Hispanic, and American Indian Studies. Within the four years from 1970 to 1974, the academic and student affairs program, then named "The Minorities Groups Studies Center" (MGSC), had four faculty members of color representing the four major minority groups. Between the years 1970 to 1980, this new program, the MGSC, under the leadership of Dr. Fagin, established four minor programs in African American, Asian American, Hispanic American, and American Indian Studies. The two individuals in the early 1970s that assisted Dr. Fagin in establishing basic academic and service programs for students of color were Dr. Jayne Larsen and Ms. Hanh Huy Phan. Dr. Jayne Larsen's special interest was in Native American Affairs, and she assisted in the establishment of the American Indian Studies Minor. Ms. Hanh Huy Phan, as a sociologist, assisted in establishing of the minor in Asian American Studies, and she contributed substantially to the overall success of the program.

Mankato State College (it later became Mankato State University in 1975, and now is Minnesota State University, Mankato, having changed its name again in 1999) was thus a leader in the state university and colleges system in establishing academically sound courses and academic minor programs with a diversity emphasis that all students were able to enroll in. Mankato State University was subsequently the first in the state university system to offer a major in Minority Studies and a master's degree program in Minority Studies.

The creation of a cultural diversity graduation requirement in 1992 grew out of the movement to transform the Mankato State University curriculum into a comprehensive curriculum that reflected diverse cultures and provided diversity education for all students. A subcommittee of the University Undergraduate Curriculum Committee, co-chaired by Dr. Fagin, established this graduation requirement. The purpose of the committee was to develop guidelines for the approval of Cultural Diversity core courses by the University Undergraduate Curriculum Committee. Starting in the fall semester of 1992, all students had to demonstrate that they had successfully completed core and related cultural diversity courses approved by the Universities Undergraduate Curriculum Committee.

To further increase representation of minority faculty and staff at MSU, Mankato, Dr. Fagin then created and implemented the highest paid pre-doctorial fellowship program in the United States in the first decade of the twenty-first century. This program allowed women and persons of color to teach at the college level while earning their doctoral degrees in diverse fields of study. The pre-doctorial fellowship program was presented in a paper presentation at the Higher Learning Commission Annual Meeting in Chicago, IL, in 2009. Since its inception, this initiative has successfully enrolled eleven students and helped diversify the faculty at MSUM.

What has been most interesting in the journey to help make higher education more inclusive for members of all under-represented groups, and to help all living in our ethnically diverse global society, has been the hard work of many faculty, students, staff, and administrators in trying to develop a sense of fairness and equality for all people. The need to put in place measures that will become institutionalized and thereby perpetually promote equality in access and opportunity was, and still is, a constant challenge for higher education and society in general. Although we have seen substantial gains made over the past forty years in promoting the positive qualities of a multicultural, integrated global society, the foundations of oppression and resistance to change still remain in place. The social diseases of racism and sexism remain deeply embedded in today's society, and thus there is yet a great deal of work remaining to be done.

It is imperative that leaders in higher education take a firm stance in putting in place programs that will institutionalize the concept of equal opportunity and access to college for all. If this is done in more than just name only, it will yield results in increasing the numbers of members of under-represented groups in completing their degrees. Such measures not only help in recruitment and retention efforts, but they also significantly increase the numbers of minority students who graduate. Additionally, the institution must balance and have a fair representation of minorities and women holding the positions of college and university presidents, faculty, and staff at predominantly White institutions (PWIs). When an institution does so, it will continue to make improvements in a stepwise manner in the number of students of color recruited, retained, and graduated.

Most important in higher education today is the need to create a new cultural diversity philosophy of education. The philosophy of higher education today must prepare students to live effectively in a multicultural global society. Higher education today can no longer allow itself to graduate students with limited multicultural skills and a weak understanding of diversity. The bottom line for higher education today is to produce students that can successfully function as productive individuals in a highly diverse, technological, multicultural world. Although there remains much work to be done, we have seen some gains having been made in today's multicultural society.

Over the past four decades, we have seen some of the positive elements of a multicultural integrated society evolve and grow. However, we have a long way to go. The election of the first Black President of the United States of America, President Barack Obama, certainly helped to make all of us acknowledge that a highly educated black intellectual could be a world leader and president of the United States. Unfortunately, having a black Commander in Chief of the world's most powerful nation does not stop a Dr. Henry Louis Gates from being subjugated to the institutionalized impact of racism and stereotypes that have often led to discriminatory behaviors (Dr. Gates was the distinguished Black Harvard University professor arrested in his own home by police who responded to a suspected break-in). Higher education must take the lead role in transforming our institutions so that we graduate greater numbers of individuals that have multicultural skills and are able to see beyond the kind of stereotypes that led to Dr. Gates' arrest. We can no longer tolerate a society that creates and conditions individuals that respond to learned stereotypes of the kind that have for generations caused the tragic deaths of our minority youth, such as what recently happened to Trayvon Martin in Sanford, Florida (a suburb of Orlando). Our educational system must hold itself accountable to help prevent the development of the George Zimmerman's of the world who are also victims of a society that has not changed and therefore has failed to produce skilled multiculturalists who can see beyond racial profiling and stereotyping.

In looking at society today and the challenges we face in higher education, I am often reminded of a statement made by Bobby Seals, a founder of the Black Panther party. Bobby Seals, while visiting the home of Dr. Fagin prior to his lecture at the annual Dr. Michael T. Fagin Pan African Student Leadership Conference, stated that, "Everything had changed, but nothing has changed." During his keynote address, Mr. Seals reiterated his earlier comments while speaking about the relative gains of the Civil Rights Movement of the 1960s. And in true African American discursive style, he stated once again that, "Everything had changed, but nothing has changed."

If society is to change and we are to benefit from the fruits of a multicultural pluralistic society, we must first change each other and ourselves by creating a system of higher education that touches all the components of today's society in a real and meaningful way. We must begin to institutionalize equity in all of our practices and institutions, and in so doing we can imbue the youth who are our future leaders with an ingrained sense of fairness that promotes equal opportunity and equal justice for all. It is the dream of countless numbers of people like myself, eloquently articulated by Dr. Martin Luther King, Jr., where Red, Black, Brown, Yellow, and White people who have dedicated themselves to making our nation and our world a better place will have the fair chance to do so. And if we work hard and do that, we can all witness one of the greatest dreams ever articulated as it comes true in this social and political pluralistic experiment called the United States of America.

SECTION
One

RACE/ETHNIC RELATIONS

Perspectives on Institutional Discrimination, Bigotry, and Ethnocentrism

Kebba Darboe and Avra Johnson

Introduction

Alexis de Tocqueville (1831), a young French magistrate, who wrote his classic book: *Democracy in America,* asked President John Quincy Adams: "Do you look on slavery as a great plague for the United States?"

"Yes, certainly," Adams answered. "That is the root of almost all the troubles of the present and the fears for the future" (Rodriquez 2007, 41).

Adams' observations are prophetic. Since the seventeenth century, through American slavery, emancipation, segregation, and the modern Civil Rights Movement, the issues of race and ethnic relations have been among the most salient issues in American civic life.

In this context, then, state agencies through administrative fiat have identified four racial minorities: African Americans, American Indians, Asians, and Hispanics (Lowry 1982). These groups have suffered discrimination in the process of American nation building. For instance, African Americans are victims of slavery; American Indians are victims of genocide—for example, there were the Trail of Tears and the destruction of their life ways through the establishment of reservations and the boarding school system; Asian immigrants are victims of racial exclusion—for example, the Chinese Exclusion Act of 1882 and the internment of the Japanese during World War II; and the Hispanics, who were conquered and segregated after the Mexican-American War following the signing of the 1848 Treaty of Guadalupe Hidalgo, which ceded what is now the southwest region of the United States—west Texas, New Mexico, Arizona, California, Utah, Nevada, and parts of Oregon and Colorado (Schaefer 2012).

The Mexican-American War was justified on the basis of "Manifest Destiny"—the idea of "Jefferson's homogeneous republic." American expansionism resulted in the conquest of the southwest region of the United States, with Mexicans landholders there becoming "foreigners on their native land" (Takaki 1993, 176, 178). It is in this historical context that Mexicans on either side of the border consider themselves today as migrants and not immigrants (Alvarez 1973). The contemporary chant, "we didn't cross the border, the border crossed us," epitomizes the life experiences of a racialized group: Chicanos/as—Americans of Mexican descent. And their justification for this view can be found in the provisions of the 1848 Treaty of Guadalupe Hidalgo, which guaranteed them their land, language, and culture after their incorporation into the U.S. (Fennelly 2007, 2). The early Chicanos, however, were a colonized people but today many have immigrant roots—this is to say, they are Mexican émigrés (Blauner 1994).

One can apply colonial and immigrant models to this situation, but one must keep in mind the fact that they are differentiated by "centrifugal and centripetal" social relationships with the dominant group (McLemore, Romo, & Baker 2001, 457). For instance, Chicanos as colonized people have a *centrifugal* social relationship with the dominant group, characterized by struggle and resistance to assimilation. By contrast, Mexicans as an immigrant group have a *centripetal* social relationship with the dominant group, characterized by some resistance to assimilation while still aspiring through education and employment to achieve the American dream (McLemore, Romo, & Baker 2001). As a consequence, the nuanced experiences of discrimination by the aforementioned racial minority groups in American life have become institutionalized over time, resulting in the imposition of institutional discrimination, racism, bigotry, and ethnocentrism on members of their respective groups.

Institutional Racism and Bigotry

In *The Souls of Black Folk,* Du Bois (1903, 3) described a troubled Black consciousness that is created by White racism: "It is a peculiar sensation, this double consciousness, this sense of always looking at one's self through the eyes of others . . . One feels his two-ness—an American, a Negro; two souls, two thoughts, two unreconciled strivings; two warring ideals in one dark body, whose dogged strength alone keeps it from being torn asunder. The history of the American Negro is the history of this strife. . . ." Similarly, the history of strife experienced by African Americans is, in many ways, identical to that experienced by many individuals and diverse populations who also undergo racism.

This article uses questions and answers surrounding these issues to shed light on the impact of institutional racism, bigotry, and ethnocentrism on diverse religious, racial, and ethnic groups.

What Is the Difference Between Individual and Institutional Discrimination/Racism?

In order to understand individual and institutional discrimination, a review of the working definitions of prejudice, discrimination, bigotry, and racism are important. For instance, prejudice is a negative attitude or feeling, such as hatred or anger, that is expressed toward racial/ethnic minorities. The term *minority* refers to groups such as American Indians, African Americans, Hispanics, Asians, women, and gays who lack access to wealth and power. They might happen to be the numerical minority but in the case of women, who reveal what it is really all about because they are the numerical majority in the United States, it is about access to power and not sheer numbers. When institutions and laws support racial prejudice, it leads to the perpetuation of racism. Thus, the formula for racism: racism equals race prejudice plus power to control systems and institutions (Zenobia 2006).

Discrimination, on the other hand, means behavior that unfairly treats individuals on the basis of race. It is the most commonly understood manifestation of racism because, due to institutional racism, there can be individuals who are not prejudiced but engage in discrimination because it is promoted by the institutions they live and work in. A civil rights activist, Stokely Carmichael, and a political scientist, Charles Hamilton, introduced the concept of institutional racism, which is embedded in social institutions but is perpetuated by overt and covert acts committed by individual Whites against individual Blacks (Schaefer 2012).

Bigotry means both a negative attitude and behavior, such as hatred and intolerance, toward an individual or various racial/ethnic groups in American society (Levin & Nolan 2011). For example, many Americans hate Russians, which is a kind of bigotry even if both are White. Similarly, many Americans are homophobic, and that is bigotry but NOT racism. Arguably, all racists are bigots but not all bigots are racists because bigotry can be directed toward many kinds of categorical affiliation other than race, such as religion, ethnicity, sexual orientation, class, disabilities, or age.

Consistent with the preceding conceptual definitions, this study applies the logic of agency and structure, as shown in Figure 1, to explain the similarities and differences between individual and institutional discrimination (Ritzer 2011).

Figure 1

Agency and Structure

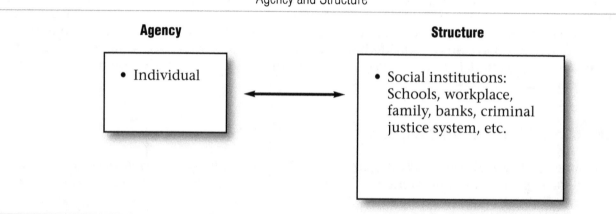

Individual discrimination occurs when individuals treat other individuals unequally because of their group membership, such as in the case of race, ethnicity, or gender. Individual discrimination can be *overt* or *adaptive* (Mooney, Knox, & Schacht 2008). For example, in overt discrimination, a White landlord may refuse to rent to an African American because of his own prejudicial attitudes against African Americans. On the other hand, adaptive discrimination is based on circumstances like the prejudice of others. For example, if the landlord is not prejudiced, he or she may still discriminate for fear that renting to an African American will mean that other tenants may move out who are prejudiced against African Americans. However, both overt and adaptive can coexist. For example, the landlord may not rent to African Americans because of his or her own prejudice combined with his fear that other tenants may move out. Additionally, the following are examples of individuals discriminating against other individuals because of group membership other than race: a landlord who refuses to rent an apartment to a single woman; a police officer who beats a person he suspects of being an undocumented immigrant; a group of teenagers who decide to paint a swastika on a Jewish temple; a man who assaults someone he suspects of being gay.

Racism is often described as the actions and attitudes of a group of people; for example, WASPS, the members of whom have the economic, political, and social powers to control the systems and institutions of a society such as schools, access to employment, the criminal justice system, banks, etc. These institutions positively/negatively affect the daily lives of everyone, especially racial/ethnic minority groups. When such institutions have policies and practices that result in and perpetuate prejudice, discrimination, and racism, this is institutional racism.

In this connection, institutional discrimination occurs when normal operations and policies of social institutions result in unequal treatment as regards job opportunities for racial minorities and women. Institutional discrimination can be overt and insidious, or it can be covert and subtle (Pincus 1994). For example, discrimination can occur indirectly in the workplace when businesses move out from inner-city Minneapolis to the suburb of Bloomington not because of economic reasons but because they do not want to hire minorities, resulting in reduced employment opportunities for minority groups, especially the youth.

When a national sample of U.S. adults was asked, "Do you feel that racial minorities in this country have equal job opportunities as Whites?" more than 53 percent said "No" in the Gallup Organization 2007a survey (Mooney, Knox, & Schacht 2008). The Civil Rights Act of 1964, which prohibited discrimination in public accommodations and employment, was the first modern legislation to address these barriers. A section of the Act known as Title VII, which specifically banned discrimination in employment, laid the groundwork for the subsequent development of affirmative action (Darboe 2009). The Equal Employment Opportunity Commission, created by the Civil Rights Act of 1964, and the Office of Federal Contract Compliance became important enforcement agencies for the program.

Affirmative action is a proactive set of legal policies that ensure that qualified and historically underrepresented groups, especially African Americans and women, are given preference in the hiring, promotion, and admission in colleges and universities. It is designed to correct present effects of past institutional discrimination against racial minorities and women (Darboe 2009). Arguably, affirmative action is intended to create a more level playing field by eliminating the unfair privilege that is enjoyed by many Whites. Today, despite laws forbidding discrimination against racial minorities, it still occurs in all phases of the employment process, from recruitment to interview, job offer, salary, promotion, and firing decisions. Additionally, glass ceilings are erected, which are barriers that block social upward mobility thereby limiting opportunities for advancement to decision-making positions for racial minorities and women (Schaefer 2012). Since the terrorist attacks of September 11, 2001, workplace discrimination has increased against individuals who are Arabs and/or Muslims.

Another example of institutional discrimination is in education. The funding of public schools through local tax dollars results in less funding for schools in poor racial minority school districts. Racial minority students are isolated from their counterpart White students because of a segregated school system predicated on *de facto* discrimination—it is not legal but structural. This means to say, it is embedded in the social institutions of residential patterns. And even though it is not *de jure* discrimination—embedded in law—it is reminiscent of the Plessy case from 1896, the separate but equal doctrine, that epitomized the Jim Crow period of heightened racial segregation in all facilities (Schaefer 2012). A study by Harvard University found that U.S. schools in the 2000–2001 school year were more segregated than they were in 1970 (Orfield 2001). The struggles of women to enter the Virginia Military Institute and the Citadel are good examples of institutional discrimination because both state-supported institutions denied admission to women until 1996 (Adams 2000).

Another example is the criminal justice system, which penalizes crimes committed by racial minorities disproportionately. For example, penalties for crack cocaine (the crystallized form of the drug) often used by racial minorities are more severe than powder cocaine, which is used more often by upper middle-class Whites like Hollywood stars. The events surrounding the Rodney King beating by five White Los Angeles police officers in 1991 and the resulting riot provide a good vehicle to discuss the differences between individual and institutional discrimination. For instance, if the beating was an isolated incident of four White police officers brutalizing an African American suspect, it could be called individual discrimination (Levin & Nolan 2011). However, the beating became institutional discrimination because the leadership of the Los Angeles Police Department tolerated and often condoned anti-African American activities. According to the conflict theorists, majority group members tend to make laws that favor their own group.

The lending practices of banks also show evidence of institutional discrimination because African Americans and Hispanics are less likely than Whites to get loans or home mortgages (Bradsher 1995, Dl 8). In other words, White loan officers tend not to trust minority applicants. Further, mortgage lending is divided into primary markets, in which banks make loans directly to borrowers, and secondary markets, which sell loans to investors (Ross & Squires 2011). It is the growth of secondary markets that paved the way for subprime and predatory lending practices that resulted in higher interest rate loans for low-income and minority borrowers. In general, some banks made loans to many borrowers who should not have received the loans that they did. For example, Countrywide and Bank of America did so, which led to mortgage default or foreclosure (Verbruggen 2008). The preceding legal but discriminatory lending practices illustrate structural discrimination because those practices have had disproportionate negative impacts on low-income racial minority groups.

How Should One Address Both Individual and Institutional Discrimination in Your Community?

As we demonstrated previously, discrimination can occur both individually and institutionally. Addressing racial prejudice and racism is a complex task that varies from community to community. Some possible approaches are:

1. One needs to examine one's personal actions such as beliefs and stereotypes about other races.
2. Learn about community efforts to improve race relations through welcoming newcomers, discussion groups, cultural exchanges, education programs, and other social activities.
3. Organize an alliance of leaders from diverse communities and the local media to discuss how they can work together to address the way people from different cultural and ethnic backgrounds are presented in the media.
4. Form a diversity taskforce or club that recognizes holidays and events relating to diverse cultural and ethnic groups. This can be done in the community, a school, or university setting.
5. Examine the recruitment, application, and admissions process of students, teachers, and staff from different racial and ethnic backgrounds in the schools and university in the community.
6. Form a committee to welcome anyone who moves into the community regardless of their racial/ethnic background.
7. Organize an alliance of community leaders from the different cultural and ethnic groups, as well as different community sectors such as police, schools, businesses, and local government to examine their existing policies and determine what needs to change.
8. Periodically re-examine the strategies to ensure that dialogues on individual and institutional discrimination lead to action.

In summary, changing people's attitudes and institutional practices is hard but necessary work. A commitment among individuals and institutions to valuing diversity is essential for healthy communities. Changes will not happen overnight, but one can begin to take small steps towards making a difference. These small steps build the foundation for more organized efforts to build inclusive communities. Social institutions provide material goods, opportunities, resources, services, and job satisfaction. Since most institutions have been structured to discriminate in the past, the change in policy will not lead to a change in results unless there is also a change in the institutions. Therefore, reducing prejudice first, and individual and institutional discrimination second, in a step-wise manner is important because it can lead to support for both policy and structural change.

How Can Ethnocentrism Be Both a Positive and a Negative Force?

The term *ethnocentrism* was coined by William Graham Sumner in his book *Folkways* (1906). His viewpoint on ethnocentrism was that "one's own group is the center of everything," against which all other groups are judged (Sumner 1906, 12–13). It is in this context that human social arrangements are differentiated into in-groups and out-groups (we-they distinctions), which shape people's values and standards of behavior. People can have so much pride in their culture or religion or race that they become racist and discriminate against out-groups. But now that the world is becoming globalized, such attitudes and behaviors are untenable. Different cultures are coming together for the purposes of trade, travel, and social and cultural exchanges. People are learning to overcome their self-centered thinking and see human society from a broader, more inclusive global perspective. Thus, diversity is not just an ideal in a globalized world but it is also extremely practical.

Ethnocentrism is often defined as the tendency to evaluate the values, beliefs, and behaviors of one's own culture as being more positive, logical, and natural than those of other cultures (DeVito 2009). In summary, ethnocentrism is the belief that one's culture is superior to another. This belief can be applied to race, ethnicity, gender, religion, and nationality. However, it can be both a positive and negative force. The positive force, for example, to be proud of one's culture, which includes: (1) patriotism—having a sense of pride in and love for one's country like the United States; and (2) military training, that is, American soldiers are some of the most well trained, disciplined, and cohesive, and therefore the best, in the world.

Conversely, it can be a negative force. For example, of the Commonwealth of Virginia's Governor, Bob McDonnell, wants to declare the month of April 2010 as the Confederate Soldiers' History Month, without any reference to slavery, which was the main cause of the American Civil War 1861–1865 (Quigley 2010). In addition, extreme ethnocentrism can lead to hate crimes and racism. For example, in 2010, the Tea Party Movement rallies were characterized by disparaging remarks and anti-government sentiments, possibly because the president is Black. But words have consequences. For example, ". . . we want our country back . . ." But the real question is, from whom? Unfortunately such remarks imply the government and government representatives are the enemy when, in fact, in America the government is of the people, by the people, and for the people. So the Tea Partiers' contentious remarks can make some lunatics, or sociopaths, commit hate crimes against government officials who are simply trying to serve our society.

In February 2009, the Tea Party Movement emerged out of popular unrest over the economic downturn of 2008 and the economic agenda of President Barack Obama. Consequently, the Tea Party Movement quickly captured the imagination of disenchanted conservatives, who perhaps not coincidentally are predominantly White (Von Drehle, Newton-Small, Jewler, O'Leary, Yan, & Malloy 2010). Another example is the Occupy Wall Street movement, which emerged on September 17, 2011, as a loosely organized movement. It began as mass demonstrations and protests against corporate greed and wealth disparities, but once again there were some criminal activities carried out by protesters (DeWayne 2011).

CONCLUSION

In summary, Noel (1968) identified three key factors that contribute to ethnic stratification: ethnocentrism, competition between different ethnic groups for scarce resources such as jobs and land, and differential power, or the fact that one group has more power than its competitor. In essence, Noel pointed out that competition for scarce resources is the basis for stratification to exist, and ethnocentrism channels this competition along gender, racial, and ethnic lines. It is a zero-sum game; therefore, the group with a power advantage wins the competition, justifying its exercise of power with ethnocentrism and establishing itself as a dominant group. Arguably, institutional discrimination, bigotry, and ethnocentrism will continue to be perennial concerns because of the social, economic, and political inequalities in a diverse and globalized world.

REFERENCES

Adams, Maurianne. (2000). *Readings for Diversity and Social Justice: An Anthology on Racism, Sexism, Anti-Semitism, Heterosexism, Classism, and Ableism.* London: Francis & Taylor Ltd.

Alvarez, Rodolfo. (1973). "The psychohistorical and socioeconomic development of the Chicano community in the United States." *Social Science Quarterly* 53: 920–942.

Blauner, Robert. (1994). [1972]. Colonized and Immigrant Minorities. In *From Different Shores:* Perspectives on Race and Ethnicity in America, ed. Ronald Takaki, pp. 149–160. New York: Oxford University Press.

Bradsher, K. (1995). "A Second Ped Bank Study Finds Disparities in Mortgage Lending." *The New York Times,* July 13, Dl, DiS.

Darboe, Kebba. (2009). "Historical perspectives on affirmative action, diversity and multiculturalism in United States Higher Education." *Great Plains Sociologist* (20): 6–25.

DeVito, J. A. (2009). *The Interpersonal Communication Book,* 12th ed. Boston: Pearson Education.

DeWayne, W. (2011). "Occupy Wall Street is a 2nd American revolution." *http://www.usatoday.com/news/opinion/forum/story/2011-10-11/occupy-wall-street-revolution/50721480/1 USA Today.*

Du Bois, W. E. B., H. Louis Gates, and Oliver T. Hume. (1999). *The souls of Black folk: authoritative text, contexts, criticism.* New York: W.W. Norton.

Feagin, J. R., & H. Vera. (1995). *White Racism.* New York: Routledge.

Fennelly, Katherine. (2007). U.S. Immigration: A historical perspective, Cover Story, *National Voter,* January 2007 *www.hhh.umn.edu/.../immigration_historical_perspective.pdf*

Harris, Zenobia. (2006). "Undoing Institutional Racism: Defining Terms; Moving Forward." *City Lights* (15) 1 Omaha, NE: City-MatCH.

Henslin, J. M. (2010). *Sociology: A Down-to-Earth Approach,* 10th ed. Boston: Pearson Higher Education.

Levin, Jack, & Jim Nolan. (2011). *The Violence of Hate: Confronting Racism, Anti-Semitism, and Other Forms of Bigotry,* 3rd ed. Boston: Pearson Higher Education.

McLemore, S. Dale, Harriett D. Romo, & Susan Gonzalez Baker. (2001). *Racial and ethnic relations in America,* 6th ed. Boston: Allyn & Bacon.

Mooney, Linda A., David Knox, & Caroline Schacht. (2009). *Understanding Social Problems,* 6th ed. Wadsworth, Cengage Learning.

Noel, Donald L. (1968). "A Theory of the Origin of Ethnic Stratification." *Social Problems,* 16 (2): 157–172.

Orfield, G. (Ed.). 2001. *Diversity Challenged: Evidence on the impact of affirmative action.* Cambridge, MA: Harvard Education Publishing Group.

Pincus, Fred L. 1994. "From Individual to Structural Discrimination," in Fred L. Pincus and Howard J. Ehrlich, eds. *Race and Ethnic Conflict,* Boulder, CO: Westview, pp. 82–87.

Quigley, P. (2010). Refighting the Civil War, yet again: Virginia's Confederate History Month melee. *American Nineteenth Century History* 11(3): 351–359. doi:10.1080/14664658.2010.520931

Reavis, D. J. (1995). "What really happened at Waco." *Texas Monthly* 23(7): 88.

Ritzer, George. (2011). *Sociological Theory,* 8th ed. New York: McGraw Hill.

Ross, L. M., & G. D. Squires. (2011). "The Personal Costs of Subprime Lending and the Foreclosure Crisis: A Matter of Trust, Insecurity, and Institutional Deception." *Social Science Quarterly* 92 (1): 140–163. doi:10.1111/j.1540-6237.2011.00761.x

Schaefer, Richard T. (2012). *Racial and Ethnic Groups,* 12th ed. Upper Saddle River, NJ: Pearson Education Inc.

Sumner, W. G. (1906). *Folkways.* New York: Ginn.

Verbruggen, R. (2008). Straw Predators. *National Review* 60 (8): 24–28.

Von Drehle, D., J. Newton-Small, S. Jewler, K. O'Leary, S. Yan, & W. Malloy. (2010). Tea Party America. *Time* 175 (8): 26–31.

Workplace Challenges of African American Managers and the Need for Effective Diversity Management

Sandra King

ABSTRACT

As proponents of workplace diversity tout its well-documented benefits, there is recognition of the problems that often accompany it. Minorities, especially African American managers, continue to deal with discrimination and other barriers to success in today's organizations. Despite the efforts of some companies to recognize and seize the opportunity to view diversity as a competitive advantage, effective diversity management in the workplace is not always a reality. The purpose of this work is to examine secondary sources in an effort to identify benefits and problems associated with diversity, including the unique challenges experienced by African American managers. Recommendations for effectively managing diversity are offered. Implications for research and practice will also be discussed.

Introduction

As today's workplaces become increasingly diverse, employers are faced with the daunting task of maximizing the benefits of diversity while running the risk of being overcome by the problems that can accompany it. Although some organizations have learned to view diversity as a competitive advantage, thereby reaping its full benefits, many have not (Cox & Blake 1991; Thomas & Ely 1996). Employment discrimination based on race, sex, and other protected characteristics continues to occur in twenty-first century organizations. The Equal Employment Opportunity Commission (EEOC, n.d.) handles tens of thousands of cases annually where employees complain of both overt and covert forms of racism and other forms of bias that creep into employment decisions. Racial discrimination, although now largely subtle, remains a problem requiring an innovative solution (EEOC 2011). Subtle discrimination, albeit less blatant than overt discrimination, is no less painful or destructive (Deitch et al. 2003).

There is a growing body of research highlighting the reality that majority and minority employees experience workplaces differently (Bell & Nkomo 2003). In fact, nearly forty years ago, Jones (1973) offered a compelling view of what it is like to experience the workplace as a Black manager. In this instructive work, he recounted example after example of a workplace that contained obstacles for minority managers because of its lack of readiness to embrace them. Years later, Caver and Livers (2002) offered a contemporary view of "what it's really like to be a Black manager" (p. 77). This letter gave voice to racial bias and everyday prejudice that often unwittingly make their way into the workplace and wreak havoc on the psyche and career outcomes of minorities.

For decades, research has raised awareness of the different ways in which numerical and racial minorities are treated in workplaces dominated by the majority. Moreover, the glass ceiling has become a familiar and frequently used descriptor for the invisible barrier that plagues women and minorities and bars them from top leadership positions in the organizations. However, the term fails to adequately capture the difficulty encountered by similarly situated African American and other minority employees. The comparable term in the literature reserved for that description is brick or concrete wall (Federal Glass Ceiling Commission 1995).

While a great deal of research has been done on the challenges women face at work, not enough has been done on those that minority managers, specifically African Americans, continue to face. The purpose of this paper is to identify benefits and problems associated with diversity and the unique challenges experienced by African American managers.

Workplace Diversity

Defining diversity, as it pertains to the workplace, is not a straightforward undertaking. Consequently, researchers often provide different perspectives regarding its meaning. Generally, diversity is viewed from two angles—surface-level and deep-level (Ivancevich & Gilbert 2000; Phillips & Gully 2012). Surface-level diversity, as the name implies, represents the kind that is on the surface and can be seen, such as race, gender, or abilities. By contrast, deep-level diversity represents the type of diversity that cannot be readily seen, such as veteran's status or education level. Using a broad definition that encompasses both levels of diversity, Ivancevich and Gilbert (2000) defined diversity as "the commitment on the part of organizations to recruit, retain, reward, and promote a heterogeneous mix of productive, motivated, and committed workers including people of color, whites, females, and the physically challenged" (p. 77).

Allen and Darboe (2010) defined diversity as "an inclusion process designed to foster an environment where talents, uniqueness, and differences of all people are respected and valued in schools and workplace situations" (p. 167). Both of the definitions offer enlightened and aspirational perspectives that have yet to be fully realized as the typical experience for racial minorities in today's workplaces. Moreover, many organizations continue to struggle with achieving organizational outcomes with its diverse human capital (Jayne & Dipboy, 2004). As a result, these employees still face numerous barriers that often prevent them from being able to do their best work (Bateman & Snell 2009; Bell & Nkomo 2003).

It is well documented that when it comes to the workplace, diversity yields both benefits and problems (Bateman & Snell 2009; Jayne & Dipboye 2004; Kochan, et al. 2012). Even organizations that view diversity as a competitive advantage recognize the myriad challenges it can trigger for both employees and employers (Gilbert & Ivancevich 2000; Ivancevich & Gilbert 2000). Catalyst's (2004) study of female African American managers further demonstrated the gravity of this problem. While some of the women in the study held high-level managerial positions and had been an asset to their organizations, they still encountered a variety of workplace barriers that were designed to prevent them from reaching their full potential. African American women are considered double minorities, as they often encounter discriminatory workplace behavior because of both race and gender (Combs 2003).

Challenges

Although it is illegal to discriminate against someone based on race, discriminatory employment decisions and behaviors are not uncommon. Discriminatory workplace behavior often manifests itself in the form of a variety of workplace barriers, including stereotypes (Ivancevich & Gilbert 2000), glass or concrete ceiling (Federal Glass Ceiling Commission 1995), lack of support, higher levels of scrutiny (Bell & Nkomo 2003), and other obstacles (Caver & Livers 2002; Chen & Kleiner 1999). These more subtle forms of racial discrimination are more difficult to detect and prove, but are no less painful or significant (Deitch et al. 2003). Not surprisingly, these actions may go unchallenged and unaddressed. Consequently, these frequently experienced slights are allowed to become commonplace and run rampant. In fact, the EEOC continues to receive a large number of race-based discrimination claims in the twenty-first century (EEOC, n.d.).

By the nature of their role as organizational leaders, managers are charged with addressing discrimination if it occurs. However, it is often the African American managers who must deal with additional racial maltreatment themselves (Catalyst 2004; Combs 2003). In addition to encountering the workplace challenges faced by other minorities, they also frequently have to deal with problems unique to their status as managers. James (2000) found race-related differences in work-related experiences and outcomes of African American managers when compared to similarly situated Caucasian managers. Even after the researcher attempted to determine if education and training would mediate the negative effect of slower promotion rates, race was still found to have an impact on promotion outcomes. Moreover, James also found other types of organizational support to be lacking.

Knight, Heibl, Foster, and Mannix (2003) asserted that because of aversive racism, a subtle form of racism, discriminatory actions could be justified using seemingly nonracist reasons. To illustrate this point, Knight et al. conducted a study using undergraduate students to evaluate the hypothetical performance of African American managers and other employees. The results showed that employees who held stereotypically non-managerial roles were rated more positively than those who held managerial roles. Furthermore, trivial reasons were offered as justification for the low ratings.

Similarly, Combs (2003) studied African American female managers to determine the impact the duality of race and gender had on these individuals at work. Specifically, she sought to determine if access to informal socialization was different for African American women than for African American men or Caucasian men. Additionally, she wanted to ascertain whether a discovered difference impacted the career advancement opportunities of the managers. Combs concluded that the combined effects of race and gender adversely affected African American women as it pertained to their career advancement.

Benefits

Despite problems that unfortunately accompany diversity, there are a variety of benefits that, if effectively managed, employers can expect. Diversity in and of itself, or simply having the right numbers, cannot yield potential benefits (Thomas & Ely 1996). However, many researchers concluded that diversity is good for business (Carnevale & Stone 1994; Cox & Blake 1991; Gilbert & Ivancevich 2000; Jayne & Dipboye 2004; Pfeffer 1995; Robinson & Dechant 1997). Gilbert and Ivancevich (2000) conducted a study comparing the experiences of two organizations with diversity management efforts and found that one organization was able to reap a number of benefits resulting from having a diverse workplace. Common benefits often mentioned in association with diversity include better use of human resources, potential for improved customer understanding, better creativity, innovation, and problem solving, and better ability to attract talent (Cox & Blake 1991).

Clearly, the frequently acknowledged value of workplace diversity has moved beyond being the morally right thing to do. It is now largely viewed as a necessary component of an organization's strategy for achieving a competitive advantage (Carnevale & Stone 1994; Cox & Blake 1991). Researchers acknowledged the benefits of diversity and highlighted its merits while calling for more research to ensure organizations can fully realize its potential benefits (Kochan et al. 2003).

Existing management literature, a sometimes-overlooked source of guidance on effective management practices for today's workplaces, contains additional theoretical guidance that could aid in facilitating recognition of the lack of wisdom in allowing discriminatory behavior to continue. Allowing even unintentional racial discrimination to continue prevents organizations from leveraging diversity in ways that will actually benefit the organization.

Insights from the Management Literature

Management literature can be quite instructive to leaders in addressing the challenges of workplace diversity. In fact, a number of theories that may seem unrelated to the diversity debate are applicable to these workplace situations. For example, organizational change, theories of motivation, and attribution theory could be used to offer organizational leaders guidance for examining diversity challenges within the context of the workplace.

There is a growing body of literature that recognizes the difficult task of diversifying a workforce as an organizational change and as a change in the organization's culture (Thomas & Ely 1996). Therefore, using what is known about the difficulty of organizational change in general and in changing an organization's culture specifically, leaders can anticipate a lack of readiness and resistance to the change on the part of some employees. This knowledge can then be used to identify appropriate strategies to navigate around these hurdles. Organizational change in general is difficult for people, with culture change often cited as one of the most difficult aspects of an organization to change (Nelson & Quick 2011). Yet, it is a change that frequently must accompany workplace changes (Carnevale & Stone 1994). For decades, organizations have operated in ways that were centered on certain deeply embedded assumptions. An influx of minorities, some of whom fill leadership roles, represents a significant departure from these long-held assumptions about organizations. Understandably, many who have benefitted or expected to benefit from this traditional system may be resistant to changes designed to expand opportunities to others. An organization's culture will not automatically adjust overnight simply because the makeup of the organization's human resources has changed. Yet, change it must if everyone is to have an equal opportunity for success. Changing an organization's culture, while difficult, is no less necessary in order for the full potential of diversity to be achieved.

Another insight from the management literature involves theories of motivation, specifically, equity and expectancy theories. These theories provide guidance on what compels employees to work enthusiastically toward organizational goals (Nelson & Quick 2011). According to equity theory, if people believe they are not treated fairly, they will be less motivated. Depending on the situation, if this perception of unfavorable treatment is not satisfactorily addressed, minority employees could reduce their work effort or even leave the organization. According to expectancy theory, in order for a person to be motivated, he or she must believe there is a link between effort and performance and between performance and reward (Nelson & Quick 2011). If a minority manager's performance is not evaluated fairly, he or she cannot believe with certainty that quality performance will be assessed as such or lead to a valued reward (i.e., higher pay or a promotion). Since a responsibility of organizational leaders is to motivate staff, application of these theories within a diversity context can help illuminate the reasons why some workplace actions may adversely affect the motivation level of minority employees.

Finally, attribution theory is often used in management textbooks to explain how managers view causes of performance success or failure ascribed to employees. Depending on an employee's past performance and other factors, an aspect or totality of one's performance is attributed to internal or external causes. In accordance with the theory, it is possible to make a fundamental attribution error by attributing poor performance to the employee when external factors may have played a role (Phillips & Gully 2012). As Jones (1973) and Caver and Livers (2002) pointed out, it is not uncommon for African American managers to receive inaccurate performance evaluations. If leaders want to get the most out of their employees, at the very least employees should be able to expect fairness and honesty in performance evaluations and related outcomes.

By examining diversity issues in this way, managers can draw on lessons learned regarding effective management that is appropriate in a variety of situations. Additionally, it can help encourage organizational leaders to remember to use effective management practices when dealing with diversity. This is why many organizations are beginning to focus on diversity management in order to link diversity to effective management actions, thereby ensuring everyone (regardless of differences) is able to fully participate and contribute in the workplace.

Recommendations

Recognizing the changing demographics, organizations have largely shifted their emphasis from mere legal compliance to a diversity and inclusion strategy (Bateman & Snell 2009). In that vein, the contemporary research has shifted emphasis from a moral imperative to a business imperative (Cox & Blake 1991) in making the case for the effective management of diversity. Increasingly, progressive enterprises are promoting the benefits of diversity and taking a proactive, rather than reactive, approach to leveraging it in ways that give the organization a competitive edge (Cox & Blake 1991; Jayne & Dipboye 2004; Robinson & Dechant 1997). These efforts emphasize building on an inclusive workforce that values everyone's talents and removes manufactured obstacles so that everyone can contribute. Furthermore, there is a growing recognition that in order for diversity to flourish and be truly effective, there must be a change in the organization's culture (Kochan et al. 2003).

The use of effective diversity management strategies is becoming a key component in efforts to get the greatest return on investments in human capital (Thomas & Ely 1996). Rather than treating diversity as an add-on program, an organization should view it as a key part of its mission and vision (Jayne & Dipboye 2004; Thomas 1990; Thomas & Ely 1996). Advocates for this line of reasoning contend that a need to attract the best talent and retain a workforce that mirrors an organization's current and potential customer base can lead to a higher level of performance. Jayne and Dipboye (2004) cautioned, however, that simply having a diverse workforce will not necessarily lead to better performance. Similarly, Kochan et al. (2003) advised that ". . . diversity, if managed well, may . . . enhance performance" (p. 17). Not surprisingly, effective diversity management is viewed as a critical link between diversity and the potential for enhanced performance.

Based on the literature, employers can take various actions to facilitate more effective management of diversity. However, there is not always agreement on what a list of effective actions should include. Actions that are often suggested as necessary components of any efforts to manage diversity are leadership and commitment from top management and accountability (Kreitz 2008; Thomas 1990; Thomas & Ely 1996). Without leadership from the top, others in the organization will not fully understand the commitment to diversity. Consequently, employees may not act in ways that are consistent with top management's view of the organization's diversity philosophy. In addition, top management will need to hold other managers accountable for leading on the issue of diversity and ensuring all employees are treated fairly.

What top management pays attention to is of utmost interest to everyone in an organization; accountability will convey this message like nothing else. While other best practices (i.e., diversity training, mentoring, employee involvement, ongoing assessment of progress toward diversity goals, and similar efforts) are often touted as effective, a key starting point is leadership from the top (Kreitz 2008). As these actions are taken, the workplace challenges African American managers and non-managers face regarding race should diminish. Similarly, as scholars conduct new research, the list of effective diversity management actions will continue to grow.

Implications for Research and Practice

More research that captures the voice of African American managers should be undertaken to better illuminate concerns and suggested solutions from their perspectives. Additionally, the research should be in a format that is usable for organizations. For example, a quantitative study that compares the workplace experiences of Caucasian and minority managers may offer insights about needed workplace adjustments and include recommendations for translating academic research into guidance for organizational practice.

Leaders can learn from what is already available on demographic trends and what these mean for twenty-first century workplaces. Those organizations that take proactive steps to shape their approach and make an effort to build on strengths and minimize the weaknesses of diversity can create a competitive edge. In contrast, those organizations that allow their human capital to suffer from the challenges of diversity going unchecked can run the risk of waiting until it is too late to address the problem. This inaction results in leaving the organization vulnerable to lawsuits and damaged reputation stemming from mistreatment of minority employees (Cox & Blake 1991; Goldman, Gutek, Stein, & Lewis 2006). Removal of barriers that prevent full workplace participation of all employees, including African American managers, will pave the way for everyone to contribute more fully to organizational goals. In this economic climate, organizations can ill afford to waste valuable resources.

Leadership and management courses for both business and public management students should include a greater focus on diversity management and the role of diversity in the workplace. These courses could aid in the preparation of aspiring managers for the responsibility of leading diverse staff and providing quality goods and services to diverse customers. Moreover, students should be introduced early to diversity management practices that are deemed effective in improving performance in diverse environments. Students also need to understand how changing demographics will impact the workplace and the implications of those changes for their ability to lead effectively in light of this new reality.

CONCLUSION

Ensuring that all employees are free to do their best is a critical task for today's organizational leaders. At a minimum, employees should be able to do their work without fear of discrimination or harassment. It is only after this critical first step takes place that employers can hope to realize a return on the investment in human capital as it pertains to diversity. African American managers, along with other employees, have a lot to offer. They should not have to constantly bump up against countless obstacles on their path to pursuing the basic opportunity to do their jobs.

Forward-looking organizations that really want to reap the full benefits of diversity will work to remove workplace obstacles and learn from their and others' mistakes. Until these unnecessary hurdles are removed and a commitment to effectively managing diversity is demonstrated, getting the most out of an increasingly diverse workforce will continue to be a challenge.

REFERENCES

Allen, W. E., & K. Darboe. (2010). *Introduction to Ethnic Studies: A new approach.* Dubuque, IA: Kendall Hunt Publishing Co.

Bateman, T. S., & S. Snell. (2009). *Management: Leading & collaborating in a competitive world.* Boston: McGraw-Hill Irwin.

Bell, E. L., & S. M. Nkomo. (2003). "Our separate ways: Black and White women and the struggle for professional identity." *The diversity factor* 11 (1): 11–15.

Carnevale, A. P., & S. C. Stone. (1994). "Diversity: Beyond the golden rule." *Training and Development 48* (10): 22–39.

Catalyst (2004). *Advancing African American women in the workplace: What managers need to know.* New York: Catalyst.

Caver, K. A., & A. B. Livers. (2002). "Dear White boss." *Harvard Business Review* 80 (11): 75–81.

Chen, S. H., & B. H. Kleiner. (1999). "Racial harassment in the workplace." *Equal Opportunities International* 17 (5/6): 48–53.

Combs, G. M. (2003). "The duality of race and gender for managerial African American women: Implications of informal social networks on career advancement." *Human Resource Development Review* 2 (4): 385–405.

Cox, T. H., & S. Blake. (1991). "Managing cultural diversity: Implications for organizational competitiveness." *Academy of Management Executive* 5 (3): 45–56.

Deitch, E. A., A. Barsky, R. M. Butz, S. Chen, A. P. Brief, & J. C. Bradley. "Subtle yet significant. The existence and impact of everyday racial discrimination in the workplace." *Human Relations* 56 (11): 1299–1324.

EEOC (n.d.). "Charge statistics FY 1997 through 2011. Retrieved January 10, 2012, from *http://www.eeoc.gov/ eeoc/statistics/enforcement/charges.cfm.*

EEOC (2011). "EEOC Enforcement Litigation Statistics." Retrieved January 10, 2012, from *www.eeoc.gov/ statistics/index.cfm.*

Federal Glass Ceiling Commission (1995). *Good for business: Making full use of the nation's human capital.* Washington, DC: Government Printing Office. Retrieved March 16, 2005, from *http://www.ford.utexas.edu/ library/speeches/990909.htm.*

Gilbert, J. A., & J. M. Ivancevich. (2000). Valuing diversity: a tale of two organizations. *Academy of Management Executive* 14 (1): 93–105.

Gilbert, J. A., B. A. Stead, & J. M. Invancevich. (1999). Diversity management: A new organizational paradigm. *Journal of Business Ethics* 21 (1): 61–76.

Goldman, B. M., B. A. Gutek, J. H. Stein, & K. Lewis. (2006). "Employment discrimination in organizations: Antecedents and consequences." *Journal of Management* 32(6): 786–830.

Ivancevich, J. M., & J. A. Gilbert. (2000). "Diversity management: Time for a new approach." *Public Personnel Management* 29 (1): 75–92.

James, E. H. (2000). "Race-related differences in promotions and support: Underlying effects of human and social capital." *Organization Science* 11 (5): 493–508.

Jayne, M. E., & R. L. Dipboye, R. L. (2004). "Leveraging diversity to improve business performance: Research findings and recommendations for organizations." 43 (4): 409–424.

Jones, E. W. (1973). "What it's like to be a black manager: Equal opportunity is more than putting a Black man in a White man's job." *Harvard Business Review* 51 (4): 108–116.

Knight, J. L., M. R. Hebl, J. B. Foster, & L. M. Mannix. (2003). "Out of role? Out of luck: The influence of race & leadership status of performance." *Journal of Leadership & Organizational Studies* 9 (3): 85–93.

Kochan, T., K. Bezrukova, R. Ely, S. Jackson, A. Joshi, K. Jehn, J. Leonard, D. Levine, & D. Thomas. (2003). The effects of diversity on business performance: Report of the diversity research network. *Human Resource Management* 42 (1): 3–21.

Kreitz, P. A. (2008). "Best practices for managing organizational diversity." *The Journal of Academic Librarianship* 34 (2): 101–120.

Nelson, D. L., & J. C. Quick. (2011). *ORGB2.* Mason, OH: South-western Cengage Learning.

Pfeffer, J. (1995). "Producing sustainable competitive advantage through effective management of people." *Academy of Management Executive* 9 (1): 55–72.

Phillips, J., & S. M. Gully. (2012). *Organizational behavior: Tools for success.* Mason, OH: South-western Cengage Learning.

Robinson, G., & K. Dechant. (1997). "Building a case for diversity." The *Academy of Management Executive* 11 (3): 21–31.

Thomas, D. A., & R. J. Ely. (1996). Making differences matter: A new paradigm for managing diversity. *Harvard Business Review* 74 (5): 79–90.

Thomas, R. R., Jr. (1990). "From affirmative action to affirming diversity." *Harvard Business Review* 68 (2): 107–117.

Multiple Perspectives on the Nature of Black and Latino/a Intergroup Relations

Raj Sethuraju

Introduction

Demographers around the country have continued to assert that by 2050 the faces that make up the American population will be more diverse. The factors involved in majority-minority relations will be a significant reality, with the Hispanic (I will use terms like Hispanic, Latino/a and Chicano/a interchangeably throughout this paper) population leading the charge, followed by African Americans (I will use the term Black and African American interchangeably from here on) and Asian Americans. Robert Suro (2009) also stated that in twenty-five years the Hispanic population, given its current growth rate, would be double the population of Blacks and permanently obscure the nature of Black and White race relations.

Historically, when we discuss the nature of race relations in the United States of America, we have generally presented it as a discussion about the nature of White and Black relations. As Ronald Takaki in his work, "A Different Mirror" declared, "African Americans have been the central minority throughout our country's history" (2008, 7). Furthermore, in his work, W. E. B. Du Bois also declared that despite the civil war and the declaration of emancipation, Blacks continued to be subjected to Jim Crow segregation, lynching, and other forms of racism (Takaki 2008, 7). W. E. B. Du Bois called this a great tragedy and declared that the problem of the twentieth century is "the problem of the color line" (1965). Again, this emphasizes that much of the debate about the nature of race relations in the United States of America is populated by discourse that emphasizes Black and White relations.

Demographic Realities

As stated previously and confirmed by the census data that follows, dynamic changes in the growth and makeup of the population of the United States of America call us to attend to growing minority populations and the nature of the minority intergroup relations, especially between Hispanics and Blacks.

Race and Hispanic/ Latino origin	Census 2010, Population	Percent of Population	Census 2000, Population	Percent of Population
TABLE 1 Population of the United States by Race and Hispanic/Latino Origin, Census 2000 and 2010				
Total Population	**308,745,538**	**100.0%**	**281,421,906**	**100.0%**
Single race				
White	196,817,552	63.7	211,460,626	75.1
Black or African American	37,685,848	12.2	34,658,190	12.3
American Indian and Alaska Native	2,247,098	.7	2,475,956	0.9
Asian	14,465,124	4.7	10,242,998	3.6
Native Hawaiian and other Pacific Islander	481,576	0.15	398,835	0.1
Two or more races	5,966,481	1.9	6,826,228	2.4
Some other race	604,265	.2	15,359,073	5.5
Hispanic or Latino	50,477,594	16.3	35,305,818	12.5

NOTE: Percentages do not add up to 100% due to rounding and because Hispanics may be of any race and are therefore counted under more than one category.

Source: U.S. Census Bureau: National Population Estimates; Decennial Census. *Population of the United States by Race and Hispanic/Latino Origin, Census 2000 and July 1, 2005*—Infoplease.com *http://www.infoplease.com/ipa/A0762156.html#ixzz1ex3Eh7wE*

TABLE 2

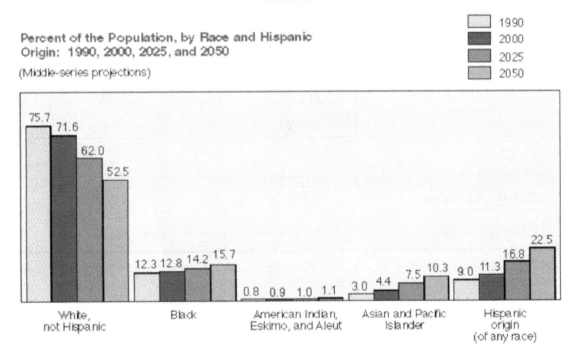

Percent of the Population, by Race and Hispanic Origin: 1990, 2000, 2025, and 2050

(Middle-series projections)

Legend: 1990, 2000, 2025, 2050

Source: http://www.census.gov/population/www/pop-profile/natproj.html

TABLE 3   U.S. Hispanic/Latino Population

Here is data from the 2000 Census and 2010 Census for the Hispanic and Latino populations in the United States.

National origin	Population, 2000	Percent	Population, 2010	Percent
Total	**35,305,818**	**100.0%**	**308,745,538**	**100.0%**
Mexican	**20,640,711**	**58.5**	**31,798,258**	**63**
Puerto Rican	**3,406,178**	**9.6**	**4,623,716**	**9.2**
Cuban	**1,241,685**	**3.5**	**1,785,547**	**3.5**
Dominican (Dominican Republic)	**764,945**	**2.2**	**1,414,703**	**2.8**
Central American (excludes Mexican)	**1,686,937**	**4.8**	**3,998,280**	**7.9**
Costa Rican	68,588	0.2	126,418	0.3
Guatemalan	372,487	1.1	1,044,209	2.1
Honduran	217,569	0.6	633,401	1.3
Nicaraguan	177,684	0.5	348,202	0.7
Panamanian	91,723	0.3	165,456	0.3
Salvadoran	655,165	1.9	1,648,968	3.3
Other Central American	103,721	0.3%	31,626	0.1%
South American	**1,353,562**	**3.8**	**2,769,434**	**5.5**
Argentinean	100,864	0.3	224,952	0.4
Bolivian	42,068	0.1	99,210	0.2
Chilean	68,849	0.2	126,810	0.3
Colombian	470,684	1.3	908,734	1.8
Ecuadorian	260,559	0.7	564,631	1.1
Paraguayan	8,769	(1)	20,023	(1)
Peruvian	233,926	0.7	531,358	1.1
Uruguayan	18,804	0.1	56,884	0.1
Venezuelan	91,507	0.3	215,023	0.4
Other South American	57,532	0.2	21,809	(1)
All other Hispanic or Latino	**6,211,800**	**17.6**	**3,452,403**	**6.8**

NOTE: Hispanics may be of any race.
1. Less than 0.1%.

Source: U.S. Census Bureau, Census 2000; Census 2010. U.S. Hispanic/Latino Population, Census 2000—*Infoplease.com*
http://www.infoplease.com/ipa/A0779064.html#ixzz1ewuiQMEL

National Population Projections (by Jennifer Cheeseman Day)

The graphs provided show a very different picture about the population distribution in America today. For the purpose of this article, I will focus on the changes between Hispanics and Blacks. According to Table 1, in the year 2000, the Hispanic population was 12.5 percent and African Americans represented 12.3 percent of the overall population makeup in the United States of America. However, according to the census in 2010, the Hispanic population stood at 16.3 percent and the African American/Black population stood at 12.2 percent overall. Furthermore, Table 2 illustrates the changes that have taken place as well as those predicted to take place. Here we also witness a dramatic shift in the population size of Blacks and Hispanics. The Hispanic population is predicted to rise to about 22.5 percent of the population, meaning they will represent up to a quarter of the overall population, meanwhile the Black population is slated to rise up to 15.7 percent.

Martinez (1993) states that the African American and White relationship is due to historical events, and because of this it has become entrenched in the nation's collective memory. However, that framework is not sufficient to examine the growing multiplicity of race-related issues that are becoming part of our dynamic society (Sethuraju 2000). This dynamic and its complex nature was brought to the general public through the movie *Crash* produced by Paul Haggie. A film reviewer described the movie as a tour-de-force exploration into the themes of prejudice and racism by using a cause-and-effect narrative style where chance and coincidence, and tragedy, are used to create a wrenching metaphor concerning the collision of interests between strangers in the course of a single day in Los Angeles, CA. The movie is, therefore, a social commentary on the interconnectedness of life in a big modern city where race, religion, ethnicity, class, and gender all intersect to create scenarios of conflict and reconciliation that must be negotiated daily by people living there.

A Different and Dynamic Story

Many would simply look at the numbers presented in Tables 1–3 and recognize them as part and parcel of population growth and nothing more. However, if one takes the time to examine the sociological implications of these shifts, there might be a story that needs telling. As I wondered about a research topic for my dissertation in the mid-1990s, I came across several news media articles about the growing tension and arguments regarding school board decisions and the conflicts they engendered among African Americans and Hispanics. It caught my attention because much of my study and research focused on the nature of Black and White relations. Other scholarly works have also focused on White and Hispanic relations (e.g., Blea 1988; Feagin and Sikes 1994), African American and Korean American relationships (e.g., Choy 1979), as well as African American and Jewish relationships (e.g., Azoulay 1997). However, there was no substantive research that explored the nature of African American and Hispanic relationships, so at the time I began searching to understand what was happening (Sethuraju 2000). What I found in my research seemed relevant, even today.

Before I discuss my findings, I would like to look at what I was able to find both in the mass media and in some scholarly quarters about the nature of Black and Latino relationships, then and now. I found the works by Gurwit (1993) and Harris (1995) to be interesting because they observed that the growth of the Hispanic population was already affecting the labor market, social welfare services, housing markets, and the education systems of California and Houston, TX. Harris (1995) observed that demographic changes were pushing the two communities, Black and Hispanic, to face each other and struggle for the limited resources available. Harris also observed that though Hispanic population growth was making its presence known, they were largely absent in the voting arena and, as such, were neglected by politicians. Other authors like Gurwitt (1993); Jackson, Gerber, and Cain (1994); and Harris (1995) also stated that the language barrier and cultural differences were causing some of the tensions, and thus they did not see a future for fostering coalitions between these two communities.

Blauner stated that many citizens of the Unites States were not aware that "Chicanos have been lynched in the Southwest and continue to be abused by the police, exploited economically, dominated politically and raped culturally" (1972, 166). Furthermore, Martinez stated that Hispanics have been discriminated against by the mainstream culture primarily because of their "cultural differences (language and religion) and nationality" (1993). Takaki points to the fact that after the conquest of Texas and California, and the signing of the Treaty of Guadalupe Hidalgo with Mexico, the new border was established between the United States and Mexico with the cession of the Southwest territories; California, Utah, New Mexico, Arizona, Nevada, and parts of Colorado and Oregon. After the formal separation from Mexico, Mexican communities that fell within the borders of the United States of America were treated as second-class citizens and servants by the White immigrants and the ruling government (2008, 155–176). In order to suppress the Mexican citizens, though they had the right to be politically involved under the 1848 treaty, the Whites used the law to undermine their rights, often treating them as slaves because of their language and cultural differences. Many of the studies pointed out that Whites, from the very beginning of their occupation, began to form group stereotypes about Mexicans and discriminated against them when it came to owning land, housing, and participating in politics and employment (Martinez 1993; Takaki 2008). I propose that such aggression and discriminatory practices employed against the Mexican community by Whites made it possible for others who were subjected to similar tyranny, like the Irish and Blacks, to continue discriminating and undermining the Hispanic (majority Mexican, Table 2) population in their pursuit to maintain their own identity.

The Anatomy of Tension

My own literature review highlighted several points of departure between the Hispanic and Black populations. The states that began to see a tremendous population growth and presence of Hispanics were California, New York, Texas, Illinois, Florida, New Jersey, Colorado, Arizona, and New Mexico and, according to Griffin (1992, 931) ,Hispanics made up 18 percent of the overall populations of these states. Portes and Zhou in their analysis in 1992 stated that the tension between these two minority groups was based on the idea of viewing things from a "zero sum perspective" (Griffin 1992, 935). This again implies that these two communities view the available resources as an all or nothing variable because of the limited amount that is available to them despite their growing numbers. So instead of looking at the structure that is fanning the flames of racial strife, the communities began to turn their focus on to each other. Some African Americans tended to view Hispanics as "free riders" and Hispanics claimed that African Americans were unwilling to accept them on equal terms (Griffin 1992, 936).

Griffin used the Martin Luther King Jr. Hospital in South Central Los Angeles to illustrate the tension. The hospital was built to meet the needs of poor African American communities, however as the neighborhood gets displaced by Hispanics the hospital was serving more Latinos compared to African Americans. In another similar case study by Garcia and De La Garza (1997, 128), we see tension between the two communities surrounding the usage of Casa de Amigos Health Clinic in Houston, Texas. The clinic staff remained predominantly African American despite a shift in the patrons who were largely Hispanics. The Hispanic population demanded more Hispanic doctors and nurses but the Black community asserted that "we worked for it [Civil Rights], we were beaten, and spat upon, we will work with you for it but giving or having the jobs taken from African-Americans is unacceptable" (Gurwitt 1993, 34). Gurwitt also stated that there were differences in perceptions between these groups. According to African Americans, Hispanics are more socially accepted and thus are discriminated against less because of their skin color, and Hispanics are able to assimilate faster. On the other hand, the Hispanic community viewed African Americans as part of the majority culture—language—and they believed they were the ones who are most often excluded (Gurwitt 1993, 36). Such perceptual differences were driving the nature of the tension. Gurwitt observed that both groups have "every reason to stick together and only one reason not to: power" (1993, 32).

Jack Miles in his observations stated that much of the tension between Hispanics and Blacks in Los Angeles was economically driven. The presence of migrants created a cheap labor pool, and this drove the wages down and thus the Black presence in jobs like gardeners, busboys, chambermaids, nannies, janitors, and construction workers has almost disappeared. Along with these factors, we also were told that many employers were hiring Hispanics because they considered them less hostile and alienated (1993, 52). Miles described this situation as "the largest affirmative action program in the nation and one paid for, in effect, by African Americans (1993, 54). Miles also stated that the April 1992 Los Angeles riots was largely a result of the frustration that African Americans were feeling as a result of the rise of the Hispanic and Asian communities (1993, 51).

Peter Skerry (1993, 370) asserted that the tension between the two communities was a direct result of the broad application of affirmative action regulations. The call for equal representation of race and gender in the workplace continues to set in opposition the two majority minority groups. As the numbers of Hispanics grow and compete for jobs, the representation of African Americans is falling behind. According to Skerry, racial tensions were a result of economic competition and until both groups have enough resources and access the tensions will continue to grow. The cleavage between the two groups centers on access to economic, educational, cultural, and physical resources (Sethuraju 2000, 12). Piatt observed that there are apparent differences between these two groups in terms of culture, language, and experiences, and unless these variables are addressed and integrated in our discourse and solutions the tension will continue to escalate (1997).

Contemporary Literature Review about the Nature of the Black-Latino Relationship

According to law professor, Tanya Hernandez (Rutgers University Law School), much of the tension between Latinos and Blacks is a result of longstanding prejudices and not a creation of economic competition (Hernandez 2007). She stated that the violence in the Chino state prison and in the Highland Park neighborhood were not isolated racial tensions but a real depiction of the growing tension between the two communities. She stated that the nature of the Black-Latino relationship has a long history. According to her research, the tension is a "pervasive and historically entrenched reality of life in Latin America and the Caribbean" (2007). Historical documents show that approximately 10 million slaves were brought and distributed among the Caribbean, and in North and South America as well. Large proportions of them ended up in Mexico and many others throughout South America.

These distributions of slaves created a sense of White privilege among Latinos in these South American and Caribbean countries. This, according to Professor Hernandez, is very pronounced in Mexico and spills into America as many undocumented workers arrive here. The signing of the NAFTA treaty was meant to increase job prospects for the Mexican community in Mexico, but unfortunately it also brought a huge number of undocumented workers to America. Their arrival and the population increase among native Latinos began to be felt in every major city in the country. There has been a population boom among Latinos between 1980 and 2000, going from 14.6 million to 35.3 million, and by all accounts, that number, has risen to 46 million in the year 2010. During this same period the African American population rose from 26 million to 33.7 million and, in 2010, the Black population stands at 39 million people. Professor Hernandez pointed to studies done to determine how each (Latinos and Blacks) view the other.

Surveys about social distance conducted by Professor Mindiola in Houston among 600 Hispanics and Blacks showed that the Black community had a greater regard for the Hispanic community compared to the Hispanic community in relation to Blacks. Only a small minority of Hispanics who are citizens had a good or favorable regard for the Black community; however, the majority of the undocumented community expressed distrust for the Black community. Professor Hernandez also pointed out that the studies conducted by Professor Charles at the University of Pennsylvania indicated that Latinos preferred not to have Blacks as their neighbors, and another study conducted by the Lilly Survey of American Attitudes between 1999–2000 also indicated that Latinos had a low desire to have African Americans as marriage partners. On the other hand, African Americans were more accepting of Latinos as marriage partners (2007).

Professor Hernandez concluded by stating that though the stereotypical image is that African Americans/Blacks are the ones who reject the Hispanic population, it is not often the case.

The historical experience of the Latino community with slaves and other stereotypical caricatures in Latin America and the Caribbean countries contributes much to the division between the two communities, more than what most media and other observers have indicated (2007). As stated earlier, most observers tend to state that the growing tension between the Black and Latino community is a result of economic pressures. However, according to Professor Bobo of Harvard and Hutchings of the University of Michigan, referenced by Professor Hernandez, the undercurrents of historical prejudices against Blacks and the ensuing animosity dictates that Blacks are an economic threat to Latinos and not vice versa.

The Carnegie Reporter published a further examination of the nature of the Latino and Black relationship in the spring of 2009. Roberto Suro, states that ". . . . Color alone becomes a weak vehicle for understanding the ways racial and ethnic groups interact" (2009). Suro suggested that we look at the population shifts in this country to determine the conversation about minority intergroup race relations. The demographic advantages Whites possessed are slowly changing and thus they are predicted to dwindle down to 50 percent of the population by 2035; the "other" will play a prominent role in dictating "policies, attitudes and social constructs" (2009). As was stated earlier, much of the conversation of Hispanic growth was witnessed in certain regions (the nine states, namely California and Texas), however Suro calls for the conversation to take into consideration the national growth of Hispanics. He stated that by 2035, "the Hispanic population will be twice as large as the African American population . . . and they have not historically played the role of the outsider in American society" (1990).

Suro does point to various examples of social distance between African Americans and Latinos. He states that the research conducted by New American Media (NAM) in 2007 points to the fact that though these two communities have geographically moved closer, the proximity is not reflected in the types of intimate relationships. The NAM survey points to the fact that "substantial majorities of Hispanics (73%) and blacks (67%) said that most of their friends were of their own race or ethnicity" and in terms of marriages "only two percent of Latino marriages and three percent of African American marriages involve spouses from the other population" (2009). Furthermore, the survey also pointed out that ". . . Blacks took a somewhat more positive view of relations between the two groups, with 70 percent saying they got along 'very well' or 'pretty well' compared to only 57 percent of Hispanics." The negative views were more ostensible, "30% of Latino responded by saying "not well" or "not at all well" compared to 18 percent of blacks" (1990). These are significant gaps that can determine the nature of the relationship between these communities. The NAM survey also pointed out that a significant number (61%) of Hispanics stated that they were more comfortable doing business with Whites and only 3 percent favored doing business with Blacks. On the other hand, only 47 percent of Blacks stated that they were more comfortable doing business with Whites and 10 percent said that they favored Hispanics (Suro 2009).

The Pew survey (quoted by Suro) about perceptions of discrimination and opportunity again showed a gap between Blacks and Latinos. A majority of Blacks (67%) stated that they do experience discrimination when they apply for a job as opposed to only 36 percent of Latinos. Another series of questions asked by NAM clearly showed a divide between the Black and Latino communities. Seventy-four percent of the Hispanics believed that "if you work hard, you will succeed in the United States" and only 44 percent of Blacks bought into this pronouncement. Suro asserted that these two large minority groups had many things in common; for example, the poverty rates between these two communities were high compared to the White community. But these fundamental differences need further examination if we are to have a better understanding of the nature of the Black and Latino relationship (2009).

Claudia Sandoval of the University of Chicago looked at the nature of the Latino and Black relationship from a political science perspective. She proposed that the Black and Latino relationship rests on the "understanding of who belongs and does not belong in America" (article was presented at a conference at the University of Chicago). Blacks, though, feel removed and disenfranchised in America (dual consciousness according to W. E. B. Du Bois) and are unable to unite around the issue of immigration with Whites under the banner of "nativist ideology"(2010). Not all Hispanics are here as undocumented workers; however, many are perceived as non-citizens by the mainstream society because of ignorance and other historical experiences. According to Sandoval, Blacks are invited to "exercise the power to marginalize another oppressed group; they are placed under the umbrella of rightful 'American' whose civil rights legacy is undercut by an undeserving immigrant group" (2010). Again, her thesis points to an important reason for the ongoing division and alienation of these two groups. "In spite of [their] social, political and economic commonalities that keep both of them subordinate to the rest of American society" they are unable to come together because of the "different notions and framing of citizenship. . . . " (2010).

Research Findings

As promised at the beginning of the chapter, I will now discuss my findings. The purpose of my study was to find out the nature of African American and Hispanic relations at two universities in northern Texas. The participants were students, faculty, and administrators from Texas Woman's University and the University of North Texas. A total of ninety-five students and thirty-eight faculty and administrators from both universities participated in the study.

As you recall, earlier I mentioned that some of the researchers have pointed out that there is social distance between these two groups. In my study, though, it was done between 1999 and 2000, and when students were asked about social distance, they did say there is a social distance between these two groups. Students desired a more active interaction between the groups. A majority of the participants also stated that on an individual level they are involved with one another; however, they would like to see more at a systems level.

Earlier, we learned that a majority of African Americans tend to see Hispanics in a positive light but less than a majority of Hispanics see African Americans in a positive light. Concerning my study, however, please keep in mind that the study was done in a university environment, and this points to the fact that both groups hold each other in a more positive light. This was true for both the students and faculty and administrators. However, when asked about the group's ability to work, the respondents in general perceived Hispanics to be better workers than African Americans. We know, from a historical perspective, both of these groups were seen as cheap labor. Today in many cities we know that the African American community is suffering from double digit unemployment and if the perception about their work continues, it might very well cause a rift between the two communities and ultimately those in power. From a historical perspective, when the minority communities competed against each other, the primary community that benefited from this divided reality was the White landowners. Thus, those who control the resources tend to be the beneficiary.

The two communities were united in their perceptions about law enforcement. They both agreed that law enforcement does not treat either group equally in relation to Whites. From a functionalist perspective, this perception can serve to bring the communities together when facing social concerns, such as discrimination and prejudice from the mainstream society. However, it is important to note that this is a strong perception and law enforcement should pay attention to such a divide.

Another important observation from the study was the perception about who is likely to get a faculty or administrator position. A majority of the African American faculty and administrators stated that both groups had equal chances; however, 47 percent of the Hispanic faculty and administrators stated that African Americans stood a better chance than Hispanics. Further study is needed to understand such perceptions, but it is important to be aware of this reality. As the population of

Hispanics grows, I am afraid such perceptions might cause a division among the two communities, especially if they are fighting for limited resources. Institutions of higher education are very much dominated by White males and females (95% of all faculty were Whites in 1972 and, in 1997, 83% were Whites), and the representation of African Americans in higher education went from 4.4 in 1975 to 5 percent in 1997, and as for Hispanics, the number went from 1.4 percent to 2.8 percent between the periods of 1975 to 1997 (Tower and Chait 2002). Thus the perception that African Americans have better chances, especially with the Hispanic population explosion, might lead to more rift among the two communities of color.

Implications

The findings presented here were some of the highlights of my research conclusions. The implication is that the nature of African American and Hispanic race relations is not as well defined as the historical Black and White relations in this country (Sethuraju 107). It is important to keep in mind the environment in which I conducted my research as opposed to some of the research I referenced here. Their findings were based on their research in cities like Los Angeles, where the number of Hispanics and their presence continue to slowly eclipse the nature of African American and White race relations. According to Bobo and Johnson (2000), ideologies, stereotypes, prejudice, perceptions of group threat, conflict, and competition over community resources in an environment of structural inequality are all factors that characterize intergroup minority relations in the city (Camarillo 2007, 285).

Camarillo reminded us that though intergroup relations, especially among Blacks and Hispanics, are rough, as her work and observation of Compton reflects, the demographic changes are real and palpable. She stated that "between 1990 and 2000, the non-Hispanic White population in the 100 largest cities declined from 52 percent to 44 percent, and in the fifty largest cities in 2006, Whites were the minorities, in thirty-five of them" (2007, p. 292). Furthermore, according to Camarillo (2007), Berube (2003), and Frey (2006), the Latino population and other minorities in the largest cities went from 38 percent of the population to 60 percent in 2000, and both Hispanics and Blacks combined make the largest population in eight of the ten largest cities in the country (Camarillo 2010, 292).

Given this reality, it is important to continue exploring ways to deal with the ongoing strife between communities of color. Given the population growth of Hispanics and Blacks, intergroup relations will be tested and it will evolve and add an important chapter to the nature of race relations in this country. The historical significance of race relations between Blacks and Whites will always be present as one of the main narratives; however, with population changes, the proximity between minority groups continues to disappear especially in major cities, and this amplifies the call for an in-depth exploration of the complexities of intergroup relations in our country. In an effort to maintain a multicultural society we have to address the complex issues of cities of color, and this initiative cannot wait until we witness race riots like the 1992 incident in Los Angeles.

It Is All about the Economy

These reviews of literature, though not all encompassing, have given us multiple perspectives about the nature of intergroup minority relations in this country. African Americans were forcefully brought to America to meet a growing demand for cheap labor, and the majority of Latinos came here, albeit voluntarily, to meet a growing demand for cheap labor (Suro 2009). From an historical perspective, we also know that many poor English workers were brought as indentured servants to serve as cheap labor. Over the years, White farmers and land owners continued to bring workers or invite workers from all over Europe, South America, China, Japan, and even the Philippines to compete for work thus allowing the owners to benefit from the competition. During the Second World War, the Bracero program was launched to bring in Mexican workers to meet the demand for labor in the United States. This also kept the various ethnic and racial groups apart from one another (Takaki 2008). The labor was used to compete against each other, thus driving the wages and the need for control down, which in turn benefited the White community at large.

This insatiable need for labor and maximum profit (largely an economic factor) set the framework for the race and ethnic relationship initially and seems to continue to this date. If one were to examine the nature of Latino and Black intergroup relations, we simply need to look at our history of how the various communities were treated to maintain White superiority and economic advantage. Following the example of the dominant narrative, every other group seems to continue the grasp on power and undermine each other. Following is an example that will help illustrate this point.

At a city council meeting in 1998, a Latino community member attempted to remind the all-Black council about African Americans' exclusion from the city's political life a generation earlier and how they [the all Black council] were perpetuating exclusion against Mexican Americans: "It was not that many years ago when Black people were at this podium saying the same things [lack of representation, absence of affirmative action, discrimination, etc.] of white folks [who were in power]. How could you forget?" (Fears 1998, quoted by Camarillo 2010, 287).

This example seems to illustrate how patterns of discrimination and exclusion become cyclical, and if we are to break that cyclical pattern we will have to understand each other and the historical roots of segregation and discrimination and work to consciously rebuild new patterns of communication, acceptance, and integration. Sandoval offers us yet another perspective, this time political in nature. She asserts that the division between the Latinos and Blacks is a result of how issues are framed in a political context. The political disobedience (Civil Rights Movement) used by Blacks during their quest for political representation and the disassembling of institutional racism was seen as a political tool and not a philosophical measure that painstakingly questioned the ethics of discrimination and segregation. The Civil Rights Movement led by many took various measures (boycotting business, occupying lunch counters, marching and protesting against wage discrimination and legally challenging practices of school segregation, etc.), and with the help of such measures, the Black community began to reframe the discourse about race relations. Though at the time when the Black communities across the country were fighting for representation, their actions were constantly seen as illegal, violent, animalistic, and even unnatural because it was presented as the will of god that Blacks serve the White community. The discrimination and segregation were institutional, systemic, and flamed by mass media. Sandoval stated that this same form of action is now employed to undermine Latinos. She states, "since the white power structure is vested in preventing minority political alliance, Latinos' views of Blacks are also colored by it" (2010). She further introduced us to Sawyer's et al. presentation at UCLA in 2008, in which they say that the present day conflicts between Blacks and Latinos are intentional ways the White majority exerts control over the political and ideological aspirations of Latinos, and thereby prevent a Black and Latino coalition (Sandoval 2010). She urges both the Black and Latino communities not to ignore this larger narrative as they work towards understanding each other and establishing coalitions between them.

Let us not forget that Professor Hernandez also offered a micro-level analysis to explain the nature of Black and Hispanic relations. She attributed the acrimonious relationship between these two communities to the large presence of slaves both in Latin America and the Caribbean. The migrant communities have been introduced to undermine Blacks in their respective countries and they were told that White skin is superior. Due to the large presence of Blacks in colonial Mexico (370,000 by 1793), their language and way of life has been shaped to consider Blacks as inferior, ugly, and violent. According to Professor Hernandez, these symbolic aspects of the Latin cultures cannot be excluded when examining the nature of Black and Latino relations.

Application

My findings in 2000 seem out of place today when examining other recent publications. However, if the intention is to bring the Black and Latino communities from acrimony and strife, then my research has a functional and practical message for our contemporary environment. Educating each other and promoting multicultural awareness and offering ethnic studies curricula—where issues and concerns of race and ethnicities and their complexities are explored openly and critically—can and will help these two communities from colliding with each other. Furthermore, it will help us examine the multiple perspectives and narratives (both macro and micro narratives as presented throughout this reading) that tend to be ignored when looking at everyday race relations, especially minority intergroup relations. Cultural celebrations tend to invite people into one another's inner lives and break the isolation of these ethnic enclaves, which if isolated can at times help stereotypes to thrive without any check. We are all largely products of the various agencies (values, belief systems, norms, capitalism, etc.) of our society, and as such we tend to repeat the cycle of oppression and divide and conquer without closely examining the foundations of the messages introduced to us through the various agencies that we come to take for granted. An educated population can help understand the complexities of race and ethnic relations and undo the conflicts facing our country and cathartically address the arduous dilemmas of the dynamic color lines in America.

REFERENCES

Azoulay, Katya Gibel. (1997). *Blacks, Jewish, and Interracial: It's not the Color of your Skin, but the Race of your Kin, and Other Myths of Identity.* Durham, N.C.: Duke.

Berube, Alan. (2003). "Racial and Ethnic Change in the Nation's Largest Cities." In *Redefining Urban & Suburban America: Evidence from Census 2000,* Bruce Katz & Robert E. Lang, editors, 2003, pp. 137–153. Washington, D.C.: Brookings Institution Press.

Blauner, Robert. (1972). *Racial Oppression in America.* New York: Harper & Row.

Blea, Irebe I. (1988). *Toward a Chicano Social Science.* New York: Praeger.

Bobo, Lawrence, & Devon Johnson. (2000). "Racial Attitudes in the Prismatic Metropolis: Identity, Stereotypes, and Perceived Group Competition in Los Angeles." *Prismatic Metropolis: Inequality in Los Angeles,* pp. 83–166. New York: Russell Sage Foundation.

Camarillo, Albert. (2010). *Doing Race: 21 Essays for the 21st Century.* Standford, CA: W.W. Norton & Company.

Feagin, Joe R., & Melvin P. Sikes. (1994). *Living With Racism: The Black Middle-Class Experience.* Boston: Beacon.

Frey, William. (2006). "The United States Population: Where the New Immigrants Are." Center for Social and Demographic Analysis, State University of New York at Albany. New York.

Garcia, F. C., & R. O. de la Garza. (1977). *The Chicano Political Experience: Three Perspectives.* North Scituate, Mass.: Duxbury Press.

Griffin, R. D. (1992). "Hispanic Americans." *Congressional Quarterly Researcher* 2: 929–952.

Gurwitt, Rob. (1993). "Collision in Brown and Black." *Governing* 6: 32–36.

Hernandez, Tanya. (2007). "Latino Anti-Black Violence in Los Angeles: Not Made in the USA." *Harvard Journal African American Public Policy:* 37–40.

Martinez, Elizabeth. (1993). "Beyond Black/White: The Racism of Our Time." *Social Justice* 20 (51): 22–34.

Miles, Jack. (1993). "Immigration and the New American Dilemma: Blacks vs. Browns." *The Atlantic* 270: 42–68.

Moya, Paula, & Hazel Rose Markus. (2010). *Doing Race: 21 Essays for the 21st Century.* Standford, CA.: W.W. Norton & Company.

Piatt, Bill. (1997). *Black and Brown In America: The Case for Cooperation.* New York: New York University Press.

Portes, Alejandro, & Zhou Min. (1992). "Gaining the Upper Hand: Economic Mobility Among Immigrants and Domestic Minorities." *Ethnic and Racial Studies* 15(4): 491–522.

Sandoval, Claudia. (2010). "Allies or Aliens? Black-Latino Relations and Perceptions of Political Membership in the U.S." Ethnic Studies Conference. University of Chicago.

Sawyer, Mark, Anani Dzidzienyo, & Suzanne Oboler. (2008). "Racial Politics in Multi-Ethnic America: Black and Latino Identities and Coalitions." In *Neither Enemies Nor Friends Latino/as, Blacks, Afro Latinos.* New York: Palgrave Press.

Sethuraju, Nadarajan. (2000). "Race Relations on Campus: African Americans and Hispanics in Two Educational Institutions." Ph.D. dissertation. Texas Woman's University, Denton, TX.

Skerry, Peter. (1993). *Mexican Americans: The Ambivalent Minority.* Cambridge, MA: Harvard.

Suro, Robert. (2009). "Blacks and Latinos: Still an Evolving Relationship in the U.S.," *Carnegie Reporter:* 24–33

Takaki, Ronald. (2008). *A Different Mirror: A History of Multicultural America.* Black CA: Bay Books/ Little Brown, and Co.

Trower. C., and R. Chait. (2002). Faculty Diversity: Too little for Too Long. *Harvard Magazine* (98): 33–37.

U.S. Census Bureau: National Population Estimates; Decennial Census. *Population of the United States by Race and Hispanic/Latino Origin, Census 2000 and July 1, 2005—Infoplease.com http://www.infoplease.com/ipa/ A0762156.html#ixzz1ex3Eh7wE)*

The Transformation of Hispanic Identity in America: Ethnicity and Race

Raj Sethuraju, Sherrise Truesdale, and Martel Pipkins

The Encounters

When I first arrived in the United States, my port of entry was Los Angeles, California. I began to look for a place to stand so that I could be checked in to officially enter the United States of America. While I was looking for a place to stand, I was approached by a police officer on duty and he asked me, "Where are you from?" and before I could finish my sentence, he pointed to a line and said, "You belong to the alien category; go there and stand to be checked in boy." I dutifully followed his instructions but could not help wonder why "alien." I have been introduced to that term through movies and understood that to be non-human species usually hostile in nature. But over the years, I simply accepted the term and stopped exploring the context.

As I was reading David Roediger's recent work *Working Towards Whiteness: How America's Immigrants Became White* (2005) and Ronald Takaki's work, *A Different Mirror: A History of Multicultural America* (2008), I could not help but wonder about that question by the officer at the airport and my deliberation about the term *alien*. Ronald Takaki introduced us to his own experience of being asked by a cab driver "Where are you from because your English sounds really good?" Professor Takaki proceeded to tell him that he is from California. The cab driver was not satisfied with the answer, and he said, "No, where are you really from?" and this time Professor Takaki said he was from Berkeley, California. Again, the cab driver asked where is his homeland and then it dawned on Professor Takaki that the cab driver, like many, did not view him as an American because he is not "White." This sent Professor Takaki on a quest to find out about who we are and why is it that the image of an "American" continues to be defined by whiteness, though he is a third generation American citizen (2008, 3).

Biological Myth

So what is race and ethnicity? According to sociologists, race is a socially constructed phenomenon that helps to establish a hierarchy and determines patterns of interactions and the distribution of power and resources. On the other hand, you, the reader, often associate the term race to skin color, hair texture, nationality, culture, accents, and a whole host of other variables. These associations come streaming to us via media, stereotypical depictions, and cultural images. Institutions also succumb to such representations.

For example, a congregation in St. Louis, Missouri, sponsored a group of young men, often referred to as the "lost boys of Sudan." When these young men arrived at the airport, the members of the congregation enthusiastically received them. After a few warm exchanges, they loaded up the vans and took the men to their new dwellings. The church members helped unload the Sudanese men and carried their bags to their apartment. The sun had set and so the new arrivals did not get a chance to see their new neighborhood. The church members left and the new arrivals went to bed. The following morning they woke up excited to get acquainted with their neighborhood. They found themselves in a largely "Black neighborhood." In an interview, later, the young men said they were surprised by this and over the next few weeks they realized that they could not get along with the residents of their new neighborhood. They also stated that they did not feel like they were in the United States of America because of the dilapidated condition of the neighborhood.

When the church members were asked why they selected the largely Black neighborhood without any questions, they said they wanted the young men to feel at home among people who look like them. The new arrivals did not feel welcome, and they had constructed their understanding of Blacks in America based on what they had learned from others and via songs and other media depictions. So here is an example of a good intention that went wrong. African Americans in the neighborhood immediately knew they (the Sudanese) were outsiders and had very little connection to their way of life and culture.

One of my former students at Gustavus was asked to pick up a foreign student at the airport. She was given a packet with information about the student, apart from the mundane details the packet stated that this student was coming from Sweden. She got to the baggage claim area and waited for the announcement and was excited about meeting a young man from Sweden, who was also a hockey player. She saw a crowd heading towards the baggage claim area and her excitement level increased. People started to claim their bags and started to meet their parties, but the young Gustavus student was still waiting for her client. There were a few new arrivals still mingling around the baggage claim area. The Gustavus student nervously looked at the few remaining new arrivals, one young man approached her and asked if she saw a college representative waiting around here. She looked at him with a startling look and asked him, "What college are you going to?" and he said, "Gustavus Adolphus College." She nervously asked him if he was from Sweden and he said, "Yes, I am. Are you from Gustavus?" He was pleased that he found his ride. However, the young woman from Gustavus was simply thrown of balance because the student from Sweden simply did not match her imagination. She was expecting a blonde and blue-eyed young athlete with a European accent. The new arrival did not match any of her expectations—he was from Sudan and a Muslim who grew up for the better part of his life in Sweden. However, he is wedded to his Sudanese roots and is very comfortable in his "skin."

Both these incidents demonstrate how entranced and entrenched we are when it comes to the physical markers of race and ethnicity. We are very aware that these symbols are socially constructed, meaning they do not have any biological determination even though we have been pushed and pulled towards accepting this fundamentally unscientific assertion that was floated by Jefferson in his writings, and by the Supreme Court in its many decisions (Lopez 1995), and by media in its depictions of characters that emphasized the biological composition of race and ethnicity. I have come to recognize the power of such depictions after hearing from an international student from Japan.

One day while walking to the library at Texas Woman's University, my friend (student from Japan) asked me why are "Black people so loud—they remind me of the hyenas in The Lion King." This association immediately struck me and I asked her where she got that association. She said, "Isn't it obvious? The producers used the culturally constructed norms to capture the imagination of its audience." Again, this example simply demonstrates the role each of the institutions discussed played in reifying and reinforcing the biological myth about race and ethnicity.

Ethnicity and Race

David Roediger's work also introduced us to a little-known fact about how even Eastern Europeans were not initially invited into the whiteness club. Many of the immigrants from Eastern Europe and Ireland had to work towards being defined as White over a period of time. Jewish communities also took some drastic measures to be invited in and defined as Whites. They changed their names and adopted many of the mainstream practices in order to escape anti-Semitism and gain acceptance into the mainstream society (Takaki 2008, 280).

Faced with new immigrants arriving here and applying for citizenship, the courts and the political arena began to define people and construct an identity for them so they would not infringe on "whiteness." Many figures of all walks of life—politicians, census directors, sociologists, biologists, and institutions of higher education like Harvard University, as well as leaders like Theodor Roosevelt, Francis A. Walker, Edward A. Ross, and E.D. Cope—respectively promoted and socially constructed an ideology of a supreme race juxtaposed against the "alien" other (Roediger 2005, 64–72). Race, according to Markus, though, is a socially constructed phenomenon that was historically born out of the need to distinguish people into groups with characteristics that were "used to establish a hierarchy and to accord one group a higher status and the other group a lower status" (Moya and Markus 2010).

The historical experience of racial hierarchies continues to dictate power relationships between members of our society, where privileges are accorded to certain members in our society, as well as how each population is represented in our society. Race becomes a historical marker on how certain groups were classified and treated by others. This was obvious in South Africa, where people have been classified into various categories, with those who were Afrikaans being the ruling White majority until 1990. And to this day, they are considered wealthy and have access to resources. Colored People are those whose ancestors came to South Africa as indentured servants from India, etc., and Blacks are the native people of South Africa, who, until the 1990s, were in a disempowered and minority status.

Markus draws a keen difference between race and ethnicity when she states that those who identify as an ethnic group often focus on differences within their group—intra-ethnic differences. Their focus is often on what members of the group think about each other. However, when race is used to describe his/her group, the focus then draws on how others tend to view the group—the interracial differences. Their focus is on how people's perspectives about them affect their opportunities and access in the greater community (Moya and Markus 2010).

However, as we examine the Latino community and its many racial representations in both the 2000 and 2010 census, the issue of race and ethnicity becomes much more complex and social. The Hispanic or Latino community, prior to 1980, despite what they wrote on the census report—'Mestizo,' 'Mexican,' 'Chicano,' "Mexicano,' or 'La Raza' got collapsed into "White" (Massey and Denton 1992). The social construction of race and ethnicity becomes obvious as the Latino community was asked to identify itself starting with the 1980 census as a racial group (Spanish Race) and after the 1990 census, they were no longer considered a racial group. They were asked to identify as an ethnic group that fell under a specific racial group: White, Black, Asian, mixed race and/or some other race since the 2000 census.

Short History of Occupation

Given these differences, it is important to examine Hispanic identity fluctuation. According to Ronald Takaki, Jefferson's dream of manifest destiny, of a continent populated by people who spoke the same language and were governed by the same laws, began to take shape when the White slave holders began to settle in *Tejas* (Texas) (2008, 155–156). The demand for products like cotton saw the arrival of Whites into Mexican territories. Though John Quincy Adams in 1826 offered to buy the territory, the Mexican government refused to sell it. But the White slave holders began to settle in these territories for the vast open land and because they had the tacit support of the United States government.

When the cotton industry expanded many of the farmers began to move into Mexico. These territories of Mexico were sparsely populated and largely unregulated. This allowed many White farmers to move into these territories and begin to occupy the land and start asserting their norms. Many of the Mexican populations in these communities received the newcomers with open arms primarily because of potential employment. When the Whites began to assert their independence and employed the help of the federal government to wage a war against the Mexican nation, many of the Mexican inhabitants supported the White community in its drive for independence because they were promised citizenship and recognition. However, the inhabitants were silenced in their pursuit to establish themselves because of language barriers. There was contention over land ownership so institutional racism began to be employed when banks and other institutions marginalized the native Mexican population based on racial categorization. According to Ronald Takaki, the native Mexican population was subjected to diminished status because they were evaluated by colonizers like Stephen Austin as a "mongrel Spanish-Indian and negro race." And he further referred to Whites as the "civilized and the American-American race" (Takaki 2008, 157). Whites also had their eyes on California and, according to Richard Henry Dana, who authored a famous book *Two Years Before the Mast*, ". . . Mexicans lacked the enterprise and calculating mentality of Americans . . . they spent much of their time in pleasure giving activities such as festive parties called fandango" (Takaki 2008, 162). He further described Whites as industrious, frugal, and sober people with strong work ethics; however, the Mexicans were viewed as less than human (Takaki 2008, 162).

Though the Whites were motivated by the desire to occupy the large land reserves for economic gains, their justification was couched by religious and racial ideologies. Both religious and racial justifications made it possible for the war between the Mexico and the United States in 1846. The war ended in 1848 with the signing of the Treaty of Guadalupe (Takaki 2008, 163). This treaty also subsequently allowed the American government to annex many more thousands of acres of land, which included the present states of California, New Mexico, Arizona, Nevada, Texas, and parts of Colorado and Utah (Takaki 2008, 163). Many Americans considered this "manifest destiny," which was "divinely designed" (ibid. 163). Such notions led to thousands of Mexicans who chose to remain on their land, now under the jurisdiction of the United States, having become "foreigners in their own land" (Pablo de la Guerra, quoted by Takaki 2008, 165). Though the occupied Mexicans were disenfranchised by the courts, politics, racism, and language, they fought hard to establish a "Mexican-American identity—a proud attachment to the culture south of the border as well as a fierce determination to claim their rights and dignity in 'occupied' Mexico" (ibid. 176). As stated previously, the United States Hispanic population predates the emergence of the American Nation, and their continued population growth and immigration from Latin America, has made them a critical mass that cannot be ignored. Nelson and Tienda pointed out that unlike "European immigrants of the 19th and 20th centuries, the majority of Hispanics have not become structurally integrated into the broader society" and thus their racial and ethnic identity "presents a challenge for students of ethnic stratification" (1984).

The Contemporary Definition of Hispanics

Until the 1980 census, race for the most part remained a polarity between Whites and Blacks (Bergad and Klein 2010, 370). Upon the directives issued in 1976 under the Nixon administration, "the U.S. congress mandated the collection of data on 'Americans of Spanish origin or descent' and in 1997 the U.S. office of Management and Budget issued a directive on gathering data on race and ethnicity" (ibid. 369). Furthermore, people were asked to self-identify and declare their racial identity since the 1980 census. This policy effectively removed the polarity between Black and White and widened, in theory, the definitions of race and ethnicity. Latinos, with this new policy, began to display a variety of ways of defining themselves. However, we can see based on the analysis presented by various authors and the census bureau—Bergad and Klein (2010); Sonya Tafoya (2004), and the 2010 census brief (issued May 2011)—that a majority of the Hispanics defined themselves as either White (58% in 1980, 51% in 1990, 48% in 2000, 54% in 2005, and 53% in 2010) or some other race (40% in 1980, 46% in 1990, 50% in 2000, 44% in 2005, and 36.7% in 2010) (ibid. 370). Furthermore, it is important to note given the history of slavery in both South America and the Caribbean countries and the racial mixture, the reference to being Black continues to remain under 3% between 1980 and 2000, and in 2005 the reference to being Black based on self-declaration dropped to 1.5% and 2.5% in 2010. Bergad and Klein conclude that there was no significant difference between foreign-born and domestic-born Latinos when it comes to declaring themselves as Whites, some other race, or Black (371). According to Tafoya, who examined the Pew Hispanic Center microdata surveys and focus groups, "more foreign-born Latinos say they are some other race (46%) than native-born (40%)" (2004). Tafoya's analysis focuses on various aspects and one of the interesting findings indicated that a majority of those who identified as White Hispanics also stated that they consider themselves to be Republicans and they are overwhelmingly registered voters (2004).

Historical Insights about the Contemporary Hispanic Community

Bergad and Klein (2010) stated that the construct of race has a very different and complex meaning and association in Latin American and Caribbean cultures compared to the United States, and this is even true of the "foreign and domestic-born population in the United States" (364). In the United States race was seen from the extremes of Black and White, however, and because of the constant mixing of races, Europeans, Blacks, and indigenous women "voluntarily or through the use of force" led to mixing where the definition of the race of their offspring has never been clear. Since the fifteenth and sixteenth centuries race mixing has been going on in Latin America and the Caribbean and this is referred to as "*Mestizaje*—race mixture" (Bergad and Klein, 365). As the indigenous community dwindled, the larger presence of the *Mestizos* began to dominate in Latin American countries. The question of race was not seen as a dichotomy in Mexico, but rather as a continuum that ran from Peninsulare to Criollo to Mestizo to Negro to Indian, and race was simplified as a "tripartite categorization of whites, Indians, and Mestizos" (Massey and Denton, 1992). The Mestizos were a mixture of Amerindians and Spanish colonists. The race mixture was further complicated when massive numbers of slaves were introduced in the sixteenth and early seventeenth centuries, which in turn "furthered the process of race and cultural mixture" (Bergad and Klein 2010, p. 365). Soon there emerged the notion of "mulatto," or person of mixed African/European heritage, or the "zambo," of mixed indigenous/African heritage. This further adds to the complexity of race in Latin America.

The Caribbean also saw a massive introduction of slaves because many of the indigenous communities were destroyed by the diseases introduced by Europeans (Bergad and Klein p. 365). Brazil, another Latin American country, functioned as the "largest destination of transatlantic slave trade." However, over a period of time Brazilian society became dominated by the mixture of race (ibid. 366). The United States maintained the dichotomy because "90% of its people of African descent were slaves and Black then became synonymous with slave." However, this distinction did not survive in the Latin American and Caribbean countries and thus did not become "part of the vocabulary on race and social or legal status" (ibid. 366). As these countries evolved into nations and states, the notion of race also evolved and became intertwined with class and status in Latin and the Caribbean countries (ibid., 366). According to many authors like Padilla (1985), Garcia (1981), and Rodriguez (1990), cited by Massey and Denton, when race became a self-identification process rather than one based on skin color or phenotype in the United States, many began to see this as a social and psychological construct (1992) similar to what was already happening in Latin America and the Caribbean countries.

In Mexico, the presence of White dominance continued even after Mexican independence in 1821 from Spain. The Mexican community was still controlled and dictated by "peninsular Spaniards with native-born Creoles (Whites of Spanish descent)" (Massey and Denton, 1992). According to Massey and Denton, the dominance reached its acme under the rule of Porfirio Diaz (1876–1910), who promoted European dominance at the expense of the Mestizos. But after the 1910 revolution, the educated and middle-class Mestizos came to power and re-established the pre-Columbian culture and contributions along with valuing the mixture of Indian and European communities.

Theoretical Examination of Identification

Though race was a difficult subject to define given the mixing of communities both in the Caribbean and Latin American countries, as people moved to the United States from the Caribbean and Latin American countries, they became enamored by the advantages of Whiteness. As Roediger points out, "five leading historians of immigration have recently concluded as much in their magisterial article on 'the invention of ethnicity; in the United States . . . they write that new immigrants and the children of immigrants quickly learned that "the worst thing one could be in this promise land was 'colored' " (2005, 119). Bergad and Klein presented a clear example of this. They said that though many Cubans and Puerto Ricans may be mulattos or even be defined by outsiders as Black, define themselves as "whites irrespective of skin color" (2010, 367).

Massey and Denton's work on Hispanic racial identity and spatial assimilation concludes that the assimilation theory can help us understand the "propensity (of Mexicans) to identify oneself as White rather than Mestizo" (1992). As the socioeconomic status among native-born and foreign-born Mexicans increases, their tendency to identify themselves as Whites also increases. Furthermore, as the Mexican immigrants stay here longer and their exposure and experience increases they are also more likely to identify with Whites (Massey and Denton 1992). However, Nelson and Tienda challenge the conception of the political term "Hispanicity" by examining the experiences of Cubans, Mexicans, and Puerto Ricans (1984). These authors further examine the social construction of ethnicity unlike the cultural definition of ethnicity, which relies on common cultural heritage such as language, food, religion, etc. They invoked William Yancey's work (1976) that emphasized ethnicity is a product of "conditions that affect immigration; availability of wage labor; urban ecology; technology and the changing structure of industry" (cited by Nelson and Tienda 1984). Thus, ethnic identity should be defined in terms of economic and political structure and not based on individual or cultural preference.

The Mexican population that stayed behind after the war between the United States and Mexico was focused on agricultural work and remained rural. Many of the early immigrants from Mexico also began as a rural community. When they did transition into urban areas after the 1950s, Sigelmann and Tienda point out that the economy was "characterized by periods of restricted growth coupled with dramatic changes in the structure of production" and the ongoing institutionalization of racism posted a challenge to their integration (cited by Nelson and Tienda 1984).

Meanwhile, Puerto Ricans were also colonized and Puerto Rico gained commonwealth status. Puerto Rico had a rural and plantation status, but it began to implement changes to its plantation economy. The industrialization of Puerto Rico also brought a massive number of Puerto Ricans to the United States. They primarily settled in the northeastern cities of the United States in the 1950s (Nelson and Tienda 1984). However, their status remained at a very low level despite their possible access to the rights of the citizens of the United States. Many of the Puerto Ricans were employed in low-skilled jobs, and as the economy transitioned into service industries and companies moved away or to suburbs, many of the Puerto Rican communities were left behind (ibid., 1984). Their situation was dire and very much reflected the experiences of many of the Blacks who migrated to the North after the Civil War. The Black community escaped slavery and Jim Crow laws in the south only to find themselves in an apartheid condition in the north (Takaki 2008, 311–325). Like the Black community that moved to the north, "Puerto Ricans were relegated to the lowest levels of the socioeconomic ladder, and often fared much worse economically . . . they also have the lowest labor force participation rates, the highest unemployment levels, the highest incidence of poverty, and the lowest levels of education" (Tienda 1984, cited by Nelson and Tienda 1984). Nelson and Tienda conclude that their "colonial status" affected migration patterns between the United States and the island, which in turn contributed to managing split values and working in jobs that were strictly low wage and separated from the dominant race. All of these factors have contributed to structural classification of ethnicity for the Puerto Rican communities, similar to the Mexican communities.

The authors further examined the Cuban community and illustrate how they escaped the structural conditions and have been able to stay above the minority ethnic groups. Cubans have easily assimilated into the majority community despite their late arrival to the United States. The Cuban community arrived here as political refugees after the coup d'état staged by the communist party. Cuba was very much an island frequented by Americans, but the siege by the communists also brought political exiles who were successful and driven from Cuba to the United States. Because they were not saddled with expectations of colonialism or subordination, they were primed to succeed. Many of the new arrivals were the "professional, white-collar urban and highly educated" individuals according to Bach (1980, cited by Nelson and Tienda). Unlike other minority communities and European communities, the Cuban community received massive help to get settled here and many of the arrivals accepted low-wage work to begin their journey. However, they were not stranded in the low-wage work sector, and they had a thriving ethnic enclave that began to grow and support each other in their development (ibid., 1984). Unlike the Mexican and Puerto Rican communities, the Cubans who were initially exiles had much more social capital that allowed them to succeed in a culture that promoted individualism, capitalism, and one that provided the necessary resources for their establishment (ibid., 1982).

REFERENCES

Bach, Robert. (1980). "The New Cuban Immigrants: Their Background and Prospects." *Monthly Labor Review* 103: 39–46.

Delgado, Richard, ed. (1995). *Critical Race Theory: The Cutting Edge.* Philadelphia, PA: Temple University Press.

Ennis, Sharon R., Merarys Ríos-Vargas, and Nora G. Albert U.S. Department of Commerce. (2010). "The Hispanic Population: 2010." May, 2011 C2010BR-04

Bergad, Laird W. & Herbert S. Klein. (2010). *Hispanics in the United States: A Demographic, Social, and Economic History, 1080–2005.* Cambridge: Cambridge University Press.

Massey, Douglas S., & Nancy A. Denton. (1992). "Racial Identity and the Spatial Assimilation of Mexicans in the United States." *Social Science Research* 21(3): 235–260.

Moya, Hazel, & Paula M. L. Markus. (2010). *Doing Race: 21 Essays for the 21st Century.* New York: W.W. Norton & Co.

Roediger, David R. (2005). *Working toward Whiteness: How America's Immigrants Became White: The Strange Journey from Ellis Island to the Suburbs.* New York: Basic Books.

Tafoya, Tonya. (2004). "Shades of Belonging." Pew Hispanic Center.

Takaki, Ronald. (2008). *A Different Mirror: A History of Multicultural America.* New York: Back Bay Books/Little Brown, and Co.

Tienda, Candace, & Marta Nelson. (1985). "The Structuring of Hispanic Ethnicity: Historical and Contemporary Perspectives." *Ethnic and Racial Studies* 8 (1): 49–74.

Tienda, Joachim, & Marta Singelmann. (1984). "The Process of Occupational Change in a Service Economy: The Case of the United States, 1960–1980." In *Labour Markets.* Manchester: University of Manchester Press.

Yancey, William, E. P. Erickson, & R. N. Juliani. (1976). "Emergent Ethnicity: A Review and Reformulation." *American Sociological Review* 41: 391–403.

Opportunities and Challenges: Managing College Access Programs for Underrepresented Students

Michael T. Fagin, Tonya Fagin, and Dalton Crayton

Introduction

It is imperative that higher education takes a leading role in making the concepts of equality and fairness a fundamental part of its mission by embedding affirmative action structures and practices in the institution, especially where it concerns equal access and equal opportunity for students from underrepresented populations. In today's multicultural society, we live with the negative consequences of racism and sexism that have been embedded and institutionalized into mainstream American culture. James Jones has suggested that racial bias in North American culture might be termed *cultural racism*. Jones has pointed out that the norms, traditions, values, and assumptions upon which all institutions have been formed, especially educational institutions, are contaminated with systemic, institutional racism and sexism. The impact of institutional prejudice and discrimination affects all people in the socialization process in America from the cradle to the grave.

If America is to heal itself of the evils found in institutional racism and sexism, it must change many of the traditional practices found in higher education that have limited underrepresented groups from being admitted to four-year institutions. One of the ways that society can begin to create a general climate of equality, fairness, and equal opportunity is to expand educational opportunities to underrepresented groups by creating programs that will increase the number of students of color attending and graduating from college. The expanding opportunities for members of underrepresented groups to complete college will increase the amount of integration and social-cultural interactions between minority and majority groups.

MSU CAP—A Successful College Access Program

A Bridge Program that has helped to expand educational opportunities and access to college was initiated at Minnesota State University, Mankato (MSUM) in the academic year 2005–2006. This program allowed MSU to move in a direction that provided first generation, low-income students of color and new immigrants an opportunity to attend a four-year university. The structure of the program was designed to be aggressive in providing educational support, both financial and instructional, to improve both the admission and graduation rates for students of color. It was designed with a strong mentorship and guidance component intended to improve recruitment by giving students of color who come from structurally disadvantaged backgrounds an opportunity to work with university faculty and student support staff in a guided mentorship setting prior to entering college, and then to continue that collaborative guidance and mentorship once they entered university as a means for the retention of these disadvantaged students of color.

According to the National Center for Education Statistics (2003), minority youth are less likely to complete a degree when enrolled in post-secondary education. It has been noted that among students who started college and universities in 1995, five years later 27.8 percent of White students had completed a bachelor's degree compared to only 14.5 percent of Black students completing a bachelor's degree. Acknowledging that Black students' graduation rates during the late 1990s was approximately 50 percent of the White students' graduation rates makes it clear that interventionist educational academic support programs and specialized college Bridge programs are needed to close the gaps between Black and White students' graduation rates. The research shows that disparity in graduation rates is not necessarily attributable to performance capabilities but rather to structural disparities in opportunities because of the disadvantages of institutional racism facing students of color. Interventionist educational academic support programs and specialized college Bridge programs are a proactive way to compensate for these structural disadvantages in an affirmative manner.

The College Access Program (CAP) at Minnesota State University, Mankato, was established in the late spring of 2006. The primary purpose of this endeavor was to provide an alternative admission procedure and college Bridge Program for low-income, first-generation, underrepresented students of color. In this way, these students could be mentored and guided in a culturally friendly academic boot camp setting the summer prior to fall admission. The intent was to make up for any deficiencies prior to being admitted to the university, as well as to provide a friendly yet disciplined cultural setting to assist with their transition to university life. The design of the program was structured to provide a systematic means for students transferring from high school to college to prepare them with the basic academic skills, social development, cultural support, and financial aid information they need to be successful in college. This twelve-month program provided two years of online tutorial and mentoring services during students' junior and senior years of high school. Students could be admitted into the College Access Program during the first semester of their junior year of high school.

The College Access Program maintained, as its theoretical base, Tinto's social integration theory (Tinto 1975), in which structured academic design and interventionist academic social-cultural tutoring, counseling, and mentoring were put in place to help College Access Program students become familiar with and connect to university community life. For underrepresented students, this program helped to overcome the culture shock associated with attending predominantly white institutions (PWIs) by connecting with each other and university student teaching assistants of color. Supportive faculty and staff that understood their unique situation stood at the ready and helped them gain the skills necessary to transition into university community life. Experience had taught the CAP professionals that proactive intervention had to be early and aggressive, beginning in the students' junior year of high school and accompanied with continuing follow-up. Connecting students to the university meant placing an emphasis on group immersion experiences on campus accompanied by teaching them the basic skills necessary to be successful in navigating through the college experience.

The CAP director, the CAP staff, and collaborating faculty and administrators found several basic factors that successfully connected the underrepresented students of color to the university. These were as follows:

- Understanding the college financial aid process
- Understanding the requirements for completing general education and specific majors
- Developing students' particular interests by motivating them to be involved in student government, student activities, and service learning

Since the inception of the College Access Program in 2006, 300 CAP students have been admitted to the university. The first class of College Access Program students, consisting of fourteen entering first-year students, was admitted in the summer of 2006. The second class of forty students was admitted in the summer of 2007; the third class of forty-six students was admitted in the summer of 2008; and the fourth class of sixty students was admitted in the summer of 2009. In 2010, sixty-five students were admitted, and in 2011 eighty-five students were admitted. The 89 percent retention rate for students in the program from their first to second year far exceeded the retention rate of the university's general student population. The persistence rate for College Access Program students was equal to the graduation rate for the general student population. The first class of College Access Program students going into their senior year in the fall of 2009 had twelve of the original fourteen students on target to graduate spring of 2010, where an overall retention rate of 89 percent compared favorably to the university's overall retention rate of 79 percent.

The success of the College Access Program can be attributed to the discipline and guidance structure embedded in the program, where administrators, staff, and faculty of color functioned as mentors and role models who provided a setting where the conditioning and strengthening of basic academic skills went hand in hand with creating a culture of acceptance and ownership on the part of the prospective students of color. The program was structured to create a welcome setting for students and their families when they first came to and experienced campus life, as well as to provide an early assessment of the students' basic communication and computation skills so that intervention could be undertaken early and often when needed. Students in their junior year of high school were able to attend a four-week residential academic program held in the summer along with the new entering students who had been enrolled in the program since their junior year of high school. Students were enrolled in six credits of general education during the four-week residential academic program.

All students, both high school juniors and new entering first-year students, were given the *Accuplacer* test to evaluate their basic skills. The testing provided an academic profile of each student's communication and computational skills. Testing also allowed the staff to determine the level and need for tutorial services that would be required for juniors returning to high school, as well as for the seniors who were enrolled as first-year students. It is interesting to note that more than 95 percent of the entering students in the College Access Program require tutorial services in math. All students in the program receive tutorial services, both in person and online.

The founders of the MSU CAP found through experience that if we are to increase the number of underrepresented students in higher education, we need to increase the number of Bridge programs creating more and better access to college. The goal of this College Access Program to assist students in making their transition from high school to college by providing them with skills to navigate through the college experience actually worked. The program was successful in its design to help students complete their general education and to prepare them for their academic majors. All students in the program were required to sign a two-year contract, requiring them to live in the residence halls and agree to mandatory tutoring and special non-credit-bearing academic and social cultural enrichment activities. These academic enrichment activities included special tutorial assistance in math and science, as well as programs in social-cultural development.

The MSU College Access Program, now in its sixth year, has been able to meet its goals in maintaining its students and having a retention rate that approximates the overall retention rate of the general student population at Minnesota State University, Mankato. While there have been over 300 students involved in the College Access Program, the results to date suggest that the program has been highly successful in assisting students through their first two years of college and in preparing them for their major fields of study. It is of paramount importance that there be institutional support on campus and that this support continues to be developed in order to help balance the scales of unequal opportunity and unequal access to college when it comes to underrepresented students of color. A program of this sort can help higher education institutions in overcoming the structural disparities that disadvantage students of color by promoting a setting where the concepts of fairness and equality in today's multicultural, multiethnic global society become part of the professional praxis of the institution. The proof is in the pudding, as they say, and the pudding is in the pie, and the pie is no longer in the sky when it comes to educating students of color like it was in days gone by. The CAP director and staff found through experience that such programs, when successful, let us all belly up to the academic banquet as equal partners, and in this way we can all begin to be fulfilled as human beings and tell embedded institutional discrimination, "Bye-bye!"

REFERENCES

Bergin, D. A., & H. C. Cooks, (2002). High school students of color talk about accusations of "acting white." *The Urban Review,* 34(2), 113–134.

Feagin, Joe, R., & Clairece Booher Feagin. (1978). *American Style Institutional Racism & Sexism.* Englewood Cliffs, NJ: Prentice-Hall.

Tinto, Vincent. (1975). Dropout from higher education: A theoretical synthesis of recent research. *Review of Educational Research 45:* 89–125.

SECTION
Two

CORRECTIONAL COUNSELING

Intellectual Power, Social Injustice, and Negotiating Tenure for Criminal Justice Faculty

Sherrise Truesdale-Moore

African American Intellectual Power and the Elimination of Social Injustice

In 1980, Clifton Wharton, in "Reflections on Black Intellectual Power," asserted that African American intellectual power is imperative to the developmental needs and the progression of the African Americans' economy and education in America (Wharton 1980). He also asserted that ideas, inventions, creations, analyses, and wisdom are the instruments by which intellectual power can flourish. But to do so, the African American community needs to develop their talent to maximize the potential offered through human capital (Wharton 1980). One significant challenge in developing intellectual power among African Americans is the limited number of African American faculty, particularly tenured faculty, in higher education. Their integration and participation in mainstream scholarship is essential if their voices are to be heard and change is to be effected. In 2007, national research results indicated that African Americans were approximately 5 percent of the full-time faculty at colleges and universities in the United States, which was a slight increase over the past decade (*Journal of Blacks in Higher Education*, 2007). At the same time, the incarceration rate for African Americans is disproportionately higher than Whites in addition to other social issues that plague the African American community (i.e., lack of educational opportunities and employment, along with family crises) (Stanford Report 2005). During a time when criminal justice issues are exacerbating the social problems present within the African American community, it is only appropriate that this article gives special attention to criminology or criminal justice faculty of color in higher education that potentially hold the means of disseminating information vital to the plight of African Americans, as well as promoting the inclusion of their perspectives within a White male-dominated discipline.

African American Faculty in Criminology and Criminal Justice

In 1993, Heard and Bing noted that there were approximately forty-eight African American faculty in the field of criminology and criminal justice (Heard & Bing 1993b). By 2000, the number of African American criminologists had doubled to approximately eighty-six. At the same time, approximately 21 percent had attained tenure, approximately 38 percent were associate professors, and approximately 39 percent were assistant professors (Heard & Bing 2000). The low number of African

American faculty in criminology and criminal justice is exacerbated by a disproportionate lack of their important contributions to scholarly work in criminology and criminal justice.

In 1991, Vernetta Young and Anne Sulton pointed to the exclusion of African American scholastic perspectives in criminology and criminal justice. Their argument is that while the ideas of White criminologists are regularly praised and rewarded by lucrative research opportunities and journal publications, and then utilized in the policymaking process, the ideas of African American scholars are at the same time either ignored or excluded (Young & Sulton 1991). In hopes that the academic environment for supporting African American criminologists has improved over the last decade, Gabbidon, Greene, and Wilder (2004) revisited this issue to determine whether significant progress has been made toward the inclusion of African American perspectives in the field of criminology and criminal justice. Their conclusion noted an improvement, giving attention to the citations of African American criminologists (particularly Elijah Anderson, Jeanette Covington, Laura Fishman, Darnell Hawkins, Coramae Richey Mann, Ruth Peterson, Lee Ross, Katheryn Russell, and William Julius Wilson) in a little more than half of the theoretical articles reviewed in their research. Unfortunately, these scholars only represent a few of African American criminologists, which suggest that the African American perspective in the field of criminology and criminal justice continues to be substantially ignored (Gabbidon, Greene, & Wilder 2004).

Personal Reflections on the Challenges of African American Criminal Justice Faculty in the Tenure Process at Predominantly White Institutions

Along with the problems concerning research, publications, and policymaking, African American faculty struggle with barriers that interfere with the attainment of tenure, such as experiencing discrimination, negotiating family matters, maintaining large teaching loads, overindulging in committee duties, and having inadequate support systems and/or professional mentoring needed to help navigate the tenure process (Gregory 2001). Additionally, White students at predominantly White institutions (PWIs) have indicated some resistance towards African American perspectives in criminology and criminal justice because of the challenges they bring to their personal cultural norms, values, and beliefs. In such cases, disgruntled students may be encouraged to give a poor teaching evaluation, which affects the tenure process for African American faculty negatively. On the other hand, African American students typically find the African American perspective refreshing, as well as an opportunity for successful mentoring. Culturally friendly mentoring has been a vehicle for the academic success of African American students at predominantly White institutions, but this relationship can be exhaustive, placing excessive demands on the limited number of faculty of color in such settings (Strickland 1975). In an effort to help produce more African Americans in the field of criminology and criminal justice, particularly by helping students of color gain doctoral degrees in the subject area, limited numbers of African American faculty may have to overextend themselves when assisting in creating supportive academic environments for African American students to help ensure student success (Gabbidon, Greene, & Wilder 2004). To help alleviate this shortfall, African American criminology and criminal justice faculty seek to create a larger pool of African American scholars in the discipline to function as role models and help assist in the dissemination of vital information.

However, going beyond the call of duty can take its toll on faculty of color who oftentimes have to overextend themselves above and beyond the normal teaching and research duties of White faculty in the same setting. Beyond mentoring and academic support, African American criminology and criminal justice faculty may be called upon to advocate on behalf of African American students and colleagues experiencing social injustice (i.e., unjustified arrests, police brutality, etc.). Unfortunately, ignoring these issues may make African American faculty appear to be deserters of their own race, which may create discriminatory practices among African American colleagues. Moreover, people within the community may act against you, making it very difficult to consult or gain research projects.

Recommendations for Dealing with the Challenges in Higher Education

First, non-tenured faculty requesting assistance need to be mindful of the career damage that can occur when extending themselves beyond the daily duties of academia. Additionally, tenured faculty should protect non-tenured faculty from engaging in practices that may interfere with the tenure process. Second, non-tenured faculty should learn how to say no. This enables the faculty member to maintain focus on personal teaching and research goals. Third, utilize support networks by referring people to others that can better serve their needs. Fourth, non-tenured faculty should learn whom to trust and avoid being used; not everyone is working with the best interests of the faculty in mind.

CONCLUSION

Structural disparities occur across the spectrum in African American communities, and the field of criminology is no different. These disparities can be seen in incarceration rates for African Americans at one end of the spectrum as well as in the low numbers of tenured faculty of color in the field at the other end. Proactive measures need to be implemented to address these telling structural disparities at both ends of the spectrum in criminology, and only by creating a context where African American scholars can succeed and get their voices, ideas, and initiatives into the policymaking arena will this ever change.

REFERENCES

Gabbidon, Shaun, Helen Taylor Greene, & Kideste Wilder. (2004). "Still Excluded: An Update on the Status of African American Scholars in the Discipline of Criminology and Criminal Justice." *Journal of Research in Crime and Delinquency* 41 (4): 384–406.

Gregory, Sheila. (2001). "Black Faculty Women in the Academy: History, Status, and Future." *The Journal of Negro Education.* 70 (3): 124–138.

Heard, Chinita, & Robert Bing. (1993b). *African American Criminology and Criminal Justice Directory.* Arlington: University of Texas at Arlington.

Heard, Chinita, & Robert Bing. (2000). *Directory of Minority Ph.D. Criminologists.* Prairie View, TX: Prairie View A & M University.

Journal of Blacks in Higher Education. (2007, November 19). "Black Faculty in Higher Education: Still Only a Drop in the Bucket." http://www.jbhe.com/features/55_blackfaculty.html

Stanford Report. (2005, May 25). "Higher Incarceration Rates Harm Social Stability, Scholars Claim."

Strickland, Edward. (1975). "Black Faculty Members at Multiracial Campuses: Some Problems of Modeling Roles." *Journal of Black Studies* 6 (2): 200–207.

Wharton, Clifton. (1980). "Reflections on Black Intellectual Power." *Journal of Black Studies.* 10 (3): 279–294.

Young, Vernetta, & Anne Thomas Sulton. (1991). "Excluded: The Current Status of African American Scholars in the Field of Criminology and Criminal Justice." *Journal of Research in Crime and Delinquency* 28: 101–116.

Counseling Racial Minorities in the Correctional System

Sherrise Truesdale-Moore

Introduction

In the twenty-first century the United States is more diverse than at any other moment in history (U.S. Census Bureau 2010; Nassar 2010). According to the most recent 2010 census data, the United States has approximately 308.7 million people, which is an increase from 281.4 million in 2000 (U.S. Census Bureau 2010 and 2000). Minorities comprise 49 percent of births in the United States, which is nearly half of the population (Nasser 2010). To date, the minority population has grown from 80 percent (year 2000) to 89 percent (year 2010), showing Hispanic and Asian populations as the fastest growing during the last decade. On the other hand, Whites still remain as the largest racial group in the United States, but their population showed the slowest growth rate among all racial groups (U.S. Census Bureau 2010; Nasser 2010).

The unfortunate reality is that racial minorities, African Americans and Hispanics, experience the greatest disparities educationally, socially, economically, and politically. And this set of disparities has profound consequences because both African Americans and Hispanics represent the majority of the offenders incarcerated and in community corrections. To improve the life circumstances of these racial minorities requires that professionals who are working with these individuals have competencies not only in correctional counseling but also in multicultural counseling perspectives. This topic has received little attention in the criminal justice field (Shearer & King 2004). In fact, a survey conducted by Cintron and Lee (2002) found that most community corrections departments were not well versed, knowledgeable, or current in their understanding of multicultural trends. This included the fact they did not understand the need for the employment of bilingual professionals and those with skills in multicultural awareness, as well as those skilled in the interpretation of assessment instruments that are racially biased (Smykla 1986, as cited in Whiteacre 2006, 331).

A review of the literature shows that the Eurocentric practice within the correctional system is a "one-size-fits-all" model applied to all offenders, regardless of race or ethnicity. Unfortunately, this builds barriers to effective assessments, counseling, and case planning for those who are racial minorities. Therefore, this article addresses the need for multicultural counseling as well as cultural sensitivity and cultural awareness in the correctional system, while giving special attention to other problems that impact successful counseling such as assessments and misdiagnoses of racial minorities, particularly as regards African Americans who are disproportionately represented in the correctional system, comprising the highest incarceration and probation rates of any racial minority groups.

The Foundation of Race Oppression

Perhaps the best approach to understanding problems surrounding the counseling of minorities in corrections is to first understand the root of oppressive racial ideologies. Since the seventeenth century, the issue of race has permeated every aspect of the American society; it is rooted in economics, politics, culture, and social movements. There are two prominent definitions of race. First, race is defined biologically, which means that physical characteristics place boundaries on various groups. Second, race is defined as a social construction; it is formulated by societal forces, giving rise to racialized groups and social thought that reinforces those group categories. According to Ian Haney Lopez (1995), the fabric of race is constructed on four important factors. First, race is a human construction. By this, Lopez means that humans define the boundaries of racial groups, and they often use physical characteristics to do so. And while this decision seems to be based on inherent biological attributes, it in fact is not. Rather, it is often based upon the context of dominant ideology, economic interests, and political controls. The biological premise alone provides little contextual relevance because human groups have been intermingling substantially for centuries, which convolutes any possibility of defined biological boundaries for racial groups. Thus, to understand the proper groupings of race, we would have to first deconstruct notions of the biology of race by analyzing genetic and phenotypic characteristics, all of which would reveal greater distances among individuals within racialized groups rather than between such groups (Todorov 2000).

Second, race is fundamentally tied to other categorical groupings like gender and class relations, which suggest that the race construct cannot be examined without analyzing the intersectionality of race, class, and gender. It is in this vein that dominant ideology, economic interests, and political controls can help to explain how notions of racial and gender categories are constructed and maintained.

Third, the meaning of race is not static. In other words, how society views a race at one point in time may change over time, and sometimes very quickly.

Fourth, race is constructed as a social relationship, and thus it is never an isolated phenomenon but a social one. The idea that race is a social relationship means that where there is an attempt to define and explain the subjugation of one race, one must also pay equal attention to the subjugator because the two are inextricably tied together. This means that race is only significant as a coexistent factor between two or more groups.

Oliver Cox (2000) argues that race exploitation and race prejudice resulted from Europeans' development of capitalism, utilizing labor around the world to exploit the natural resources of America. Many people believe that Indians and Africans were exploited as slaves because of their obvious skin color and other physical outer appearances that made them readily recognizable and distinguishable. But these factors say more about *how* they were exploited than why. Why they were exploited is because Europeans in a pre-mechanized world needed them to do the work in mines and plantations across the Atlantic. In fact, Cox argues that if Whites who were ethnic others had been found in sufficient numbers, their "otherness" would have been reified through a social construction and they would have been exploited equally as oppressively. Moreover, in some parts of the West Indies, White servants were exploited and characterized in the same terms as Africans. It was thus the Europeans' need to exploit others for labor, as well as their ability to ethnocentrically rationalize and justify their social construction of exploitation and oppression, that gave rise to the early emergence of race prejudice in race relations. Race prejudice is, therefore, an extension of the ideology used to rationalize and justify the exploitation people of color for slave labor.

Early capitalist exploiters justified their mistreatment of other human beings by arguing that West Indians, North American Indians, and Africans were innately inferior and immoral, and therefore less human, making them well suited for slave labor conditions because they were more like draft animals than human beings. But there was a problem, and it had to do with justifying one group over another because the religious principles of the Roman Catholic Church opposed the brutal enslavement of Indians. So an ideology that reconciled the conflict between their religious principles and their pragmatic brutality was needed to justify the enslavement of others while still holding out the possibility of some degree of redemption, which would come through the slaves' conversion to Christianity (Cox 2000; Taylor-Greene & Gabbidon 2012). Thus, the capitalist exploiters rationalized the reconciliation of their conflicted consciences by degrading and dehumanizing West Indians, North American Indians, and Africans into degenerates in need of religious instruction and conversion to Christianity. The Europeans' race ideology, supported and reinforced through their effective control of firearms and other technologies and structures of oppression, led to their successful overthrow of almost every social and political system of people of color they encountered.

Racial oppression of the indigenous people of North America (American Indians) and people of African origin by Whites in the United States continues to be a reality. American Indians, upon the arrival of Christopher Columbus (Clarke 1992, as cited in Taylor-Greene & Gabbidon 2012) were viewed as inferior inhabitants of an abundant frontier. As such, they were subjected to brutality and massacres that resulted in the genocide of American Indians. The reality of these events reduced the population from approximately 15 million American Indians at contact during the seventeenth century to approximately 250,000 by the end of the nineteenth century. The remaining American Indians were eventually placed on reservations and forced to adhere to government policies seeking to assimilate and control them. Blaumer (1972) refers to this as internal colonialism.

One of the problems with enslaving American Indians was that their exposure to the new populations arriving into the American colonies established by the Europeans included diseases that were brought by colonists that nearly decimated the American Indian population (Clarke 1992, as cited in Taylor-Greene & Gabbidon 2012). Historians point out the fact that the first Africans that arrived in America in the early 1600s were not considered slaves. Rather than Black or White, the distinction was Christian or non-Christian. The only kind of slavery at that time consisted of indentured servitude (Taylor-Greene & Gabbidon 2012). Some Africans were explorers (Van Sertima 1976), but the desperate need to produce labor for the growing of labor-intensive crops like tobacco and cotton led to colonial legislation that placed Africans into slavery. This set in motion events that created a heinous system of slavery that lasted until the Emancipation Proclamation in 1863 that ended human bondage for Africans in the United States (Blauner 1972). Although slavery officially ended in America with the Emancipation Proclamation in 1863, the issue of racism persisted throughout reconstruction (1865–1877), and then during the Jim Crow Era (1877–1964), including enactments of Black codes among southern states and lynchings of Blacks by Whites as a method of strongholding, controlling, and suppressing any economic or political agenda promulgated by African Americans (Taylor-Greene & Gabbidon 2012). And it has continued in more contemporary forms like separating the races through segregation in school, housing, labor, accommodations, and in restricting voting access through poll taxes right up into and through the first half of the twentieth century. The vestiges of this dark chapter of American history can still be seen in the twenty-first century in obvious disparities in housing, education, income, and incarceration rates (Carr & Kutty 2008).

Many Whites think the oppression of racism is over but Blacks live with the vestiges of it every day, and these holdovers still continue to present chronic problems in the civic life of the United States in the twenty-first century. The vestiges of slavery and racism continue to adversely affect individuals and communities of color by inhibiting prosperity in almost every aspect of their lives (Constantine 2006; Carr & Kutty 2008). Racism is a continuation of the institution of slavery that was entrenched in American life for several hundred years, and its continued expression reflects institutionalized patterns of White power and social control to subordinate people of color based on their racial or ethnic group. Government policies, such as Affirmative Action and school desegregation, were aimed at addressing institutional racism, but the infection of racism was so ingrained in American life that these policies have done little to change White male domination and control of government institutions, corporations, and media, which unconsciously (and some might even say, unintentionally) gives rise to the perpetuation of prejudice (an expression that affirms bias toward a particular group), discrimination (an expression of bias through exclusionary practices), and stereotypes (a conceptualization and overgeneralization of a particular group that serves to repress members of that particular group) (Allport 1954, 3–4).

What most individuals understand nowadays about racism is overt racism; it is the intentional and disclosed racist action that seek to oppress or harm people of color (Ridley 2005), such as the most recent incident in Jackson, Mississippi, concerning Mr. Daryl Dedmon. Mr. Dedmon went searching for an African American to kill, and finally he saw Mr. James Craig Anderson, whom he beat severely, ran over, and killed for being Black (Griffin 2011). Although this sort of incident is traumatic and was all-too-often practiced during the Jim Crow Era, the most prevalent and dangerous type of racism of the twenty-first century is covert racism. It includes unintentional racist acts that oppress people of color. However, what is most significant is that the oppressors fail to connect with their racist thoughts and feelings, so they tend to deny and negate that they are engaging in racism, and therefore are racist (Sue, 2003, 5–6).

Both overt and covert racism, according to research, have been noted to be painful experiences for people of color; it is traumatic, stressful, stigmatizing, and leads to low self-esteem (Constantine & Sue 2006). However, covert racism when, operationalized in a collective context where individual, institutional, or cultural racism occurs through policies and systematic practices, can be very oppressive towards people of color. It manifests in social, economic, and political disparities, such as educational achievement gaps and disproportionate incarceration rates, and it therefore reinforces and perpetuates the cycle—in fact, oftentimes a downward spiral—of negative treatment and false perceptions.

Despite our society's official policies of separatism, America pushed to have a society that embraced one common culture, "the melting pot," which was imposed by White dominance. The melting pot is a metaphor for a diverse cultural society transitioning into a monolithic cultural society. White leaders called it *e pluribus unum*—"out of the many, one." But the many meant differing White folks uniting around privilege and power, and the one meant whatever those White folks in power said it was. The idea was to extinguish diverse values and norms, and thereby create an America that would assert one way of life for all Americans, regardless of their cultural heritage. But the melting pot ideology was a racist perspective that viewed cultures other than European as inferior; and its implicit assumptions were disseminated through mass media, art, research, and literature primarily to maintain White dominance (Abrahams 1971).

Scholars have argued that the "melting pot" ideology was a failure for anyone who was not defined as "White." One reason is that it failed to recognize that some groups continued to live by separate cultural values within their communities—values that pertained to their family, religious worship, and heritage celebration. Second, race exploitation and oppression (i.e., slavery, genocide, and discrimination) among some groups were so traumatic and ingrained in the social fabric of society that it could not be easily erased (Trusty, Davis, & Looby 2002). Third, the intermingling of racial groups made it possible for each to borrow elements from the other, which makes it questionable whether the melting pot ideology was actually attainable (Abrahams 1971).

The Need for Specialized Counseling Skills When Working with Racial Minorities in Corrections

According to the Bureau of Justice Statistics (2009), there are approximately 7.2 million people on probation, in jail or prison, or on parole. This represents 3.1 percent of all U.S. adults, which is 1 in every 32 adults in the United States (Glaze 2009). However, racial minorities, African Americans in particular, are disproportionately affected (Austin & Irwin 2001). For example, African American men are eight times more likely to be incarcerated than White men, and African American women are six times more likely to be incarcerated than White women. These statistics have led to more than three-quarters of a million African American men incarcerated and one in every 300 African American women incarcerated, compared to 1 in every 1,099 White women (Brewer & Heitzeg 2008).

This phenomenon is polarizing to the civic life of America, and especially in communities of racial minorities, particularly African Americans and Hispanics. The most important reason is that there are 70 percent (5,018,900) of offenders in the criminal justice system that are under the supervision of community corrections (Glaze 2009), and over 2 million of these offenders are African American, and over 400,000 are Hispanic (Shearer & King 2004). An overwhelming number of these offenders end up unemployed or employed in minimum wage service jobs after release, which ultimately impacts families (Truesdale 2011). In this case, counseling becomes very significant as a means to help improve the life chances of offenders involved in the criminal justice system. While counseling has in place specific standards for working with all types of clients (Master 2004), it cannot be denied that the field of counseling (regardless of the institution) incorporates practices and beliefs that are Eurocentric. What are assumed to be neutral standards for all cultural groups are in fact culturally biased standards unconsciously designed to acculturate everyone to the mainstream norm for offender reentry into society. If it does not work for minority populations, no one cares except those minorities because they are the ones to experience the brunt of those policies and practices failures when they recidivate. But those of us who are African American scholars in the field, this imposition is troubling because many people of color are negatively impacted by a system saturated with these ethnocentric practices.

Therefore, probation officers or community counselors who understand multiculturalism and cross-cultural communication must point out the fact that the criminal justice system is Eurocentric, and is therefore just another in a long line of seemingly neutral proxy representations for the oppression of dominant culture over people of color. We simply must change this system and its negative consequences, to save money if for no other reason because it is costly in this day and age to employ programs that do not work, and we must develop sensitivity for working with racial minorities by becoming culturally aware. Scholars in the field of corrections and correctional counseling like myself must point out that the diversity of offenders requires that the treatment provided to them should be individualistic and culture specific (Masters 2004; Shearer & King 2004). Failure to consider racial/ethnic culture can lead to problems with counseling and with unfortunate social, economic and mental health outcomes that we all end up paying for in the end (Masters 2004). If we do not, we will ultimately pay for problems associated with reentry of the offender in the community.

Multicultural Counseling in Corrections

According to Sue and Sue:

> Multicultural counseling and therapy can be defined as both a helping role and process that uses modalities and defines goals consistent with the life experiences and cultural values of clients, recognizes client identities to include individual, group, and universal dimensions, advocates the use of universal and culture specific strategies and roles in the healing process, and balances the importance of individualism and collectivism in the assessment, diagnosis, and treatment of client and client systems (2008, 42).

The historical social construction of race created cross-cultural barriers to building effective relationships between the correctional counselor and the client (Shearer & King 2004). As a result, many racial minorities do not take advantage of counseling services, and when they do they often cancel the service (Parrott 1997, 4; Whaley 2001, 55). One reason is that some racial minorities, African Americans in particular, are more likely than Caucasians to fear mental health treatment. A second reason is that racial minorities mistrust the mental health system because some view this form of treatment as invasive. In order for these relationships to improve, the counselor must have a competency in multicultural counseling (Pedersen 2003, 5). This means that the counselor must seek to reduce racial bias through training in the area of cultural sensitivity. Part of this training is becoming aware of their own assumptions, values, and biases; and understanding the particular worldview of clients that are culturally different; developing appropriate approaches to working with diverse cultures; understanding the clients' life relativistically; and understanding that the perceived symptoms may be a product of the clients' cultural identity and not a clinical pathology (Sue, Arredondo, & McDavis 1992; Dana 1998). The importance of these competencies will generate appropriate responses and successful outcomes. Chung and Bernak (2002) argue that appropriate responses are mirrored in the practice of cultural empathy, including an understanding that cultural diversity exists among differing families and communities within distinctive populations; recognizing that indigenous treatment practices may be more appropriate than that of the dominant culture's; acknowledging the historical and sociopolitical demography of the racial minority client; acknowledging the environmental changes that the clients experience; and empowering clients who feel disadvantaged and devalued.

Training in diversity issues is not a new phenomenon, but since its inception it has spurred resistance because many people reject someone questioning their values or trying to adjust their attitudes about others. Furthermore, if they do not think it is in their best interest or the demand is perceived as an attack on their self-image then they will resist and outcomes will be negative or non-responsive (Karp, Sammour & Hael 2000). In response to resistance, Arrendondo (1999) argues that people can be encouraged to develop multicultural competencies if they are shown how it serves to confront racism and oppression. He mentions that professional competencies in counseling should encompass:

- Knowledge of how a person's culture and heritage affect them personally and professionally
- Knowledge of how oppression, racism, discrimination, and stereotyping affect them personally and professionally
- How their negative and positive reactions toward other racial and ethnic groups may prove detrimental to the counseling relationship
- How poverty, racism, and stereotyping may affect the self-esteem and self-concept of racial and minority clients
- Knowledge of how institutional barriers prevent minorities from using mental health services
- Knowledge of the bias in assessment procedures
- Acting proactively to eliminate biases, prejudices, and discriminatory contents in conducting evaluations and providing interventions
(Arrandondo 1999, 5)

These competencies can be examined using a number of instruments: 1) a Diversity Awareness Assessment Instrument (Tulin 1995), a Multicultural Counseling Knowledge and Awareness Scale (Ponterotto 1997; Wong 2003). Furthermore, the most productive exchange ultimately happens when both the client and the counselor are functioning at a mature level of racial identity. Helms and Cook note:

> The therapist's expression of her or his underlying racial identity statuses influences his or her interaction to the client, and the client's underlying statuses, in turn, influences his or her reactions to the therapists. . . . Each complimentary response to the other person's observable expressions of his or her racial identity . . . constitutes a relationship (1999, 270).

Problems Assessing Racial Minorities in Correctional Counseling

With over seven million people on probation, in jail or prison, or on parole, and when the majority of this population is African American and Hispanic, it is important that correctional counselors do not use a one-size-fits-all approach for working with racial minorities, particularly as it relates to assessments and mental health diagnoses. To this aim, the criminal justice system has the task of identifying offenders' risk and needs and prescribing appropriate case management plans and goals designed to address these risk/need areas (Vose, Cullen, & Smith 2008). The most common assessments in criminal justice are the Level of Service Inventory (LSI) (Andrews 1995) and the Youth Level of Service Inventory (YLS) (Hoge 2002). The LSI is a fifty-four-item instrument that scores ten categories concerning the risk/needs of an adult offender, including criminal history, education/employment, financial, family/marriage, accommodation, leisure/recreation, companions, alcohol/drug problems, emotional/personal, and attitudes/orientation (Andrews 1995). The YLS is a similar instrument that scores risk/needs of a youth offender, including prior and current offenses/dispositions, family circumstances/parenting, education/employment, peer relations, substance abuse, leisure/recreation, personality/behavior, and attitudes/orientation (Hoge & Andrews 2002).

Despite the fact that these LSI and YLS have been widely used, scholars have raised concerns pertaining to the accuracy of the assessment outcomes when they are applied to racial minorities (Smykla 1986, 331). Research examining this issue shows that the correctional counselor would be in error if he or she too simply stated whether an instrument is biased or not. It must examine the following: the behavior that is being used to predict behavior; the cut-off scores used for the analysis; the appropriate outcome measures; and the purpose of the instrument. To this aim, results have shown that African Americans are more likely to be over-classified for program outcomes than Caucasians or Hispanics. When adjustments were made to the cut-off score, African Americans were more likely to be under-classified when predicting disciplinary incidents. This finding is significant, as cut-off scores are used to determine how an offender will be classified under security and supervision (Whiteacre 2006), which may arguably produce a biased, negative reflection on the overwhelming number of African Americans under community corrections. According to Whiteacre (2006), each facility must decide the appropriate cut-off score for that specific facility, but the problem is imposed when the administrator does not conduct the follow-up assessments to ensure the validity of the instrument for their population. Furthermore, Onifade et al. (2008) and Jung and Rawana (1999) note that beyond the cutoff scores, practitioners in assessing racial minorities fail to examine ecological variables, such as neighborhood, community policing, and gender.

Misdiagnosis of Racial Minorities

According to Navasky and O'Connor (2005), there are approximately 500,000 inmates diagnosed with mental illness, but it is unclear as to how many are racial minorities. Feisthamel and Schwartz (2009) note that there are approximately three hundred mental disorders recognized in the Diagnostic and Statistical Manual of Mental Disorders, and African Americans have been shown to have more harmful diagnoses than White Americans. For example, research has shown that African Americans who revealed suspiciousness and unusual perceptual experiences were diagnosed more often as having schizophrenia than other groups (Flaskerud & Hu 1992, 48). Fabrega (1996) examined the proportionality of mood disorders and psychotic disorders among African Americans and found that they were more often diagnosed with psychotic disorders than mood disorders. Lawson, Hepler, Holladay, and Cuffel (1994) found similar results, but the most current research results revealed more specific psychotic disorders, indicating that African Americans were more often diagnosed with schizophrenia (Whaley 2004; Foulks 2004; Neighbors, Trierweiler, Ford, & Mufoff 2003, 48).

Harold Neighbors (1997) impacted the mental health profession by arguing that many of the African Americans who were diagnosed with harmful disorders (schizophrenia namely) were misdiagnosed. Feisthamel and Schwartz (2009) note that there are many reasons why racial minorities may be misdiagnosed with various mental disorders. First, some diagnoses are racially biased, which means that some clinicians have made groundless judgments about a client based on the individual's race, which may lead to mistakes in treatment and referral decisions (Snowden 2003). Second, some bias resides in the clinician's attitudes and behaviors, the service delivery process, and intervention (Dana 2002). Third, clinicians have perceptions or stereotypes of clients, particularly African Americans, that interfere with accurate diagnosis, including biased judgments on African Americans' inabilities in articulation, competency, and sophistication (Abreu 1999; Geller 1988), or inaccurate assessment of cultural information, which can be influenced by standardized clinical training combined with a lack of cultural awareness (Neighbors, Trierweiler, Ford, & Muroff 2003). For example, the "blunted affect" is a mental health term used to describe the lack of emotional reactivity by an individual; it is a failure to express feelings either verbally or non-verbally. This affect is often influenced by cultural differences, and it is often misdiagnosed as schizophrenia, particularly among African Americans (Neighbors, Trierweiler, Ford, & Muroff 2003). Fourth, many non-African American clinicians do not have an intimate understanding of the social conditions prevalent in the communities of racial minorities, and disregard situational information in exploring their client's mental health (Trierweiler, Muroff, Jackson, Neighbors, & Munday 2005). Based on these results, the code of ethics was developed to prevent bias in counseling and misdiagnoses of racial minorities. For counselors, it articulates expectations for cultural competence (i.e., awareness, knowledge, and skills) in delivering direct and indirect services when working with diverse groups (Cartwright & Fleming 2010).

CONCLUSION

The need for correctional counselors to be culturally aware has tremendous implications because of the numerical representation of racial minority groups in the correctional system and their high rates of recidivism. This article was an attempt to briefly explain how the socially constructed phenomena of race and race ideologies tend to determine how we treat and address the needs of the racial minority population. If systematic oppression and racist ideologies inform our work with the racial minority population in our correctional institutions, then the disproportionate punishment for minorities will continue. And this is simply unacceptable in the twenty-first century. The correctional system, particularly community corrections, needs to address professional preparation for working effectively with offenders of racial minorities, as well as examining tools used to assess and diagnose these same individuals.

REFERENCES

Abrahams, R. (1971). "Cultural differences and the melting pot ideology." *Educational Leadership.* Retrieved January 9, 2012, from *http://www.ascd.org/ASCD/pdf/journals/ed_lead/el197111_abrahams.pdf.*

Abreu, J. (1999). "Conscious and non-conscious African American stereotypes: Impact on first impression and diagnostic ratings by therapists." *Journal of Consulting and Clinical Psychology* 67 (3): 387–393.

Allport, G. W. (1954). "The nature of prejudice." In *Addressing racism: Facilitating cultural competence in mental health and educational settings,* eds. Madonna Constantine and Derald Wing Sue, pp. 3–4. Hoboken: Wiley.

Andrews, D.A., Bonta, J. (1995). *LSI-R the level of service inventory revised user's manual.* North Tonawanda, NY: Multi-Health Systems Inc.

Arrendondo, P. (1999). Multicultural counseling competencies as Tools to address oppression and racism. *Journal of Counseling and Development,* 77, (1), 102.

Austin, J. & J. Irwin. (2001). *It's about time: America's imprisonment binge,* 3rd ed. Belmont: Wadsworth.

Blauner, R. (1972). Racial oppression in America. New York: Harper.

Brewer R., & N. Heitzeg. (2008). "The Racialization of crime and punishment: Criminal justice, color-blind racism, and the political economy of the prison industrial complex." *American Behavioral Scientist* 51 (5): 625.

Carr, J. N., & N. Kutty. (2008). *Segregation: The rising costs for America.* New York: Routledge.

Cartwright, B., & C. Fleming. (2010). "Multicultural and diversity considerations in the new code of professional ethics for rehabilitation counselors." *Journal of Applied Rehabilitation Counseling* 41 (2): 20–24.

Cintron, M. & W. Lee. (2002). "Bilingual workforce needs in Texas community supervision and corrections departments." Survey results, Texas Probation, 7 (1): 4–7.

Chung, R. & F. Bernak. (2002). "The relationship of culture and empathy in cross-cultural counseling." In Multicultural competencies in probation: Issues and challenges, eds. R. Shearer & P. King (2004). *Federal Probation* 68 (1): 3.

Clarke, H. J. (1992). Christopher Columbus and the Afrikan holocaust. In *Race and Crime,* eds. Helen Taylor-Greene & Shaun Gabbidon, pp. 5–6. Los Angeles: Sage.

Constantine, M., & S. Wing. (Eds.). (2006). *Addressing racism: Facilitating cultural competence in mental health and educational settings.* Hoboken: Wiley.

Cox, O. (2000). "Race Relations." In *Theories of Race and Racism,* 2nd ed., eds. Les Back & John Solomos, pp. 75–78. New York: Routledge.

Dana, R. (1998). *Understanding cultural identity in intervention and assessment.* Thousand Oaks: Sage.

Dana, R. (2002). "Mental health services for African Americans: A cultural/racial perspective, cultural diversity and ethnic minority." *Psychology* 8: 3–18.

Fabrega, H. (1996). Cultural and historical foundations of psychiatric diagnosis. In J. E. Mezzich, A. Kleinman, H. Fabrega, & D. L. Parron (Eds.), *Culture and psychiatric diagnosis: A DSM–IV perspective* (pp. 3–14). Washington, DC: American Psychiatric Press.

Feisthamel, K., & R. Schwartz. (2009). "Differences in mental health counselors' diagnoses based on client race: An investigation of adjustment, childhood, and substance-related disorders." *Journal of Mental Health Counseling* 31 (1): 47–59.

Flaskerud, J. H., & L. Hu, (1992). Relationship of ethnicity to psychiatry diagnosis. *Journal of Nervous and Mental Disease, 180,* 296–303.

Foulks, E. F. (2004). Cultural variables in psychiatry. *Psychiatric Times, 21.* April 15.

Geller, J. D. (1988). Racial bias in the evaluation of patients for psychotherapy. In L. D.

Glaze, L. (2009). *Correctional population in the United States, 2009.* Bureau of Justice Statistics Bulletin. U.S. Department of Justice, Office of Justice Programs, Bureau of Justice Statistics. (Accessed January 9, 2012 from *http://bjs.ojp.usdoj.gov/content/pub/pdf/cpus09.pdf*)

Comas-Diaz & E. E. H. Griffith (Eds.), *Clinical guidelines in cross-cultural mental health* (pp. 112–134). New York:Wiley.

Griffin, D. (2011). "Mississippi burning." *CNN.com.* (Accessed January 9, 2012, from *http://cnnpresents.blogs.cnn.com/category/james-craig-anderson/*)

Harrell, S. P . (2000). "A multidimensional conceptualization of race-related stress: Implications for the well-being of people of color." In *Addressing racism: Facilitating cultural competence in mental health and educational settings,* eds. Madonna Constantine & Derald Wing Sue, p. 5. Hoboken: Wiley.

Hartman, C. (2011). "Muslim Americans experience a mix bag." *The Huffington Post.* (Accessed January 9, 2012, from *http://www.huffingtonpost.com/2011/08/30/american-muslim-views-of-terror-policies_n_942028.html*)

Helms, J. E., & Cook, D. A. (1999). Using race and culture in counseling and psychotherapy: Theory and practice. Needham Heights, MA: Allyn & Bacon.

Hoge, R. D., Andrews, D. A., & Leschied, A. (2002). *Youth Level of Service/Case Management Inventory: YLS/CMI manual.* Toronto, Canada: Multi-Health Systems.

Jones, J. M. (1997). "Prejudice and racism." In *Addressing racism: Facilitating cultural competence in mental health and educational settings,* eds. Madonna Constantine & Derald Wing Sue, p. 5. Hoboken: Wiley.

Jung, S., & E. Rawana. (1999). "Risk and need assessment of juvenile offenders." *Criminal Justice and Behavior* 26 (1): 69–89.

Karp, H., H. Sammour, & Y. Hael. (2000). "Workforce diversity: Choices in diversity training programs and dealing with resistance to diversity." *College Student Journal* 34 (3): 18.

Lawson, W. B., N. Hepler, J. Holladay, & B. Cuffel. (1994). "Race as a factor in inpatient and outpatient admissions and diagnosis." In Differences in mental health counselors' diagnoses based on client race: An investigation of adjustment, childhood, and substance-related disorders, eds. K. Feisthamel & R. Schwartz (2009). *Journal of Mental Health Counseling* 31 (1): 48.

Lopez, I. (1995). "The social construction of race." In *Critical Race Theory,* eds. Richard Delgado, pp.192–199. Philadelphia: Temple.

Masters, R. (2004). *Counseling Criminal Justice Offenders,* 2nd ed. Thousand Oaks: Sage.

Nasser, H. (2010). Minority births drive growth in U.S. diversity. *USA Today,* June 22.

Navasky, M., & K. O'Connor. (2005). *The New Asylums.* PBS.org. (Accessed from *http://www.pbs.org/wgbh/pages/frontline/shows/asylums*)

Neighbors, H. (1997). "The Misdiagnosis of Mental Disorder in African Americans." (Accessed January 9, 2012, from *http://www.rcgd.isr.umich.edu/prba/perspectives/winter1997/hneighbors.pdf*)

Neighbors, H., S. Trierweiler, B. Ford, & J. Muroff. (2003). "Racial differences in DSM diagnosis using a semi-structured instrument: The importance of clinical judgment in the diagnosis of African Americans." *Journal of Health and Social Behavior* 43: 237–256.

Onifade, E., W. Davidson, C. Campbell, G. Turke, J. Malinowski, & K. Turner. (2008). Predicting recidivism in probationers with the youth level of service case management inventory. *Criminal Justice and Behavior* 35 (4): 474–483.

Parrott, L. (1997). "Counseling and psychotherapy." In Multicultural competencies in probation: Issues and challenges, eds. R. Shearer & P. King (2004). *Federal Probation* 68 (1): 3.

Pedersen, P. (2003). "Increasing the cultural awareness, knowledge, and skills of culture-centered counselors." In Multicultural competencies in probation: Issues and challenges, eds. R. Shearer & P. King (2004). *Federal Probation* 68 (1): 5.

Ponterotto, J. G. (1997). "A multicultural counseling knowledge and awareness scale." In Multicultural competencies in probation: Issues and challenges, eds. R. Shearer & P. King (2004). New York: Fordham University.

Ridley, C. (2005). "Overcoming unintentional racism in counseling and therapy." In *Addressing racism: Facilitating cultural competence in mental health and educational settings,* eds. Madonna Constantine & Derald Wing Sue, p. 5. Hoboken: Wiley.

Ropers, R. H., & D. J. Pence. (1995). "American prejudice: With liberty and justice for some." In *Multicultural Counseling: Context, theory, practice, and competence,* eds. J. Trusty, E. Looby & D. Sandhu. New York: Nova Science.

Shearer, R. & King, P. (2004). Multicultural competencies in probation: Issues and challenges. *Federal Probation,* 68 (1): 3–9.

Smykla, J. (1986). Critique concerning prediction in probation and parole: Some alternative suggestions. In Kevin Whiteacre (2006). Testing the level of service inventory-revised for racial/ethnic bias. *Criminal Justice* 17 (3): 331.

Sue, D. W. (2003). "Overcoming our racism: The journey to liberation." In *Addressing racism: Facilitating cultural competence in mental health and educational settings,* eds. Madonna Constantine & Derald Wing Sue, pp. 5–6. Hoboken: Wiley.

Sue, D., and D. Sue (2008). *Counseling the culturally diverse: Theory and practice,* 5th ed. Hoboken: Wiley, p. 42.

Taylor-Greene, H. & S. Gabbidon. (2012). *Race and crime.* Los Angeles: Sage.

Todorov, T. (2000). "Race and racism." In *Theories of race and racism,* eds. Les Back and John Solomos, p. 69. East Sussex, UK: Psychology Press.

Trierweiler, S., J. Muroff, J. Jackson, H. Neighbors, & C. Munday. (2005). "Clinician race, situational attributions, and diagnoses of mood versus schizophrenia disorders. Cultural diversity and ethnic minority." *Psychology* 11 (4): 351–364.

Truesdale, S., K. Darboe, & S. Leonard. (2011). *The impact of employment opportunities on the social reintegration of ex-offenders: A case study on twelve employment agencies in Minnesota.* Manuscript submitted for publication.

Trusty, J., E. Looby, & D. Sandhu. (Eds.) (2002). *Multicultural counseling: Context, theory and practice, and competence.* Hunington: Nova Science.

Tulin, D. (1995). "Diversity awareness assessment." In Multicultural competencies in probation: Issues and challenges, eds. Shearer R. and P. King (2004). *Federal Probation* 68 (1): 7.

U.S. Census Bureau, 2010. "U.S. census bureau releases new race and population data based on findings from 2010 census." (Accessed January 9, 2012, from *http://www.commerce.gov/blog/2011/03/24/us-census-bureau-releases-new-race-and-population-data-based-findings-2010-census*)

Vose, B., F. Cullen, & P. Smith. (2008). "The empirical status of the level of service inventory." *Federal Probation* 72 (3), 22–29.

Whaley, A. (2001). Cultural mistrust and mental health services for African Americans: A review and meta-analysis. In Differences in mental health counselors' diagnoses based on client race: An investigation of adjustment, childhood, and substance-related disorders, eds. K. Feisthamel & R. Schwartz (2009). *Journal of Mental Health Counseling* 31 (1): 55.

Whaley, A. (2004). "A two-stage method for the study of cultural bias in the diagnosis of schizophrenia in African Americans." *Journal of Black Psychology* 30(2): 167–186.

Whiteacre, K. (2006). "Testing the level of service inventory-revised for racial/ethnic bias." *Criminal Justice* 17 (3): 330–342.

Wong, V. S. (2003). "Evaluation of sociocultural competency training in enhancing self-efficiency among immigrant and Canadian-born health sciences trainees." In Multicultural competencies in probation: Issues and challenges, eds. Shearer R. and P. King (2004). *Federal Probation* 68 (1): 6.

Counseling the Minority Male Deviant

James Burnett

Introduction

It is important to define the term *deviant* as a starting point. Despite the negative connotations, it merely means a deviation from the norm, or simply different than what is accepted as the status quo. Howard Becker in *Outsiders: Studies in the Sociology of Deviance (1991)* states:

> Social rules define situations and the kinds of behavior appropriate to them . . . one who cannot be trusted to live by the rules agreed on by the group is regarded as an outsider . . . outsiders refer to those people who are judged by others to be deviant and thus to stand outside the circle of 'normal' members of the group. (pp. 1, 15)

Anthony Lemelle Jr. in *Black Male Deviance* (1997) says:

> The Black Male Problem has become so monumental and threatening to the institutional and cultural order in the United States that the positivistic, humanistic, pragmatic, and even phenomenological approaches to the problem of black male "deviance" has proved to be inadequate. (p. 1)

Assisting minority males to become productive members of society is an important goal. This is especially true with the election of our nation's first Black President. President Obama has raised the bar for the norm of the Black male, and it is up to those who advocate, model, and serve minority males to empower them to meet the new standards, opportunities, and expectations. It is in the deviation from this standard that minority males will find the same old stereotypes, low expectations, and more of the same outcomes (addiction, criminality, abuse, prison, and death). Advocates must learn to move them toward continuous acceptance of this new norm and thereby help break the cycle of deviation.

Breaking this cycle involves a change in thinking, perception, ideas, notions, and expectations. The minority male deviant must move beyond the invisible force field of constraints and rules and develop an identity that would not be expected in usual minority male deviant behavior and thinking. This involves moving from mainstream expectations to a personal pattern that connects him with his personal gifts and talents.

In the previous two articles in the reader, Dr. Truesdale Moore speaks to the significance of focusing on cross-cultural awareness and sensitivity when counseling the minority person in the correctional system. In this article, I draw from personal experience to discuss strategies to assist the minority male deviant in finding his inner self and making that the focus of his life rather than simply reacting to situational circumstances in his life. In the third article of this series, Dr. Williams discusses how leisure can be used to integrate the minority male deviant into society.

In this article, I will discuss five strategies that represent a rite of passage that can assist the minority male deviant in his personal growth process: Initiation, Sacred Space, The Hero's Journey, Individuation, and the Creative Process. These strategies can help the minority male deviant to transcend the deviant label by getting in touch with his inner self, which he can then develop and use as a compass to guide and direct his life so that he can become a productive member of society.

The Problem

I believe that all men share a certain level of dysfunction, but my past experiences as a minority male deviant have led me to believe that our modern cultural reality has contributed in great part to a social, ethnic, and cultural phenomenon that is oftentimes dysfunctional. Modern society creates disconnectedness that results in anomie, leaving the individual floundering for a purpose and an identity, especially the minority individual who is already at risk due to the oftentimes overwhelming and powerful forces of racism and institutional discrimination. This dysfunction has manifested itself in a myriad of problems seen in American society today among minority males. When I reflect on my life as a minority male deviant (prior to my initiation into manhood), I remember being confronted with rough living, frustration, poverty, and dysfunction all around me. Our world was full of violence, death, anger, and disillusionment. All one has to do is turn on the news to see the images of apathy, drugs, gangs, violence, and stereotypes depicting that failure is an inescapable element of the destiny of the hopeless minority male.

One way to survive in the face of a world that oftentimes seems uncaring and cruel, one where there are few employment opportunities for the minority male, is to become involved in the underground economy, usually selling drugs, making book and running numbers in illegal gambling, pimping, or some other form of crime. Money buys attention and respect in our community, but trying to get it is a risky venture. This is so much so that the experience of being locked up is an inevitable part of growing up and is often seen as a badge of merit.

When I was growing up, the hardworking men in my community did not provide a strong example for us males. We looked up to the hustlers, pimps, players, and dealers. Given that, it is not irrational that we made decisions that we later regretted. One of the most mistaken decisions I ever made, with devastating consequences, was getting involved in "street capitalism." The opportunity to sell drugs and hustle was just too enticing, and it distorted my aspirations and stunted my growth as a man. Later, though, the process of my initiation into masculinity helped me grow and to break the cycle of self-destruction. I began a personal journey that has helped me become more than just a minority male deviant, even though that is still part of who I am because it is a part of my past. It is just that, now, I own that and it no longer owns me. And I believe this gives me a unique insight into the growth process I am advocating in this paper because it is a time-tested method that has actually worked for many others and me over the generations.

Initiation

In going through my (Dr. Burnett) initiation process, I experienced an awakening to my true self, my identity, my purpose in life, my calling, and my destiny. If a man knows his vocation—his work or his calling—this can empower him and help direct his actions, his drives, his motives, and his energy throughout his life. He can then have a purpose and make a difference. It is as if there is then a map and a compass deeply embedded in him, with guideposts leading him down his personal journey towards his life goals.

According to James Hillman (1997) in the audio tape, *Character and Destiny,* if left on his own, the minority male deviant will not go where he needs to go to find out what is going on within himself. And without that, he will never truly be a man. Hillman supports helping the male go deep within himself to find his inner tiger. Hillman tells the story, "A tiger is born just as its mother is killed by some hunters and wanders off and is raised by some goats for years. They take it in because it is a little one, and they nourish it and it grows up among the goats doing what they do. Later on, a huge tiger descends on the goats and begins to eat them and notices the small tiger and asks it, "Why are you acting like a goat?" The little tiger is scared to death and does not know what to say and cannot answer. So the big tiger takes it to a lake and shows it its reflection, and the little one notices that he looks just like the big tiger, only smaller. The big one says, "You're a tiger, you're not supposed to eat grass and act like a goat. You're supposed to act like a tiger, rip throats, drink blood, and eat flesh." And it is thus that the little tiger realizes his true calling through an act of self-reflection and self-realization, having an elder role model to show him the way. He and the big tiger then go around together until it is time for him to be on his own and make his own way in life. In this same vein, those of us who have been through it can now help minority male deviants to focus on self-reflection and self-realization as a means to initiating them into manhood.

Michael Meade (2007) described the initiation process in *Initiation and the Soul: The Sacred and the Profane.* In summary, Meade said that initiation is the intentional creation of circumstances that cause a person to connect more deeply to what is already inside him. Meade believes that initiation involves transforming boy energies into man energies by going from a fragmented identity to a consolidated, structured identity. According to Meade, tribal societies had ritual processes that enabled boys to achieve maturity, but our culture has pseudo rituals like the military and gangs that initiate boys into dysfunctional, false masculinity, which does not produce real men. What these processes produce are males that are self-centered (rather than self-actualized), hostile, violent, and bent on the domination of others. What minority male deviants need is detachment from their old ways of the boy ego so that the new man can emerge.

In initiation, there are several characteristics. There is a separation from the old habits, and a new journey is taken up where the male does not recognize who he is or what is going on. The male accepts that there is an unknown outcome even though he feels vulnerable. In an initiated place, there is no turning back, others are in control and set the limits, emotions are overwhelming, imagination is fully activated, and the male recognizes that he has a wound that must be dealt with. Additionally, there are signs that the male is either in initiation or not in it. After initiation, something within the male has changed forever and things do not go back to the way they were. There is a scar or mark that represents evidence of the change. The male is more alive and involved in life than before. When trouble or danger comes, the male can go back to the initiated place. In initiation, power and control is not important but subordination and submission to a new masculine personality marked by calm compassion and clarity of vision is valued.

Robert Moore (1991), in *King, Warrior, Magician and Lover,* highlights seven stages of initiation. In these stages, the initiate moves from Unconscious Incompetence (does not even realize that he is not a man), to Conscious Incompetence (realization that he is missing something), to Conscious Competence (learning), to Unconscious Competence (effortless manhood). In stage one, the male does not know what he lacks, but he has a vague sense of emptiness, which moves him toward a quest to manhood. The second stage is a sort of idealized transference in that whatever blessings he did not receive from his family, he idealizes in a mentor and projects onto the mentor since he does not have it. The male experiences what he has been looking for in envy because he does not realize that it is also in him. However, in stage three, if the mentor is mature enough, he can manage to allow the electricity to flow between him and the initiate so that the initiate can discover the power within himself. In stage four, the mentor helps the initiate to take baby steps by forming an apprenticeship to develop what is missing. In stage five, the initiate is getting to be a journeyman. He is not ready to teach or be a mentor, but he is getting good and ready to be a sponsor. In stage six, he is a master. His flow is optimum, and he has integrated all that it takes to be a man. In the seventh stage, he is a steward and has figured out how he will serve humankind.

According to Hillman, Meade, and Some (1992), in *Images of Initiation,* the easiest way to end a culture is to have uninitiated males who do not love life become men. Mentoring minority males involves watering the seed that is planted within them and setting them on their path to growth. Specifically, the mentor might help the male with his father issues, help him deal with his grievances, help him get over his complexes, and give him outside confirmation and blessing. Minority males can work at sharpening the skills they have, but it takes the presence of a mentor working with them, telling them they did a good job, helping them to expand their field of visibility on their journey toward manhood to gain the ability to use those skills. Having someone who has already journeyed on this path and who has the desire to teach, share, and exchange fertile ideas is what mentoring is about. A mentor gives small tasks that may be difficult for the initiate to digest but tasks are given with passion.

Hillman et al. tells about the original mentor in the story *The Odyssey.* This mentor worked with Telemachus while his father Odysseus was away. The authors say that mentoring involves the kind of instruction that is beyond skill and an awareness of how to do things or make things happen. The authors also say that initiation is ongoing and that circumstances will often throw men back into the initiatory experiences, but as the mentor and not a novitiate. Another way to assist the minority male deviant is sacred space.

Sacred Space

In order to help the minority male deviant through transformation from male to man, in a sense he must be taken from an acorn to an oak tree (i.e., a process of development of self-growth). According to Fritz Kunkel (1984), this comes from suffering, the recognition of a power greater than himself, and coming to care for someone other than he. In the context that I am using sacred space, it has at its core a journey within oneself in the context of a path to manhood. As mentioned in the initiation discussion, the minority male deviant needs to separate himself to an unknown place for an unknown reason or outcome, and then submit his ego to the change process. There are three processes that can help the minority male deviant: Individuation, the Hero's Journey, and the Creative process.

The Hero's Journey

According to Joseph Campbell (1968) in *The Hero with a Thousand Faces,* during the hero's journey, it becomes apparent to the minority male deviant that if he wants to stay on a positive, growth-oriented track, he has to make a fundamental shift in how he lives life. According to Jean Shinoda Bolen (1989), in *Gods in Every Man,* the male who follows the heroic principle of integrity and faith will receive help through intuition, a dream, a creative solution, an instinctual gut level response, or a change in attitude that arises to aid his situation. Charles DuBois said that the important thing is that the male must be able at any moment to sacrifice what he is for what he could become (Keen 1989).

Once the minority male deviant decides to follow his bliss, he sets off on a track that has been there for him all the while, waiting. He is then able to get a glimpse of the life he should have been living and then he meets people who open the doors and help him to walk through them. Then, when he is ready for the Hero's Journey, he goes through six phases:

1. Innocence—During the beginning phase, he is comfortable with his life. He is relatively naïve and happy with the dysfunction in his life (drug dealing, gang banging, partying, etc.)

2. Call to adventure—Something disrupts his familiar patterns and challenges him, and within him develops a secret yearning to grow and change. He answers the call and leaps into the unknown.

3. Initiation—Spoken to in detail previously.

4. Allies—In moment of crises, strength and help will be provided. When most needed, he meets some very wise people who help him realize his breakthrough.

5. Breakthrough—There comes a time when he recognizes a deepening understanding that signals the crossing out of the world of deviancy and into the free world.

6. Celebration—In this phase the minority male deviant develops a new status quo for himself and begins to contribute to the world around him. He now has gifts and a newfound wisdom and is acknowledged as wiser, deeper and, not the same person he was before. This phase paves the way for the Individuation Process.

Individuation Process

According to Fritz Kunkel (1984) in *Fritz Kunkel: Selected Writings,* individuation is a process of becoming yourself and finding the work that you were placed on this earth to achieve. Individuation is, in a nutshell, searching for the meaning in life. It is a process by which the personality of a person is built up and the persona—a mask used to hide the person's true nature and to make a particular impression on the surrounding environment—is detached. It is based on an inner urge to find and obtain truth using a step-by-step process by diving deep into the core of the personality of the person. This involves coming to a self-understanding of aspects of the personality and increasing awareness of the aspects that were previously unconscious and unknown. Individuation helps the minority male deviant change from an egocentric person to a person who seeks harmonious leisure, meaning, and wholeness. The basic idea is that the minority male deviant seeks to fulfill his urge toward growth through a process of development.

It is as if the minority male deviant has to have a wilderness type of experience where he is in exile suffering desperate straits without intercession. It is like a journey through an unfamiliar environment that is frightening and painful where he is plunged into circumstances of sickness, or a breakdown that is designed by life to change his attitude. The minority male deviant will come out of this experience a different person than when he entered into it. The goal is for him to relinquish control from the egocentric part of him that has been in charge and things will then come together and have meaning.

The Creative Process

According to Sam Keen (1989), in *Your Mythic Journey,* the moment a minority male deviant commits himself to positive growth, providence moves in as well. He begins to operate from his soul. The realization of having more potential than he has previously shown in his life causes him to live from the most complete part of who he is. There are six stages in the creative process:

1. Preparation—Helping the minority male deviant gather information to do what he must to catch hold of his initial vision of creative possibilities.

2. Frustration—As he begins to experience unanticipated challenges he may temporarily lose sight of his goals. This stage can be a catalyst that forces him to find alternative approaches to his life and to discover talents and strengths he did not know he had. Frustration is a necessary part of the creative process.

3. Incubation—The minority male deviant begins to experience creative insight that was percolating in the back of his mind.

4. Strategizing—He then develops spiritual strategies for dealing with the challenges of his life. He does not sit passively waiting for inspiration but instead invites a breakthrough in his new life.

5. Illumination—Every so often, the minority male deviant has an "aha" experience that helped him to meet his challenges.

6. Verification—In this stage, he tests out his ideas and makes them real by applying them to his new life. He notes the reaction of others. He realizes that he has a newfound wisdom and a fresh start.

This process is specific to each person as they go through it. The minority male deviant must have faith in his creativity as it helps him to root out the voice of his inner critic. Once this is accomplished, he is able to be more observant and ask questions when needed. This also helps him to suspend a problem, which usually plagues him throughout his life: negative judgment. This causes him to open his self to unexpected insights and unknown possibilities. Awareness is a newfound skill that comes with creativity. It is important to practice precise observation by noticing what is happening around him and what the situation demands of him. This will allow him to notice clues on how to proceed and to really get at what is going on around him.

CONCLUSION

There are various methods to assist the minority male deviant, but I am speaking to the strategies my mentors used to help me become the man I am today. My mentors took me on a journey toward self-development and helped to remove the blocks to my creative energy and growth to become the man I was meant to be. In the same way, those who work with the minority male deviant can help him to catch a glimpse of life beyond his past misdeeds, help him to take responsibility for self-improvement, help guide him through his desire to make amends to those he has hurt, and to eradicate that within him which stands in his way of rising above his circumstances to tap into his potential and then connect with a new consciousness and adapt a mature way of relating to the world.

Those who work with the minority male deviant can help him get rid of the poisons of ego inflation, egocentricity, selfish behavior, and blind self-serving ambition. This is done by giving him strong medicine to cure all within him that is not fit to exist by helping him to endure pain, crises, anxiety, self-pity, and despair, and to purge him of these things by shattering their effects. In the end, the minority male deviant can come to terms with himself as a mature adult who is emotionally honest, who makes meaning out of his life by listening to his deep instinctual inner voice.

I gave myself wholeheartedly to the tasks that came my way on this journey by accomplishing the most that I could, doing the best job possible in every situation no matter how lowly it was, and by making the best of what came my way. I brought my actions and attitude in line with my inner reality, pursuing inner development, listening to my inner voice in accordance with what I learned to be my gifts and calling. And with the right mentoring and guidance, the minority male deviant of today can accomplish this also.

REFERENCES

Becker, Howard Saul. (1991). *Outsiders: studies in the sociology of deviance*. New York: Free Press.

Bolen, Jean Shinola. (1989). *Gods in Every Man*. New York: Harper Collins.

Campbell, Joseph. (1968). *The hero with a thousand faces*. Princeton, NJ: Princeton University Press.

Hillman, James, & Michael Meade. (1997). *Character and Destiny*. Pacific Grove, CA: Oral Tradition Archives.

Hillman, James, Michael Meade, & Some Malidome. (1992). *Images of Initiation.* Pacific Grove, CA: Oral Tradition Archives.

Keen, Sam, & Anne Valley Fox. (1989). *Your mythic journey: finding meaning in your life through writing and storytelling.* New York: St. Martin's Press.

Kunkel, Fritz, & John A. Sanford. (1984). *Selected Writings.* New York: Paulist Press.

Lemelle, Anthony J. (1997). *Black Male Deviance.* Westport CT: Prager.

Meade, Michael. (2007). *Initiation and the soul the sacred and the profane.* Seattle: Mosaic.

Moore, Robert L., & Douglass Gillette. (1991). *King, warrior, magician, lover: rediscovering the archetypes of the mature masculine.* San Francisco: Harper.

How Can Leisure Be Used to Integrate Young, Minority Offenders into Society?

D. J. Williams

Introduction

In this article, I introduce how leisure may be used to successfully integrate young, minority male offenders into society. Leisure is a common and important human need, yet its significance to human lives often gets overlooked in societies dominated by work and career. Nevertheless, an individual's specific leisure preferences and pursuits can be important personal strengths that counselors can utilize to help clients live crime free. I will introduce leisure as a field of study, consider how leisure is conceptualized, note the benefits of leisure, and comment specifically on how leisure may be utilized to facilitate crime-free living.

Leisure as a Field of Study

Leisure as a field of study is often called "leisure sciences" across North America, or "leisure studies" in Europe, Australia, and New Zealand. Leisure scientists are interested in studying people's lifestyles and what people do outside of their work time. The field of leisure has its roots in sociology and social psychology, and it can overlap with several other disciplines, including public health and health sciences, anthropology, social work, and criminology. Despite the fact that leisure scientists often study "things that are fun," they utilize the same research methods common to other academic fields. Researchers are discovering that a leisure perspective potentially can be very useful in understanding and addressing important social issues, including issues involving crime and deviance (Williams 2006; Williams and Walker 2006).

What is Leisure?

Most people think of leisure as being simple free time. While free time certainly fits within a broad leisure science framework, the specific term *leisure* refers to something beyond free time. Scholars agree that what counts as legitimate leisure experience must be freely chosen (autonomous) by the person who engages in it, and leisure is intrinsically motivated (Mannell and Kleiber 1997). In other words, people engage in leisure for its own sake and not for some external reason. Some professionals think of leisure in terms of time, others conceptualize it as activity, and still others think of leisure as inner psychological experience. Thus, while leisure has the essential property of being autonomous and performed for intrinsic reasons, it remains somewhat difficult to define precisely. Still, leisure tends to be associated with a number of positive psychological states, such as pleasure or enjoyment, relaxation, excitement, self-expression, and happiness (Mannell and Kleiber 1997).

Various forms of leisure can range from being casual and spontaneous to those requiring considerable training and skill development, such as mountain climbing or parachuting (Stebbin 2001). Hiking, swimming, sports, visiting a museum or art gallery, playing cards, board games, riding motorcycles, art, dancing, cooking, gardening, and bird watching are all potential forms of leisure. Specific leisure activities may be grouped into categories, such as mass media forms (i.e., reading magazines, going to movies), cultural events, sports activities (as participant or spectator), outdoor activities, social activities (i.e., parties, entertaining, dating, games), and hobbies (Ragheb 1980). The possibilities for leisure seem endless.

Common Therapeutic Benefits of Leisure

It is important for people to have frequent meaningful and enjoyable experiences; thus leisure is an important aspect of a person's overall life. Researchers have documented a wide variety of physical, psychological, and sociocultural health benefits associated with regular, active leisure experiences. Reviews of research studies suggest that leisure participation helps prevent disease and cope with stress (Caldwell 2005; Mannell 2007). Researchers have reported that leisure can bring cardiovascular benefits, control and prevention of diabetes, weight control, improved immune function, neuropsychological improvements, and better overall quality of life (Driver and Bruns 1999). Because leisure, by definition, is freely chosen and intrinsically motivated (people already want to engage in it), leisure becomes an important tool in promoting personal health and well-being.

Leisure and Deviance: Identifying Leisure and Crime Relationships

Deviant leisure refers to leisure practices that are outside of the norms of a society and can be criminal or noncriminal (Williams and Walker 2006). Crime that is committed for fun and thrills can be viewed as deviant leisure. For example, some young male offenders explain that stealing cars provides a source of excitement, utilizes specific skills in order to pull off the theft, and helps them socially connect with deviant friends. Given these characteristics of the criminal episode, it is relatively easy to begin to understand the nature of the theft from a leisure perspective. Leisure adds an additional lens with which to view certain types of deviant behavior.

It is also important to consider how "normal" leisure may be embedded in some criminal processes. For example, it is possible for a sexual offender to engage in what appear to be healthy leisure activities, yet these activities may function as part of a broader cycle of continued crime. Engaging in common, legitimate leisure activities *after* the crime may function to help the offender blend into society and avoid detection (Williams 2005). Prior to the crime, some forms of leisure may provide ideas and skills needed to carry out the crime. Using the example of vehicle theft, a leisure hobby of mechanics and auto repair could come in handy in successfully carrying out repeated thefts.

It can be valuable to consider young male offenders' behavior from a leisure perspective. Is there leisure embedded in motivation and development of the deviant behavior? If so, what leisure properties (i.e., fun, excitement, self-expression, recognition from others, social cohesion, etc.) might occur from participating in the deviant behavior? Are there alternative, noncriminal leisure activities that could provide similar psychological and social benefits, thus preventing crime instead of furthering it? If the deviant behavior does seem to be a source of leisure (or connected with leisure), then practitioners can help clients restructure leisure to help promote crime-free living.

Using Leisure as a Strength to Promote Crime-Free Living

Several scholars have proposed various ways to utilize a leisure perspective to help prevent and reduce youth offending. Dr. Brenda Robertson (2000) at Acadia University suggested that leisure education for young offenders can help reduce stress, provide healthy alternatives for drug and alcohol use, build interpersonal skills, provide access to new (crime-free) social environments, foster new interests, and develop awareness of personal needs and ways to satisfy such needs.

Dr. Steven Danish, a faculty member in Counseling Psychology at Virginia Commonwealth University, recognized that numerous psychological and social skills required for success in sport (and leisure) could be transferrable to other life contexts (Danish, Petitpas, & Hale 1995). For example, success in sport and leisure activities often require the ability to be organized, meet challenges, communicate with others, handle both success and failure, be patient, respect others, develop self-control, accept responsibility for behavior, make good decisions, work within a system, and be self-motivated. In other words, a male youth offender who enjoys and has experienced success in, say, basketball already has a repertoire of well-developed skills that can be applied to help him integrate into family and community and live crime free. The role of the counselor is to help the youth recognize these skills that have already been developed through sport and leisure and then to help the youth to apply them across social contexts. In this way, unrecognized existing client strengths and motivation are identified and used to help clients progress in other important areas of their lives, thus facilitating crime-free living.

Young male offenders who already enjoy sport and leisure games may also understand a counseling approach that considers lifestyle possibilities according to the structure of games (Williams, Strean, & Bengoechea 2002). Sport and leisure games have rules and parameters, which define the specific game and its main objective. These parameters provide an appreciation for the game and necessary skills to play well, as well as informing tactical awareness and decision-making strategies that can bring success. Just as there are many different types of sports and games with different rules and structures, there are also many different versions of the "game of life." Young male offenders may want to explore the particular type of game of life they have been playing (consciously or not), along with the "rules" and likely outcome of the game. Oftentimes, criminal lifestyles are associated with time in jail and/or prison, freedoms lost, separation from loved ones, difficulty obtaining and maintaining future employment, and sometimes health problems and early death. The rules, tactical approaches, and decisions are different when one is engaged in a crime-free game of life compared to playing criminal games.

There are several possibilities for utilizing leisure as a form of strengths-based counseling for young male offenders. Besides the general approaches described, specific programs are also being developed. Dr. Linda Caldwell at the Pennsylvania State University and her colleagues have successfully designed a specific leisure education intervention, called *TimeWise*, to help alleviate boredom, improve decision-making skills and community awareness, and participate in new leisure activities (Caldwell, Baldwin, Walls, & Smith 2004; Caldwell & Smith 2006). *TimeWise* focuses on increasing youth motivation to participate in constructive leisure activities that provide meaningful benefits, manage free time, and learn planning and decision-making skills to further positive leisure experiences.

CONCLUSION AND POINTS TO REMEMBER

Leisure may be carefully structured and paired with traditional counseling approaches to help young offenders in living crime free. Leisure experience, by definition, is personally meaningful and enjoyable, and it is associated with significant psychological benefits that are often consistent with counseling objectives. Perhaps the greatest potential benefit that leisure offers when utilized in conjunction with strengths-based counseling has to do with increasing client treatment motivation. Because leisure participants are already motivated to engage in specific activities, counseling can identify and utilize this motivation to help young offenders make positive lifestyle changes to reduce recidivism. In other words, counseling can capitalize on clients' existing leisure motivation to further therapeutic goals and process. Counselors should not impose their own preferred leisure activities onto their clients, or this will likely have a detrimental effect.

In working with young male offenders, counselors should strive to become culturally competent. Preferred leisure activities often vary across cultures, and meanings of activities can also vary. Counselor flexibility is needed when helping young clients consider therapeutic leisure possibilities. Shared leisure experiences with others, especially with those of the same culture, racial, or ethnic group, can strengthen social bonds, which then reduces the likelihood of criminal activity. Thus, healthy leisure choices may include activities that can be performed alone or with other individuals, families, groups, or communities. Indeed, leisure provides an important context wherein client behavioral change and personal growth may occur. Although leisure sciences is its own field of study, it has much to contribute by collaborating synergistically with disciplines such as counseling, sociology, ethnic and cultural studies, social work, and psychology. By considering knowledge from multiple disciplines, professionals can be more creative with clients, help maintain client motivation for positive change, and have more resources to address client issues.

REFERENCES

Caldwell, Linda L. (2005). "Leisure and Health: Why is Leisure Therapeutic?" *British Journal of Guidance & Counseling* 33: 7–26.

Caldwell, Linda L., Cheryl K. Baldwin, Theodore Walls, & Ed Smith. (2004). "Preliminary Effects of a Leisure Education Program to Promote Health Use of Free Time Among Middle School Adolescents." *Journal of Leisure Research* 36: 310–335.

Caldwell, Linda L., & Ed Smith. (2006.) "Leisure as a Context for Youth Development and Delinquency Prevention." *Australian and New Zealand Journal of Criminology* 39: 398–418.

Danish, Steven J., Al J. Petitpas, & Bruce D. Hale. (1995). "Psychological Interventions: A Life Development Intervention." In *Sport Psychology Interventions*, ed. Shane Murphy, pp. 19–38. Champaign, IL: Human Kinetics.

Driver, Beverly L., and Donald H. Bruns (1999). "Concepts and Uses of the Benefits Approach to Leisure." In *Leisure Studies: Prospects for the Twenty-First Century*, ed. Edgar L. Jackson and Thomas L. Burton, pp. 349–369. State College, PA: Venture.

Mannell, Roger C. (2007). "Leisure, Health and Well-Being." *World Leisure* 49: 114–128.

Mannell, Roger C., & Douglas A. Kleiber. (1997). *A Social Psychology of Leisure*. State College, PA: Venture.

Ragheb, Mounir G. (1980). "Interrelationships among Leisure Participation, Leisure Satisfaction and Leisure Attitudes." *Journal of Leisure Research* 12: 138–149.

Robertson, Brenda J. (2000). "Leisure Education as a Rehabilitative Tool for Youth in Incarcerated Settings." *Journal of Leisurability* 27: 27–34.

Stebbins, Robert A. (2001). *New Directions in the Theory and Research of Serious Leisure*. Queenston, ON: Edwin Mellen Press.

Williams, D. J. (2005). "Functions of Leisure and Recreational Activities Within a Sexual Assault Cycle: A Case Study." *Sexual Addiction & Compulsivity* 12: 295–309.

Williams, D. J. (2006). "Forensic Leisure Science: A New Frontier for Leisure Scholars." *Leisure Sciences* 28: 91–95.

Williams, D. J., William B. Strean, and Enrique G. Bengoechea. (2002). "Understanding Recreation and Sport as a Rehabilitative Tool Within Juvenile Justice Programs." *Juvenile and Family Court Journal* 53 (2): 31–41.

Williams, D. J., and Gordon J. Walker. (2006). "Leisure, Deviant Leisure, and Crime: Caution: Objects may be Closer than They Appear." *Leisure/Loisir* 30: 193–218.

SECTION
Three

MIGRATION THEORIES

Theoretical Perspectives on Migration

Kebba Darboe and Agnes A. Odinga

Why Do People Migrate?

Migration is the movement of people from one geographic location to another for various reasons—for example, in search of food, shelter, or freedom. Therefore, migration, as one of the three population processes, with the others being fertility and mortality, is the most controversial. While migration is as old as humanity itself, theories about migration are fairly new. One of the early scholars on modern migration is Ravenstein, who in the 1880s based his "Laws of Migration" on empirical migration data (Tobler 1995). In addition, international migration or immigration is a relatively recent phenomenon because "it was only in the early 20th century that the system of nation-states, passports, and visas developed to regulate the flow of people across borders" (Martin & Widgren 2002, 3). An international migrant is defined by the United Nations as a person outside his or her country of citizenship for over a year or more, regardless of the reason for migration or the legal status of the person (Koser 2010).

Does International Migration Lead to Development or Underdevelopment?

This study answers the preceding question through two competing theoretical approaches; for example, neoclassical economic perspective contends that migration leads to development in both the sending and receiving countries. This theoretical approach is one-dimensional because it views economic factors as the main cause of migration. Conversely, cumulative causation theory perspective contends that migration leads to underdevelopment and exploitation in the sending countries. The migration-development theories include neoclassical economics, new economics of migration, dual labor market theory, and network theory. On the other hand, migration-underdevelopment theories include institutional theory, world systems theory, and theory of cumulative causation. The migration-development and underdevelopment dynamics guide the theoretical explanations of immigration.

Theoretical Perspectives on Immigration

The theoretical perspectives through the push-pull conceptual framework explain the dynamics of migration-development and underdevelopment. Lee (1966) elaborated on the nineteenth-century geographer, Ravenstein's (1885), laws of migration and advanced a new analytical framework for migration called "push-pull factors." As shown in Figure 1, the push-pull and intervening factors conceptual framework guides theoretical explanations of international migration. What is the difference between emigration and immigration? Emigration means leaving country of origin; for example, Christopher emigrated from the Gambia to the United States in 2001. Conversely, immigration means entering the country of destination; for example, Joseph and Angel immigrated to Minnesota in 2005.

Migration theories can be categorized according to their level of analysis; for example, micro-level theories focus on individual migration decisions. On the other hand, the macro-level theories focus on aggregate migration trends. However, the meso-level is in between the micro- and macro-level, and focuses especially on the household or community level and can explain both the causes and perpetuation of migration. For instance, Thomas Faist, a sociologist, emphasizes the meso-level of migration and pointed out that social relations and social capital in households, neighborhoods, communities, and formal organizations help migrants in their migration decision-making and adaptation processes (2000). On a meso-level also, social capital, institutions and networks can help or hinder migration.

Figure 1
Push-Pull Factors: A Refined Conceptual Framework

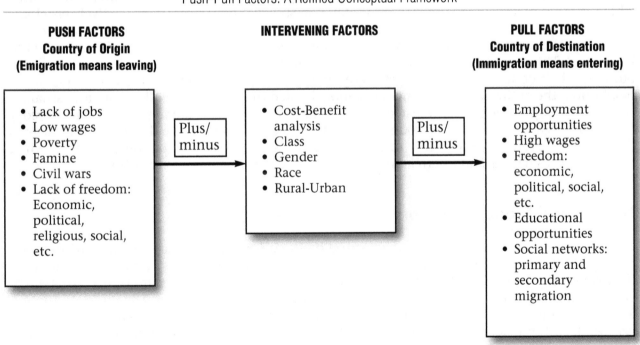

PUSH FACTORS
Country of Origin
(Emigration means leaving)

- Lack of jobs
- Low wages
- Poverty
- Famine
- Civil wars
- Lack of freedom: Economic, political, religious, social, etc.

Plus/minus

INTERVENING FACTORS

- Cost-Benefit analysis
- Class
- Gender
- Race
- Rural-Urban

Plus/minus

PULL FACTORS
Country of Destination
(Immigration means entering)

- Employment opportunities
- High wages
- Freedom: economic, political, social, etc.
- Educational opportunities
- Social networks: primary and secondary migration

The push-pull framework is a descriptive model listing different factors that affect positively or negatively (plus/minus) the migration decision-making process. Applying the logic of cost-benefit analysis, people decide to migrate, for instance, if the benefits are greater (such as employment opportunities) than the costs (like lack of jobs and low wages). Arguably, more non-White males from low socioeconomic status and developing economies migrate. However, today many new immigrants are well-educated people and women. Through social networks both primary and secondary migration can happen. Primary refers to the first place of destination; for example, Joseph immigrated to New York in 2005. After some time, Joseph relocated to Minnesota in 2006 in a secondary migration.

Migration-Development Theories

Migration can positively or negatively affect economic development in the origin and destination country thereby changing potential push and pull factors. For example, high migration flows might make labor scarce in the origin community and therefore improve the job prospects of people left behind. As a result, these people are less likely to migrate, as the benefits of migration are lower.

Modernization Theory

Modernization theory assumes that the periphery or low-income countries will develop by acquiring appropriate technology from core or high-income countries; for example, the United States (Rostow 1978). The underlying assumptions of the theory are consistent with the diffusionist model, which assumes that the migration experience tends to spread progressively from relatively developed areas to less-developed ones (De Haas 2005). The main goal of the theory was to explain how some Latin American countries, which have succeeded in economic development, could help those that have failed. This perspective derives much of its intellectual heritage from Max Weber, who pointed out that the Protestant work ethic of Western Europeans brought about the Industrial Revolution. In addition, the optimistic developmentalist model noted that through a policy from industrialized countries of large-scale capital transfers, such as loans, development aid, remittances, technology, and labor migration; developing countries could be able to economically develop and modernize (Hayes 1991). However, the theory of modernization is replaced by globalization theory, which focuses on the changes and interrelationships among countries of the world (Wang 2009).

Neoclassical Economic Theory

The neoclassical economic theory was advanced by W. A. Lewis but refined and adapted to migration by scholars like Ranis, Fei, and Todaro (Todaro 1969). This perspective pointed out that there is a relationship between income rates and international migration. For example, Christopher will emigrate from the Gambia to the United States if income rates are higher. Therefore, at a micro-level, a migrant is a rational actor who decides to move on the basis of a cost-benefit analysis (Borjas 1989). At the macro-level, neoclassical economic theory explains migration by geographical differences (rural to urban) in the supply and demand of labor (Bauer & Zimmermann 1998). The "Harris-Todaro model," advanced by Harris and Todaro (1970), elaborated on the rural-to-urban labor migration by explaining the contradictory phenomenon of continuing rural-to-urban internal migration in developing countries despite rising unemployment in cities. The preceding observations are consistent with the laws of migration advanced by the nineteenth century geographer, Ravenstein (1885), who contended that the major causes of migration are economic. However, the conclusion drawn from the Harris and Todaro model was that wage differential alone cannot explain migration—a measure of risk adversity factor also must be present.

New Economics of Migration Theory

Oded Stark developed the new economics of labor migration theory in the 1980s, and it posits migration as a family or household decision-making process (Stark 1991). The underlying assumption of the new economics of migration theory is that the migrant's remittance behavior and household's use of it is related to more migration. At the macro-level, remittances are considered a vital source of hard currency. Different from the neoclassical economic theory, the new economics perspective is a macro-level analysis because family or households faced with the greatest local market failure are most likely to adopt an international migration strategy (Stark and Boom 1985).

Further, many scholars and policymakers view migration as a development tool, and remittances play an important role in stimulating local, regional, and national economic growth. For instance, return migrants not only bring back money but also new ideas, knowledge, and entrepreneurial attitudes that they have acquired as a result of migration. In this context, return migrants become social change agents, thereby contributing to the development and modernization of their country of origin.

The Relative Deprivation Theory

The relative deprivation theory argues that awareness about income differences of other members (or households) in the sending society is an important factor with regard to migration. Therefore, the incentive to emigrate will be higher in societies that experience much economic inequality (Stark and Taylor 1991). At the meso-level analysis, migration is also more likely to take place if migration institutions, such as networks, have already been established and available to the potential migrant.

Dual Labor Market Theory

The dual labor market theory advanced by W. A. Lewis in 1954 pointed out that migration benefits both the sending and receiving country through economic development. The dual labor market approach, elaborated on by Piore in 1979, divides the labor market into primary and secondary sectors. Workers in the primary sector enjoy high wages, good benefits, and employment security. By contrast, workers in the secondary sector experience low wages, high turnover rate, job insecurity, and little chance of promotion. This perspective pointed out that immigration is driven by labor demand such as pull factors rather than supply. In addition, the dual labor market theory has focused mainly on microeconomic factors such as discrimination, poverty, and public welfare. This theory is important because it explains some of the post-war migration trends in Europe and the United States. However, the theoretical focus is too narrow with only one pull factor being analyzed and offers no great insights into the migrants' decision-making process.

Network Theory

"The probability of international migration should be greater for individuals who are related to someone, who has prior international experience or has a relative, or friend"; for example, in the United States (Mobasher & Sadri 2004, 25). This phenomenon of network migration can be best described as 'chain migration' (Massey, Arango, Hugo, Pellerino, & Taylor 1993, 448). The settled migrants become "bridgeheads," thereby reducing the costs of subsequent migration but may also function as restrictive "gatekeepers" (Böcker 1994). Further, the formation of an established migrant community at one particular receiving country will increase the likelihood of subsequent migration to that particular destination (Appleyard 1992). These social bonds explain why migrants tend to remit substantial amounts of money to their families and friends. These remittances are not taken into account by the neo-classical theory because of its individual-centered approach (Djajic 1986; Taylor 1999). The networks, however, make it difficult for governments to control immigration. Although the kinship networks are of great help in migrating, they also tend to be exclusionary for people not belonging to particular social or kinship groups (De Haas 2005).

Transitional Migration Perspective

Zelinsky (1971) advanced the mobility transition and pointed out that demographic and economic changes embodied in modernization have affected global migration patterns. Subsequently, the transitional migration perspective was refined by Martin (1993) and Martin and Taylor (1996), who argued that a temporary increase in migration, called a migration hump, is associated with the process of economic development. That is, with increase in wealth and the establishment of migrant networks, more people are able to migrate, and this process of "development" initially tends to lead to an increasing diffusion of migration across communities. Further, the transitional migration perspective has broadened migration-development focus on economic and demographic factors to include social and cultural factors (De Haas 2007b). Therefore, socioeconomic development tends to increase people's capabilities, freedoms, and aspirations to migrate (Sen 1999).

Migration-Underdevelopment Theories
Dependency Theory

In contrast to modernization theory, dependency theory focuses on European colonization and imperialism as the root causes of poverty in many countries. Therefore, dependency theory contends that the colonial process that helped develop rich nations also underdeveloped poor societies (Frank 1969). This observation is consistent with Lenin's (1939) contention that the forces of capitalism have led to the European colonization of the world. The theory is derived from the works of Karl Marx, who argued that capitalism would create an exploited class of dependent countries, just as it has created an exploited class of workers within countries. A proponent of this theory is Andre Gunder Frank, who focused on Latin American countries where dependency theory originated from the works of Pablo Gonzales Casanova (1970) of Mexico and Fernando Henrique Cardoso (1979) of Brazil.

Dependency theory assumes that poverty in periphery countries is a direct result of their political and economic dependence on core countries. It blames rich countries for keeping the poor ones dependent either through colonization, neocolonialism, or multinational corporations. As a result, the political liberation of poor countries has not translated into economic autonomy. For instance, Nigeria is the richest oil-producing country in West Africa but had no refinery capabilities, so it exported crude oil to Great Britain and then imported finished byproducts, such as gasoline, at higher prices. In addition, Great Britain colonized Nigeria and made it dependent through economic controls such as setting very low prices for oil and other raw materials so that it could not accumulate enough capital to industrialize. As a consequence, Nigeria had to borrow money from Great Britain in order to finance its economic development priorities. Nigeria's indebtedness to Great Britain increased its dependency. This form of international control without direct political or military involvement is called "neocolonialism." This new form of domination ensures the supply of raw materials and a market for British exports, thereby maintaining the dependent status of Nigeria. However, since the 1970s, Great Britain was replaced by the United States as Nigeria's chief trading partner.

World Systems Theory

Similar to the dependency theory, world systems theory explains global inequality in terms of the historical exploitation of poor societies by rich ones (Wallerstein 1974). World systems theory assumes that the world is economically divided into three positions: 1) core countries like the United States are industrialized and urbanized, 2) semi-periphery countries like South Korea and Taiwan are partly industrialized, and 3) periphery countries like Nigeria are not industrialized and largely rural. These countries are interconnected through the world market, where countries sell their products and buy products and services from other countries. However, this is not a market of equal trading partners. The world systems perspective takes into account structural factors that other theories neglect by stressing the dislocations in peripheral countries as a result of colonialism, neocolonialism, multinational corporations, and the technological advantage of core countries. World systems theory is a useful tool for understanding global inequality; however, it does not account for changes in the position of countries in the world system.

Institutional Theory

As international migration occurs on a large scale, it can become institutionalized. According to institutional theory, a large inflow of international migrants induces profit and non-profit organizations, which can be legal or illegal, to provide, for instance, clandestine transport, labor contracts, counterfeit documents, dwellings, or legal advice for migrants (Massey et al. 1993). The inequalities that exist between the supply of and demand for entry or immigrant visas into core countries leads to the erection of barriers; for example, Mexico and the United States.

Network and institutional theories explain the course of international migration flows over time. However, countries in a migration system are not only connected by people but also by historical, cultural, colonial, and technological linkages (Fawcett 1989; Kritz & Zlotnik 1992). In general, the economic, social, and political factors have an impact in both sending and receiving countries. According to Fielding (1993) society is comprised of cultural, social, and demographic components. The cultural component describes lifestyles and ethnicity. The economic and social components explain both inequality and cohesion in societies. The demographic component relates to the age and sex distribution of the population. The cultural linkages include, for instance, the colonial past or sharing the same language.

However, a large influx of immigrants can increase xenophobic reactions and institutional discrimination against them (Jandl 1994). Another negative effect of a large stock of immigrants of a particular ethnic origin is that these immigrants have more difficulties learning the language, usually live in linguistic enclaves and, as such, are less exposed to the language in the receiving country (Chiswick & Miller 1996). According to Waldorf (1994), the degree of assimilation of a migrant in the host society has a negative effect on his or her intentions to return. Whereas "ties to home," a form of social capital, is an important determinant of return migration.

In addition to specialized migration systems at the micro-level, there are several international migration systems at the macro-global level. For instance, particular regions in the developing world have specialized in migration to particular regions in the developed world. Examples are the North American migration system, which links Mexico and Central American countries to the United States and Canada; and the Euro-Mediterranean migration system, which links North African countries and Turkey to the European Union (De Haas 2007b; Kritz et al 1992).

Theory of Cumulative Causation

Cumulative and circular migration refers to the fact that once migration is in place, it sustains itself. It has been shown that migrant institutions, social capital, and networks that develop over time as more people migrate, reduce the costs and ease of migration for future migrants. Cumulative causation theory was developed earlier by the Swedish economist Gunnar Myrdal (1957). Myrdal pointed out that migration as a process serves the interests of the receiving nations in need of cheap immigrant labor, while worsening underdevelopment at the sending country. In addition, migration deprives developing countries of their valuable human and material capital resources, which are exploited for the benefit of receiving countries and capitalist elite groups within developing countries. Although the brain drain has attracted the most literature review, more significant is the lower-skilled labor migration from developing countries, which can be best described as the "brawn drain" (Penninx 1982, 793); that is, the massive departure of young, able-bodied men and women from rural areas (Lewis 1986).

Three Major Waves of Immigration to the United States

"The shift to federal control of immigration was launched in 1875, when the U.S. Supreme Court ruled that only the U.S. Congress was empowered by the constitution to regulate immigration," (McLemore, Romo & Baker 2001, 86). Politics matters in migration theory because migration laws and policy directly influence migration flows; for instance, the right to cross a border legally (Green 2002). The United States of America, despite being a nation of and descendants of immigrants, has periodically restricted immigration between welcoming and not welcoming immigrants—it has been a cyclical process. As a consequence, the United States policy responses to immigration varied from one period to another. For instance, laissez-faire policy was implemented from 1780 to 1875; then a qualitative restrictions policy was implemented from 1875 to 1920. During this period, the 1882 Chinese Exclusion Act was passed and suspended Chinese immigration, until it was repealed in 1943. Subsequent to that, a quantitative restrictions policy has been implemented since 1921. The Johnson-Reed Act was passed in 1924 and created a new national-origins quota system favoring immigrants from northern and western Europe; 4) the 1960s Civil Rights Movement struggles led to the passage of the 1965 amendments to the Immigration and Nationality Act, which eliminated the race-based admission criteria and instituted ones that favor immigrants from Africa, Asia, Latin America, and skilled people (Brunner & Colarelli 2010); 5) President Reagan signed the Immigration Reform and Control Act of 1986, which granted amnesty to undocumented immigrants and instituted sanctions for employers who hire undocumented workers (Gimpel & Edwards, Jr. 1999); and 6) following the terrorists attacks of September 11, 2001, the United States Congress passed and President Bush signed on October 26, 2001, into law the Patriot Act (Uniting and Strengthening America by Providing Appropriate Tools Required to Intercept and Obstruct Terrorism Act of 2001), which gives the federal government broad powers to indefinitely detain suspected terrorists (USA Congressional Digest 2003).

Subsequently, the attacks on September 11 intensified anti-immigration policy, and "on November 25, 2002, the Homeland Security Act of 2002 became law," which led to the creation of a new Department of Homeland Security (King III 2009, 152). The Immigration and Nationalization Service merged with the new department, and its dual responsibility was divided between the United States Citizenship and Immigration Services (USCIS), which now oversees legal immigration and enforcement of laws preventing illegal entrance; and the office of Immigration and Customs Enforcement (ICE), which is responsible for deporting undocumented immigrants. The aforementioned policy responses always informed immigration debate.

Immigrants entered the United States through two receiving ports: Ellis Island, New York, and Angel Island, California. Ellis Island received immigrants from eastern and southern Europe "between 1892 and 1954," (Desforges, & Maddern 2004, 437). Similarly, Angel Island received immigrants from the Pacific Shores "between 1910 and 1940," (Barde & Bobonis 2006, 103). Today, international airports are the receiving ports; for example, New York, Chicago, Los Angeles, etc.

Further, Portes and Rumbaut (2006) pointed out that, "immigration is a transformative force, producing profound and unanticipated social changes" (p. xv). The push-pull conceptual framework can be applied to all the immigrants; for instance, the push factors for immigrants from Ireland were poverty and potato famine, and they were pulled to the United States because of economic opportunities and freedom. According to McLemore, Romo, and Baker (2001), there were three immigration streams to the United States, especially during the Agrarian and Industrial Revolution periods, and each had different characteristics. The first immigration stream came in the early nineteenth century and included the Irish, Germans, Norwegians, and Swedes. From 1890 to 1924, the second immigration stream came from southern and eastern European countries; for example, Italy, Spain, Portugal, Greece, and Poland. Their languages and religion were further removed from the English as compared to the first stream of immigrants. From 1946 to present, the third immigrant stream or new immigration come mainly from Asia, Latin America, Africa, and refugees.

African Immigration Waves

The first African diaspora was the seventeenth-century slave trade, when Africans came involuntarily to America as indentured servants in 1619 (Hine, Hine & Harrold 2009). By contrast, in the "new diaspora," Africans came voluntarily through the stream of international migration because of push-pull factors. One response to the growing disparity between developed and underdeveloped economies is international migration. The reasons for migration to the United States are globalization of economies, liberalization of United States immigration policy, and economic and political failures in developing countries (Stieglitz 2002). The push factors are the pressures that force people to leave their own countries (sending countries); for example, internal and regional conflicts based on religion and ethnicity (Papadimitriou 1985). While a pull factor is the favorable economic conditions in the United States (receiving country); for example, the demand for cheap labor.

The first wave, called the "new diaspora" of Black Africans, came to the United States in the 1940s to 1950s and after independence in Ghana and Nigeria. Most came for education; for example, Dr. Kwame Nkrumah, former President of Ghana, and Dr. Nnamdi Azikiwe, former President of Nigeria. From the 1950s to 1960s, began the second wave, and large numbers came from Egypt and South Africa (Arthur 2000). Most outstanding students came for education; for example, Dr. Lamin Sanneh, from the Gambia, Professor at Yale University, New Haven, Connecticut, and Mr. Barack H. Obama, Sr., father of President Obama, from Kenya attended the University of Hawaii and Harvard University. Some graduates also stayed and provided a nucleus for future migration in the 1970s. The third wave came from the 1970s to 1980s; most came for educational opportunities. However, some did not succeed and instead pursued self-employment or other employment opportunities. From the 1990s to 2000s was a fourth wave consisting primarily of immigrants and economic and political refugees from Liberia, Sierra Leone, Somali, and Sudan. Both push factors at home, and the pull factors of jobs and opportunities are likely to increase African immigration to the United States.

Recommendations

Drawing on migration-development and underdevelopment theories, as well as primary and secondary readings, this study makes four recommendations. First, researchers should employ a multidimensional approach that views economic, political, and social factors as the main causes of migration.

Second, researchers should employ mixed research methods (triangulation) to collect and analyze data: that is, both qualitative and quantitative approaches to study the causes or determinants and consequences or impacts of migration. The findings informed by the answers collected from qualitative face-to-face interviews and the questionnaire can serve as a framework for developing theories.

Third, in lieu of comprehensive migration theories, researchers should do case studies on sending and destination countries. For example, "a case study on Mexico and the United States: Test of migration theories." Data collected and analyzed can help in theorizing.

Fourth, researchers should employ a combination of cross-sectional and longitudinal research designs to collect and analyze data on immigrants from sending country to receiving country. The benefits of a longitudinal study are to establish sequences of events and changes in the characteristics of the target immigrant groups at both the group and individual levels. On the other hand, a cross-sectional study can compare different immigrant groups at a single point in time.

CONCLUSION

Migration is dynamic; therefore, the causes and consequences of migration are linked. In this context, an analysis of decision-making framework on the household level can deepen the theoretical understanding of migration as an integral part of broader development processes. For instance, the factors that affect the decision-making process include cost benefit analysis; political institutions, such as immigration laws in receiving countries; pull factors like labor demand as analyzed in the dual labor market theory; and economic development as in the world systems theory. Arguably, the dynamic nature of migration, the question of why people migrate, and the development of comprehensive migration theories remain a work in progress.

REFERENCES

Appleyard, R. T. (1992). Migration from Countries of the Pacific to Australia in Solidarity in Favor of New Migrations, Vatican.

Arthur, A. John. (2000). Invisible Sojourners: African Immigrant Diaspora in the United States. Westport CT: Praeger.

Barde, R., & Bobonis, G. J. (2006). Detention at Angel Island. *Social Science History* 30 (1): 103–136.

Bauer, T., & K. F. Zimmermann. (1998): "Causes of International Migration: A Survey." In Crossing Borders: Regional and Urban Perspectives on International Migration, eds. C. Gorter, P. Nijkamp, & J. Poot. Aldershot et al.: Ashgate, pp. 95–127.

Böcker A. (1994). "Chain Migration over Legally Closed Borders: Settled Migrants as Bridgeheads and Gatekeepers." *Netherlands' Journal of Social Sciences* 30: 87–106.

Borjas, G. J. (1989). "Economic Theory and International Migration." *International Migration Review* XXIII (3): 457–485.

Brunner, L., & S. M. Colarelli. (2010). Immigration in the Twenty-First Century A Personnel Selection Approach. *Independent Review* 14 (3): 389–413.

Cardoso, F. Henrique., & E. Faletto. (1979). *Dependency and development in Latin America.* Berkeley: University of California Press.

Casanova, Pablo González. (1970). *Democracy in México,* 2nd ed. Oxford University Press.

Chiswick, B. R., & P. W. Miller. (1996). "Ethnic networks and language proficiency among immigrants." *Journal of Population Economics* 9(1): 19–35.

De Haas, Hein. (2005). Morocco's migration transition: Trends, Determinants and Future Scenarios. *Global Migration Perspectives* No 28. Geneva: Global Commission on International Migration.

———. (2007b). "Morocco's migration experience: A transitional perspective." *International Migration* 45 (4): pp. 39–70.

Desforges, L., & J. Maddern. (2004). "Front doors to freedom, portal to the past: history at the Ellis Island Immigration Museum, New York." *Social & Cultural Geography* 5 (3): 437–457. doi:10.10SO/14649. 160420002S28U

Djajic, S. (1986). "International Migration, Remittances and Welfare in a Dependent Economy." *Journal of Development Economics* 21: 229–234.

Fawcett, James T. (1989). "Special Silver Anniversary Issue: International Migration an Assessment for the 90's." *International Migration Review* 23 (3): 671–680.

Faist, T. (2000). "The Crucial Meso-Level." In *International Migration, Immobility and Development*, eds. T. Hammer, G. Brochmann, K. Tamas, & T. Faist. Oxford: Berg Publishers.

Fielding, A. J. (1993). "Mass migration and economic restructuring." In *Mass migration in Europe: The legacy and the future*, ed. R. L. King, pp. 7–18. London, England: Belhaven.

Frank, Andre Gunder. (1969). *Latin America: Underdevelopment or Revolution?* New York: Monthly Review Press.

Gimpel, James G., & James R. Edwards, Jr. (1999). *The Congressional Politics of Immigration Reform.* Boston: Allyn and Bacon.

Green, Nicole W. (2002). "CQ's Vital Issues Series: Immigration," University of Michigan. A Division of Congressional Quarterly Inc. Washington, D.C.

Harris, John, & Michael Todaro. (1970). "Migration, Unemployment, and Development: A Two-Sector Analysis." *American Economic Review* 60: 126–142.

Hayes, Geoffrey. (1991). Migration, Metascience, and Development Policy in Island Polynesia. *The Contemporary Pacific* 3(1): 1–58.

Hine, Darlene Clark, William C. Hine, & Stanley Harrold. (2009). *African Americans: A Concise History*, 3rd ed. Upper Saddle River, N.J.: Prentice Hall.

Jandl, M. (1994). "Is migration supply—or demand—determined?" *International Migration* 32 (3): 467–476.

King III, Charles B. (2009). "The Department of Homeland Security An Organization in Transition." *JFQ: Joint Force Quarterly* (55): 152–159.

Koser, K. (2010). Introduction: International Migration and Global Governance. Global Governance, 16(3), 301–315.

Kritz, M. M., & H. Zlotnik. (1992). "Global interactions: Migration systems, processes, and policies." In *International Migration Systems: A Global Approach*, eds. M. M. Kritz, L. Lim. & H. Zlotnik, pp. 1–16. Oxford: Clarendon Press.

Lee, E. (1966). "A theory of migration." *Demography* 3: 47–57.

Lenin, V. I. (1939/1917). *Imperialism: The Highest Stage of Capitalism.* New York: International Publishers.

Lewis, J. R. (1986). "International labour migration and uneven regional development in labour exporting countries." *Tijdschift voor Economische en Sociale Geografie* 77 (1): 27–41.

Lewis, W. A. (1954). "Economic Development with Unlimited Supplies of Labour." The Manchester School, XXII(2), pp. 139–191.

Martin, Philip, & Jonas Widgren. (2002). International Migration: Facing the Challenge. *The Population Reference Bureau* 57 (1): 1–43.

Martin, P. L. & J. E. Taylor. (1996). "The anatomy of a migration hump." In *Development Strategy, Employment, and Migration: Insights from Models*, ed. J. E. Taylor, pp. 43–62. Paris: OECD Development Centre.

Martin, P. L. (1993). *Trade and Migration: NAFTA and Agriculture.* Vol. 30. Washington D.C.: Institute for International Economics.

Martin PL. (1993). *Trade and Migration: NAFTA and Agriculture.* Washington D.C.: Institute for International Economics, pp. 457–476.

Massey, Douglas S., Joaquin Arango, Graeme Hugo, Ali Kouaouci, Adela Pellegrino, & J. Edward Taylor. (1993). Theories of international migration: A review and appraisal. *Population and Development Review* 19: 431–466.

McLemore, S. Dale, Harriett D. Romo, & Susan Gonzalez Baker. (2001). *Racial and ethnic relations in America*, 6th ed. Boston: Allyn & Bacon.

Mobasher, Mohsen M., & Mahmoud Sadri. (2004). *Migration, Globalization, and Ethnic Relations: An Interdisciplinary Approach.* Pearson, Prentice Hall.

Myrdal G. (1957). *Rich Lands and Poor.* New York: Harper and Row.

Papademetriou, D. G. (1985). "Illusions and Reality in International Migration: Migration and Development in post World War II Greece." *International Migration* XXIII (2): 211–223.

Penninx, Rinus. (1982). "A critical review of theory and practice: The case of Turkey." *International Migration Review* 16 (4): 781–818.

Piore, M. J. (1979). *Birds of passage: migrant labor and industrial societies:* Cambridge University Press.

Portes, Alejandro, & Rubén G. Rumbaut. (2006). *Immigrant America: A Portrait,* 3rd ed. Los Angeles: University of California Press.

Ravenstein, E. (1885). The laws of migration. *Journal of the Statistical Society* 48:167–235.

Rostow, Walt Whitman. 1978. *The World Economy: History and Prospect.* Austin: Texas University Press.

Sen, Amartya. (1999). *Development as freedom.* New York: Anchor Books.

Stark, O. (1991). *The Migration of Labour.* Oxford: Blackwell Publishers.

Stark, O., & R. E. B. Lucas (1988). "Migration, Remittances, and the Family." *Economic Development and Cultural Change* 36 (3): 465–481.

Stark, O., & D. E. Bloom (1985). "The New Economics of Labour Migration." *American Economic Review* 75: 173–178.

Stark, O., & J. E. Taylor. (1991). "Migration Incentives, Migration Types: The Role of Relative Deprivation." *The Economic Journal* 101: 1163–1178.

Stiglitz J. (2002). *Globalization and its Discontents.* London: Allen Lane, The Penguin Press.

Taylor, J. Edward. (1999). "The New Economics of Labour Migration and the role of remittances in the migration process." *International Migration.* 37 (1): 63–88.

Tobler, Waldo. (1995). "Migration: Ravenstein, Thornthwaite, and Beyond." *Urban Geography* 16 (4): 327–343.

Todaro, Michael P. (1969). "A model of labor migration and urban unemployment in less-developed countries." *American Economic Review* 59 (1): 138–148.

USA Patriot Act. (2003). *Congressional Digest* 82(4): 110.

Waldorf, B. S. (1994). Assimilation and attachment in the context of international migration: The case of guestworkers in Germany. *Papers in Regional Science* 73 (3): 241–266.

Wallerstein, Immanuel. (1974). *The Modern World-system; Capitalist agriculture and the origins of the European world-economy in the sixteenth century.* New York: Academic Press.

Wang, J. (2009). "Some Reflections on Modernization Theory and Globalization Theory." *Chinese Studies In History* 43 (1): 72–98.

Zelinsky, Z. (1971). The Hypothesis of the Mobility Transition. *Geographical Review* 61: 219–249.

Somali Immigration to the USA

Abdulkadir Alasow

Introduction

Nearly anyone can look around and notice the increasing diversity of the U.S. population. Immigration in the United States is not a new concept, but the mix and countries of origin of new immigrants are. Until recently, immigration was associated in the minds of many Americans with European immigrants getting off teeming boats at Ellis Island and settling in ethnic enclaves in major American cities. However, since the 1960s, the number of non-European foreign-born people in the United States has increased. It is now, in terms of absolute numbers, at its highest point in history. According to 2000 U.S. Census Bureau data, some 51 percent of these foreign-born persons originate from Latin America, 25.7 percent from Asia, 15.2 percent from Europe, and 8.1 percent from other regions of the world, such as Africa (Guthrie 1997).

The African foreign-born population in the United States is small but growing. According to the U.S. Census Bureau, there were approximately 364,000 African immigrants in 1990, and this population more than doubled to over 881,000 by 2000. The most recent estimates put the number of African foreign born at over 1 million. Despite their growing numbers, African immigrants as a population, particularly Somali immigrants, are among the least understood populations among the new immigrants (Guthrie 1997).

Emigration to the United States has always been a destination for Somali immigrants, but since 1990 their numbers increased when refugees escaping the civil war in Somalia began to come to America in larger numbers than ever. Waves of Somali immigrants came to America from different parts of the world through resettlement programs, family sponsorship, or as asylum seekers. According to McLemore, Romo, and Baker (2001) there were three great immigration streams to the United States, and each had different characteristics.

First Wave

Somali immigrants came to the United States in the 1920s and settled in the New York area (Kusow 1998). The majority were sailors although some worked in steel mills, and most came from northern Somalia (Somaliland) similar to the first Somali immigrant group to the United Kingdom. These early immigrants became naturalized Americans.

Second Wave

The second wave of Somali immigration was in the 1960s when Somali students began coming to the United States for school, mostly on United States government or United Nations scholarships or through the support of relatives who were now living in the U.S. (Kusow 1998). Once done with their studies in the U.S., the majority of these students returned home and contributed greatly to the development of their country.

Third Wave

The third wave of Somalis occurred in the mid-1980s, when small numbers of Somalis were admitted to the United States. Unlike the first two waves (sailors and students) of Somali immigrants, this population was comprised of refugees. And as the political situation (civil war) in the Republic of Somalia worsened, the United States saw an increasing number of Somali refugees in the 1990s. The Somali refugees resettled in the U.S were distributed in a number of different states. These refugees lived in different parts of the U.S with the larger concentrations in New York, Washington, D.C, Boston, Los Angeles, San Diego, Atlanta, and Detroit (Kusow 1998). However, the recent statistics of 2001 show that the largest numbers of Somali refugees now live in Minnesota, California, Virginia, Tennessee, New York, Connecticut, and Texas.

Somali Refugee Arrivals in the United States 1990–2004

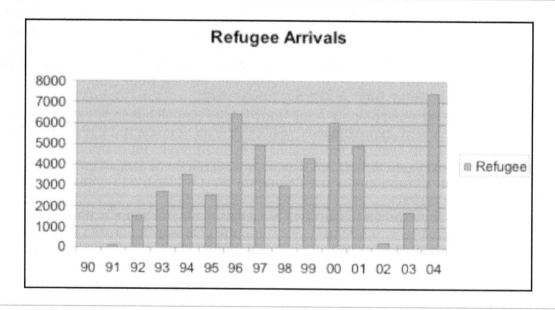

Note the dramatic reduction of number of Somali refugees admitted into the U.S. after 9/11. Admission numbers gradually increased in 2003 and eventually peaked in 2004.
(Source: Office of Refugee Resettlement, 2004)

Minnesota has always had a large number of immigrants from other places in the world, although they currently make up a much smaller percentage of the population than in the past—just 2.6 percent in 1990, compared to 28.9 percent in 1900. The most recent figures from the U.S. Census Bureau indicate an upswing in the number and percentage of immigrants, both in Minnesota and nationwide. The points of origin for these new Minnesotans have changed over time, influenced by world

Minnesota's Immigrant Population	
	State Rank
Total number of immigrants: 217,000	20
Immigration in the 1990s: 98,000	19
Immigrants as a percentage of state population: 4.6%	24
(*Source:* U.S. Census Bureau, Current Population Survey, March 1998.)	

events (war, upheaval, economic conditions) and tightly governed by national and international policies that limit how many immigrants can enter the country, from where, and for what reasons.

The Minnesota State Demographic Center also stated in the same issue: "very few African immigrants came to Minnesota before 1990, but since that time African immigrants have become a very important part of Minnesota." The office of Refugee Service of the Minnesota Department of Human Services estimates 45,000 Somalis in Minnesota, and other sources estimate 50,000–60,000. The Twin Cities has one of the largest Somali populations in the Western Hemisphere (United Way 2000). Due to continuing civil upheaval in Somalia, many Somali immigrants came to settle in Minnesota, partly because of the high demand for unskilled labor and the presence of a growing Somali community as well as a good educational system and hospitable environment for immigrants.

According to Gordon F. De Jong and Quynh-Giang Tran "urban areas with large concentrations of immigrants—and with a higher level of education—typically spread the welcome mat for newcomers more readily than smaller towns and rural areas that have little experience dealing with immigrants." Atlanta, Baltimore, Detroit, Miami, Minneapolis, Philadelphia, Phoenix, Seattle, and Washington, D.C., lead the researchers' list of cities with native-born residents expressing the most receptive attitudes toward immigrants. Chicago, New York, Pittsburgh, and St. Louis are also open to immigrants, the researchers say, but Boston, Houston and Los Angeles are less open, and Dallas, San Diego, San Francisco, and Tampa are the least receptive. Negative attitudes can crop up if residents think illegal aliens are taking unfair advantage of health and social services. Tran and Jong believe receptivity falls as unemployment rises among the nonimmigrant population.

The Somali population in Minnesota has grown from a small handful of single individuals and families in 1992 to a significant size—estimated to be approximately 55,000 people (more than 95 percent of the Somali people in Minnesota are refugees) in 2000 according to the Minnesota state department. The vast majority of these Somalis have come in the past five years mainly through secondary migration. A growing number of Somalis resettled in the United States and, to some extent in Canada, are moving to Minnesota due to some pull factors, which include the Minnesota education system, family/relative connections, and the opportunity to improve one's well-being (in comparison to Canada and Britain). Hence, Minnesota Planning estimates an increase of 1000 Somalis in the state per year (United Way 2000).

According to a news release by the Minnesota State Demographic Center, immigrants from 160 countries came to Minnesota in 2002. Immigrants born in Somalia (1,588) outnumbered all others, followed by India (1,001), Ethiopia (918), and Mexico (756). One explanation for the increased numbers in Minnesota may be changes in immigration policy. Under the family preference provision of immigration law, many Africans can bring family members to the U.S. Increases in the number of African immigrants over 2001 accounted for 70 percent of the total increase. Other large increases were recorded in immigrants from India. Refugees from Africa to the U.S. doubled between 2001 and 2002. The data for states is not available, but since Minnesota has both a large share of refugees and African immigrants, it is safe to assume that increased refugee numbers also contributed to the overall increase in immigrants to Minnesota.

According to the Census, Minnesota's share of total immigration was 1.3 percent. But 7 percent of all African immigrants came to this state, including 35 percent of Somalis, 12 percent of Ethiopians, and 13.5 percent of Liberians. About one in eight Laotian immigrants to the U.S. came to Minnesota in 2002.

Ninety-one percent of all immigrants settled in the Minneapolis-St. Paul, Rochester. and St. Cloud metropolitan areas. Nearly 24 percent of Mexicans, 20 percent of Canadians, and 12 percent of Somalis settled outside these metropolitan areas. Indian, Ethiopian, Chinese, and Russian immigrants were very unlikely to live outside metropolitan areas. Minnesota has seven metropolitan areas; however, five of them include parts of neighboring states. Only 869 immigrants settled in those four metropolitan areas, with the vast majority in the Fargo-Moorhead Metropolitan Area.

A little more than half of the immigrants (58%) came to Minnesota as their first residence in the United States. The rest lived somewhere else in the United States, and then moved to Minnesota. According to a study by the Wilder Foundation (Wilder 2000), Somalis (38%) were the least likely to have come directly to Minnesota. When Wilder Foundation researchers asked Somalis who lived elsewhere first their reasons for moving to Minnesota, they responded as follows: family or friends were here (64%); jobs were available (58%); welfare benefits were good (11%); and people were hostile or unfriendly in other parts of the United States (10%).

Somali Immigration to Minnesota

Over the past several decades, tens of thousands of immigrants have arrived in Minnesota. They have come from all over the world and settled throughout the state. They have come for the same reason that attracted immigrants in the past—opportunity. They experience the same difficulties of adjusting to life in a new country—language, social, political and economic barriers, culture shock, a sense of loss, and isolation.

Why Minnesota

During the 1990s alone, Minnesota's foreign-born population more than doubled, from 110,000 to 240,000. For many immigrants, Minnesota provides the first glimpse of life in the U.S. Others settle briefly elsewhere in America, but relocate to Minnesota because of family ties, economic and educating opportunities, or for other reasons.

Minnesota is attractive to immigrants for the same reasons it is attractive to the rest of us—a strong economy, good quality of life, educational opportunities, and a thriving civic and cultural life. Minnesota also has a history of active volunteerism regarding immigration and refugee resettlement, led primarily by faith-based organizations (United Way 2000).

In the last three decades, Africans have made up a more significant part of the immigrant flow. In Minnesota, a high proportion of immigrants come as refugees. The African refugees began coming to Minnesota in the mid-1990s and after. Due to U.S. intervention, Somalia sent the most immigrants. Other immigrants came from Eastern Europe, Vietnam, China, India, Mexico, and Ethiopia. Tens of thousands of Somali refugees have settled in Minnesota since Somalia's civil war erupted in 1991. The Twin Cities of Minneapolis and St. Paul has become the de facto "capital" of the Somali community in North America. Somalis have arrived directly from refugee camps or in secondary migrations from other U.S. cities, drawn by an attractive urban job market and refugee service agencies. Minnesota is home to the country's largest population of Somali residents.

More recently, many Somalis have begun to settle in smaller cities and towns around southern Minnesota. This diffusion is creating an "immigration hinterland" that increasingly resembles the ethnic make-up of the Twin Cities. They have been drawn by meat processing plants (and other industries that do not require advanced English language skills) in small Minnesota cities such as Rochester, St. Cloud, Owatonna, Mankato, Faribault, and Marshall. Somalis have racial, cultural, and religious gaps in these previously monoethnic rural towns, much greater than Latino meatpackers before them (United Way 2000).

Earlier Immigrant Groups in the Midwest

In recent years, the Midwest has increasingly been hosting immigrant workers, especially in the meatpacking industry. Over the past two decades, the decreasing consumer demand for meat has forced the meatpacking industry to cut costs. One of the simplest solutions is to hire immigrant workers who are typically willing to work for lower wages, but also because of a generally high employee turnover, and linguistic barriers to labor organizing.

The meatpacking industry does not hire immigrants only to save money. A plant is often forced to hire immigrants because the local American youth no longer want to there. At one point in the 1990s, half of the population in Norwalk, Wisconsin, was Mexican, due to the presence of a meatpacking plant, and its continuing need for workers.

The meatpacking industry's practice of hiring immigrant workers is not always beneficial to its bottom line. High turnover rates can end up costing the plant money due to the costs of new interviews, screening, training, and periodic labor shortages (Martinez 2001). High turnover rates can create problems in the host community, such as unstable school enrollments. Conflicts between the local population and the immigrant population often arise. These tensions arise over issues such as the immigrant workers dating local young people or perceptions that immigrant workers are taking away local jobs. Tensions are particularly acute if local workers have recently been laid off or fired from the plant.

Not only are immigrants attractive employees for the meatpacking industry, but meatpacking is an attractive job for immigrants. Most jobs in the meatpacking plants require few technical skills, and what skills they do require can be learned fairly quickly. Notably, little English proficiency is needed to successfully complete a job on a processing or packing line. Translators are often hired for the training process, but then the employee is left to do the work and not required to learn any English (some companies promise English instruction, but do not deliver). Another positive aspect of working for the meatpacking industry is its flexibility.

Other Immigrant Groups in Comparison

Midwestern states have hosted Hispanic or Latino immigrants from Mexico and Central America since the 1970s. Large meatpacking companies in Iowa, Nebraska, Minnesota, and Wisconsin have recruited and employed Hispanic immigrants. Hispanic immigrants were often recruited by the employer in order to break a strike. The Hispanic immigrant workers were willing to work for lower pay and fewer benefits than the American workers, so they were often brought in to replace workers that had gone on strike. This allowed the factory to keep its lower wages and also left some local residents unemployed, thus creating a negative feeling towards the immigrant group. Somali workers employed in meatpacking factories were not brought in to break unions, but were recruited to fill empty positions that local workers did not want. This factor, however, does not outweigh the many "negative" aspects that the Somali population has been forced to deal with which the Hispanic immigrant population has not (Martinez 2001).

For example, the majority of the Hispanic immigrant population is Christian. Therefore, they blend in with the existing religious beliefs of the American population and do not have to face the religious gap that the Somali Muslim population faces. Muslim customs and practices are not typically well known in Midwestern communities, and this lack of understanding has created several points of conflict. Somali women's Muslim dress is very different from the attire of the majority population. The Somali women wear bright-colored dresses and head coverings, and so stand out among the rest of the population (more so than Somali men). Secondly, the greater contrast in skin color makes Somali immigrants stand out more than Hispanic immigrants, and make them more easily identified as "foreign." The only other such immigrant population in northern Wisconsin is the Hmong from Southeast Asia (Martinez 2001).

Migration In and Out of the Twin Cities

There are currently between 10,000 and 60,000 Somalis residing in the Twin Cities. The ambiguous number is somewhat a result of continuously shifting populations, but mostly due to the amount of error in census data regarding Somali refugees (Black 2002). This large Somali population makes the Twin Cities the Somali capital of the United States.

There are several factors that draw Somalis to the Twin Cities, including an initially plentiful job market and refugee social service agencies. A major pull recently has been the presence of a large Somali community. This sizable community allows Somali immigrants to feel at home, and the presence of Somali restaurants and Somali shopping centers makes meeting there everyday cultural needs much easier than living elsewhere.

However, large cities do have their drawbacks. There is more crime in the Twin Cities than elsewhere in the state. The larger city is much more expensive to live in, and the unemployment rate is higher. Also, the school system in the poorer areas of the Twin Cities is not as good as the school systems in other communities. Therefore, Somalis have experienced some major pushes to leave the big city and move to the smaller communities. While the lower crime rate draws some to communities such as Rochester, Minn., the prospect of employment attracts most Somalis to the smaller communities.

Manufacturing jobs in St. Cloud, technical and janitorial jobs at IBM in Rochester, and the Jennie'O Turkey Store in Barron are just a few of the employment opportunities that pulled the Somalis away from the Twin Cities. There are many similarities in these jobs; there is a low level of English proficiency required, and they provide on-the-job training so that people can go to work right away.

Yet, employment was not the only attractive aspect of the smaller communities. The school systems in general are much better in the smaller communities than in the areas of the Twin Cities where most of the Somalis were living. The state of Minnesota requires each high school student to pass a graduation standards exam, an exam that is very difficult to pass if you are not highly proficient in English. Therefore, many young Somali students moved across the Minnesota-Wisconsin border to Barron, Wis., in order to attain their high school diploma without having to take the Minnesota graduations standards exam. The employment option at the Jennie'O Turkey Store in Barron also guaranteed that the students could afford to live in Barron, Wis., while attending school. The town is small enough that Somalis could walk to work and school without driving—a major question for immigrants without drivers' licenses.

Minnesota Communities: St. Cloud

St. Cloud, Minnesota, is a small community located 75 miles outside of the Twin Cities, and has a population of 59,200. Somalis arrived in St. Cloud, Minnesota, in 2000–2001. The number of Somalis residing in St. Cloud is in the 2,000–3,500 range, with 135 Somali children enrolled in the public school system. St. Cloud has one of the only local governments to act prior to the arrival of the Somali immigrants in order to prepare the local community. First, the city acted to educate and train public service providers and the general community about the Somali population, its culture, and Islamic beliefs. Second, the city identified the housing needs of the Somalis and was able to negotiate housing opportunities with providers. Next, the city set aside funding and space to encourage and allow the Somalis to practice their culture and religion (Franklin 2002). The proactive policies that the City of St. Cloud put into place helped to address many problems before they arose.

There were, however, still some areas that needed to be addressed after the Somali population arrived in St. Cloud. First, a basic curriculum was developed to educate the Somali population on American culture, community norms, laws, and general resources. Second, panel presentations were organized to provide educators, spiritual communities, service providers, and the general community with information about Somali culture and Islamic beliefs. Next, cultural awareness training was provided for city administrators, and Human Rights and Housing brochures were translated into Somali. Also, the mayor's office set aside funding for local nonprofit Somali organizations, "to directly serve immigrants and refugees" (United Way 2000).

There were many positive interactions between the Somali immigrants and the St. Cloud population. Several Somalis sought to become involved in the St. Cloud community, and the St. Cloud population was eager to learn about the Somali culture. However, after September 11, 2001, there were some negative interactions between Somali and American employees at one of the factories (Furst 2002). Also, in the fall of 2002, a Somali community center was vandalized with hate graffiti, and again in late 2002 a Somali-owned and an Ethiopian-owned business were both vandalized with hate graffiti. The city reacted very quickly to "denounce the hate crimes and discrimination of any kind." Several community members contributed to a fund to remove the graffiti, while the community sent letters of support, made personal contacts, and developed business relationships with the people that were impacted by the hate crime (Furst 2002).

Owatonna

Owatonna is another small community in Minnesota that is home to a large Somali population. Owatonna is 42 miles west of Rochester, Minnesota, and has a total population of 22,400. The Somali immigrants first arrived in Owatonna in 1995. They have continued to move in and out of Owatonna over the past eight years, but often move to follow different opportunities that arise in other towns.

The 2002 census estimate does not truthfully represent the number of Somali immigrants that reside in Owatonna or for that matter anywhere in Minnesota (Williams 2000). Therefore it is estimated that approximately 1,400–1,500 Somalis live in Owatonna. The majority of Somalis are employed by the factories; however, some have begun to find jobs outside of the factories. For example, several women are employed in health care jobs and in nursing homes, and Somali youth can be found working in the supermarket. There is also a halal market, which is owned by local Somali. The halal market not only provides jobs for Somalis, but also provides the Somalis a place to buy their food rather than driving to the Twin Cities.

As of 2003, there have not been any policies adopted by the Owatonna city government that specifically address the new Somali population. This is largely due to Owatonna's past experience with other immigrant groups, such as Vietnamese, Hmong, Bosnians, and other groups. The past experience with non-English-speaking immigrant groups prepared the community and the government to be open to different ethnic groups. However, in 1996, Mayor Peter Connor developed the Cultural Diversity Network, which helped supply Somali immigrants with furniture, clothing, food, and other basic needs. Today the Cultural Diversity Network continues to help the community, but through "emphasis on helping to create an environment of understanding and mutual respect." Many long-time residents and local church groups have helped the Cultural Diversity Network by helping welcome the Somalis and also supporting the English as a Second Language (ESL) and English as a Learned Language (ELL) programs.

The reaction to the Somali immigrants has not been wholly positive. Beginning in 2001, the Steele County Coalition for Immigration Reduction formed and began lobbying Congress to reduce the number of legal immigrants to pre-1970 levels. They also lobby to completely close the U.S. borders and prevent undocumented immigrants from entering. While this group's direct objective may appear national in slope, its indirect objective is "to make Owatonna an unwelcome place for those who are racially and culturally different."

The mayor contends that the vast majority of Owatonna's population, about 80 percent, is still fairly neutral with its feelings toward the Somali immigrants. The other 20 percent is divided equally into the 10 percent that welcome the Somalis and the 10 percent that do not welcome the Somalis and want them to leave Owatonna.

CONCLUSION

Refugees to a new land are invariably faced with the need to make many compromises. They must suffer changes to their traditional way of life, which must be altered to conform to the realities of resettlement. But it is also important for members of a multicultural nation to understand all other cultures that are an important part of the vitality of the host country. Considering the rapidly increasing population emigrating from Somalia it is of utmost importance for members of America to become knowledgeable about their reality, beliefs, customs, culture, and history.

As Somalis in the diaspora establish themselves in the host societies, predominantly the West, they identify themselves primarily as Muslims before identifying themselves as Somalis, Black, or along their clan affiliations. The reason for this is the fact that Somalis have always identified themselves along clan lines and never as "Somali," a generic categorical name that is assigned to them in their host countries. Thus, since they feel a stronger sense of identity and belonging as Muslims in comparison to the term *Somali,* they are prioritizing the preservation of their Muslim identity as they feel it is under the most pressure and conflict with the dominant religion within the host societies. Additionally, having suffered years of intense pain and having seen enough bloodshed in the name of clan affiliations, Somalis in the Somali diaspora are coming together around a unitary "Somali" identity in a way that they apparently never did in Somalia.

On the whole, Somalis are, by and large, people with a very strong sense of their own religious and cultural identity. While clan affiliation and animosity may still exist in some Somalis, the general consensus that now is the time to move on and work together for a common good irrespective of the clan differences, which they hope will come to pass so that Somalis can together work towards a common good of reviving Somalia. They are aiming at working together as one instead of working in small, clan-based groups, so as to collectively work towards a common good of preserving both their cultural and Muslim traditions that are central to their identity as a people. Somalia is rich in all of these areas. However, one must remember, regardless of amount of limited information presented, there is always more to learn.

GLOSSARY

Aqal
Portable, dome-shaped dwelling of nomads

Aroos
Wedding

Bakaar
Underground pit used to store grain

Beeraley
Farmers

Canjeero
Flat, unrisen bread, similar to a pancake

Cariish
Rectangular house

Clan
Upper limit of political action. Has territorial properties and often a clan head or Ugaas. *Example:* Garjante

Clan family
A group of different clans with a sense of identity when engaged in conflict against other clan families. *Example:* Hawiye

Daaqsin
Grazing areas

Dambiil
A handwoven bag

Derin/dermo
A handwoven mat

Dervish
Known as *Daraawiish* in Somali. Followers of Sayyid Mohammed Abdullah Hassan, an anti-colonial religious leader (1856–1920)

Dhobeey
Crop production areas with heavy soil

Diya-paying group
A group of men linked by lineage and a contractual agreement to support one another, especially in regard to compensation for injuries and death against fellow members

Gaal
Originally the Oromo, now used when referring to any non-Moslems

Geel
Camel(s) [generic]

Istun
Stick fighting at the start of the solar calendar

Macaawiis
Man's sarong or long wrap skirt

Masjid
Mosque or house of worship for Moslems

Muddul
A round conical dwelling used by farmers

Odkac/Muqmad
Lean, finely cut and fried meat, often kept in oil or melted butter, which lasts for a long time

Ramadan
The month of fasting for Moslems

Sar
Urban cement buildings

Soor
Porridge, often made out of sorghum, a mainstay of the diet for southern farmers

Warlords
Leaders of different militias that control portions of the country

Xaaraan
Ritually unclean, forbidden for Moslems

Xalaal
Clean or ritually pure for Moslems, including the correct slaughter of animals for food. The opposite of Haraam

Xeeb
Coastal area

Xool Raacato
Nomadic herders

Yarad
Dowry paid to the family of the bride

DEFINITION OF TERMS

Assimilation: The mainstreaming of minority populations into a dominant society that result in the loss of cultural identity by the minorities and adoption of the majority population's language, cultural, and way of life.

Brain Drain: The effort made by the dominant society to recruit and retain foreign people who have special and valuable skills. Somali immigrants who arrived after the immigration reforms of 1965 are sometimes referred to as the "Brain Drain" generation, because many of the most talented people were "drained" from Somalia.

Discrimination: An unfavorable act that result in the unequal treatment of an individual or population on the basis of race, ethnicity, religious practices, gender, or social class.

Family Reunification: The process by which citizens and legal immigrants, including refugees, are allowed to sponsor close relatives, enabling them to come live in the U.S.

Immigrant: A person who moves to a country where he or she intends to settle permanently. Legal immigrants have permission of the government to live in the U.S.

Immigration: Involves the movement of people into or out of (**emigration**) a specific geographic area or location.

Minority Groups: People belonging to populations categorically labeled as such are powerless and discriminated against by the dominant population in terms of economics, politics, and culture.

Melting Pot: The fusion of all the ethnic differences to assimilate each minority population to dominant population standards and values.

Naturalization: The process by which an immigrant becomes a U.S. citizen. With a few exceptions (such as the right to run for president), naturalized citizens have all the rights, privileges, and responsibilities of native-born citizens.

Refugee: A person who is unable or unwilling to live in his or her native country because of persecution or a well-founded fear of persecution on account of race, religion, nationality, membership in a particular social group, or political opinion.

Somali American: U.S. citizen whose ancestors are from Somalia.

Stereotype: An overgeneralization of characteristics toward a population, which often leads to discrimination.

REFERENCES

Ahmed, Ali Jimale. (1996). *Daybreak is Near: Literature, Clans and the Nation-State In Somalia.* Lawrenceville, NJ: The Red Sea Press.

Atkinson, Donald R., George Morten, and Derald Wing Sue. (1998). "American Minorities." In *Defining Population and Terms,* 5th ed., pp. 3–20. New York: McGraw-Hill.

Barone, Michael. (2001). *The New Americans: How the Melting Pot Can Work Again.* Washington, D.C.: Regnery Publishing.

Besteman, Catherine L. (1995). "The Invention of Gosha: Slavery, Colonialism, and Stigma in Somali History." In *The Invention of Somalia,* ed. A. J. Ahmed, pp. 43–62. Lawrenceville, NJ: Red Sea Press.

Black, Erick. (2002). "From Mogadishu to Minneapolis." *Minneapolis, Star Tribune,* August 3, 2002.

Boyd, M. (1989). "Family and Personal Networks in International Migration: Recent Developments and New Agendas." *International Migration Review* 23: 638–669.

Breton, R. (1964). "Institutional Completeness of Ethnic Communities and the Personal Relations of Immigrants." *American Journal of Sociology* 84: 293–318.

Brunner, Borgna (Ed.). (2000). "TIME Almanac 2000." USA: Family Education Company. *The Struggle for Land in Southern Somalia: The War Behind the War,* eds. L. V. Cassanelli, & C. L. Besteman. London: Haan Publishing.

Cassanelli, Lee V. (1982). *The Shaping of Somali Society: Reconstructing the History Of a Pastoral People, 1600–1900.* Philadelphia: University of Pennsylvania Press.

Declich, Francesca. (1995). "Identity, Dance and Islam Among People with Bantu Origin." In *The Invention of Somalia,* ed. A. J. Ahmed, pp. 191–222. Lawrenceville, NJ: Red Sea Press.

Desbarats, J. (1994). "Ethnic Differences in Adaptation: Somali Refugees in the U.S." *International Migration Review* 20 (2): 405–427.

Franklin, Robert. (2002). "Somalis work to make St. Cloud their home despite a few conflicts." *Minneapolis Star Tribune,* November 26, 2002.

Foner, N. (1985). "Race and Color: Somali Migrants in London New York City." *International Migration Review* 19: 708–727.

Furst, Randy. (2002). "St. Cloud faced with perceptions of racism, anti-Semitism." *Minneapolis Star Tribune,* December 28, 2002.

Geshekter, Charles L. (1979). "Socio-Economic Developments in Somalia." *Horn of Africa* 2 (2): 24–36.

Glazer, N. & D. P. Moynihan. 1970. *Beyond the Melting Pot.* Cambridge: MIT Press.

Great Twin Cities United Way (2000). "Somali Culture. United Way." Confederation of Somali Community in Minnesota.

Guthrie, P. (1997). "Sea Islanders." In *American Immigrant Cultures: Builders of a Nation,* eds. D. Levinson and M. Ember, vol. 2, pp. 779–784. MacMillan Reference, New York.

Hess, Robert L. (1966). *Italian Colonialism in Somalia.* Chicago: University of Chicago Press.

Kilani, Method. (2001). Ecumenism in Multi-Religious Context. (Africa). *The Ecumenical Review,* July: 1–19.

Konczachi, Z. A. (1967). "Nomadic and Economic Development of Somalia." *Canadian Journal of African Studies* [Montreal] 1 (2): 163–75.

Kusow, Abdi M. (1995). "The Somali Origin: Myth or Reality." In *The Invention of Somalia,* ed. A. J. Ahmed, pp. 81–106. Lawrenceville, NJ. The Red Sea Press.

———2001. "Stigma and Social Identities: The Process of Identity Work among Somali Immigrants in Canada." pp. 152–182 in Variations on the Theme of Somaliness, edited by M. S Lilius. Turku, Finland: Center for Continuing Education, Abo University Press.

Lewis, I. M. (1969). *The Peoples of the Horn of Africa: Somali, Afar and Saho.* London: International African Institute.

Library of Congress; Federal Research Division (1993). *Somalia: A Country study,* 4th ed., ed. Metz, Helen Chapin. United States: First.

Luling, Virginia (1976). "Colonial and Post-Colonial Influences on a South Somali Community." *Journal of African Studies* 3 (1): 491–511.

Martinez, Ruben. (2001). *Crossing Over: A Mexican Family on the Migrant Trail.* New York: Metropolitan.

McGowan, Rita (1999). *Muslims in the Diaspora: The Somali Communities of London, Toronto, and Buffalo.*

McLemore, Dale S., Harriett D. Romo, & Susan Gonzalez Baker. (2001). *Racial and Ethnic Relations in America,* 6th ed. New York: Allyn and Bacon.

M-A Pérouse de Montclos, A refugee diaspora: When the Somali go west, in K. Koser (ed), *New African diasporas,* Routledge, London, 2003, pp. 37–55.

Mukhtar, Mohamed Haji. (1995). "Islam in Somali history: Fact and Fiction." In *The Invention of Somalia,* ed. A. J. Ahmed, pp. 1–28. Lawrenceville, NJ: The Red Sea Press.

Ronningen, Barbara J. (2004). Estimates of Selected Immigrant Populations in Minnesota. Minnesota State Demographic Center.

Ronningen, Barbra J. (2000). "Immigrants in Minnesota: an increasingly Diverse Population." Minnesota State Demographic Center, December, 1–8.

Wilder Research Center. (2000). Speaking for Themselves: A Survey of Hispanic, Hmong, Russian and Somali Immigrants in Minneapolis-St. Paul, Wilder Research Center.

Williams, Sarah T. (2002). "Somalis find refuge from war in Owatonna." *Minneapolis Star Tribune,* December 17, 2000.

A South Asian Feminist Perspective

Mridusha Shrestha Allen

Women: Object or Person?

Historically, oppression has been and continues to be a serious issue of concern worldwide, both in developed and underdeveloped countries. Many feminists today argue that feminism is a grass-roots movement that seeks to cross boundaries based on universal human rights that transcend social class, race, culture, ethnicity, sexual orientation, and religion. The feminine is culturally specific, but feminism addresses universal issues relevant to the women of any particular society (for example, female genital cutting in Africa or the glass ceiling in developed economies). Feminism creates a debate that examines the extent to which certain issues, such as rape, incest, female oppression in marriage, and mothering are universal. Major themes explored in feminism include patriarchy, stereotyping, personal objectification, sexual objectification, and oppression. The following discussion looks at parallels between the issues facing Latinas, Native American, and South Asian women.

For women, the "idealized" female body has been problematic for many reasons. Within a given context, women's subjectivities are often conflated with a volatile and leaky female body and relegated to a position of less power and stature than men. For women with disabilities (or more properly, differing abilities) or body types outside the mass media norm, the idealized female body is unattainable. Therefore, the subjectivity of the minority woman feminist requires ways of locating one's *positionality* and value within a social landscape that objectifies a "differently abled colored woman" as being wounded, unhealthy, unlovable, and often less than human because our bodies do not fit the mass media idealized and objectified norm. And it seems that this is not just applicable to minority women like myself but perhaps it has some universal relevance in all societies.

Similarly, new forms of subjectivity must be examined in postmodernist research and writing. Although some feminists claim that postmodernism strips away identity and voice, even from those like myself who, having come from a Third World country, never had them in the first place, it is not possible to apply a formula like that to all women. It is especially not accurate to claim that all women have been denied these things. Many so-called Third World women beg to differ when it comes to producing this feminism of the masses, which roots itself in White mainstream culture. While Suleri's *Meatless Days* and Anzaldua's *Borderlands* address similar issues, the women's positions in different parts of the world enable oppositional subjects to emerge in relation to their life histories of interaction with fathers, uncles, brothers, cousins, boyfriends, and husbands. These complex examples of how postmodern experiences allow us to deconstruct modernist subjects, while being connected to them, in the end offer new forms of subjective positioning that move beyond the White traditional ideal into a realm women of color can begin to define and refine.

The human body has long been the object of focus for countless artists. Historically, the female body in particular has proven to be the most profitable gender for an artist to base his/her work on, especially that of the colonized colored female who has long been perceived as an object White male colonizers were free to exploit. The roots of Native American, Latino, and Hindu art celebrating the female form, on the other hand, are ancient. In fact, these are considered some of the oldest artistic traditions in the world, with Native American being the oldest in North America. The antiquity of female-oriented art such as literature, drama, music, the visual arts, and cinema can be explained in part by the intermingling of non-White and cultures after the advent of European colonialism. But more and more women of color are taking charge of their identities, as well as how those identities are constructed, represented, and exploited.

The colonized world and European artistic and folkloric customs blended from the earliest days of colonial settlement beginning in the late fifteenth century. This meeting of cultures evolved over centuries and resulted in an inextricable mingling of traditions. Recently, many feminist scholars from all colonized lands have begun to express their grief at not being able to make traditional art employing their own voices, narratives, and symbols because there was only one style of art narrative in the public arena, and, unfortunately, that narrative was White male dominated. However, not all of the women in the world were standing idly by allowing the men to dominate. Women were actively participating in decision-making processes—politically, organizationally, and artistically (Huerta 2000, 11).

The classic behavior typical of colonizing White men has been a serious obstacle to women anxious to play a role in the struggle for indigenous female liberation. The oppression suffered by Native American women, Latinas, and African and Asian American women is different from that suffered by White women in this country. Because minority women have been victimized by colonialism and racial oppression as well as by sexism, we are part of an oppressed collective that has been subjected to racism as well misogyny. Since the overwhelming majority of minority men have also been relegated to subservient roles as workers in the colonized world, minority women have also been victims of their own men who have suffered the exploitation of demeaning working class conditions foisted upon them by colonizers. But in addition to this, minority women are relegated to an inferior position because of their sex. Thus, minority women suffer a triple form of oppression: as members of an oppressed race, as menial workers, and as women.

On the other hand, minority women are starting to understand that the struggle now unfolding against the oppression of women is not only relevant to them but *is* in fact their struggle. Because sexism and male *chauvinism* are so deeply rooted in this society, there is a strong tendency, even within the women's movement, to deny the basic right of minority women to organize around their own concrete issues. We minority women are thus victims of a double whammy—we are subtly discouraged from joining the women's liberation movement on our own terms by domineering feminists as well as by our own people because it is perceived as a "White thing."

Just consider the fact that dance in contemporary Western culture is considered to be primarily a "feminine" activity when it is done by people of color. Minority women are often presented as sultry, seductive, and even sometimes lewd caricatures when they dance. Why are some minority women labeled "bad" because of the way they dance? How does the minority female dancer find empowerment and pleasure through control of her body when she is objectified as an exotic object designed for the entertainment and pleasure of both men and mainstream women from the dominant culture? Despite being viewed as an object of exotic desire and being subjected to the predatory gaze, how could the twentieth-century minority female dancer discover ways to speak her mind and express her soul in a world where the only venues were owned by White men and women and controlled by White men and women for their pleasure? Just ask yourself how Sarah Baartman, the Hottentot Venus in the nineteenth century, must have felt to be the powerless dark-skinned woman who was objectified, put on display and viewed, and degraded by both men and women.

Some minority feminists take a holistic approach to body politics—issues revolving around sexual identity, marriage, and motherhood, believing the saying of Dr. Martin Luther King Jr., "A threat to justice anywhere is a threat to justice everywhere." With that statement in mind, some self-identified minority feminists have found it useful to support other movements such as the civil rights movement and the gay rights movement. At the same time, many minority feminists criticize the women's movement for being dominated by White women, especially lesbians. But we minority women have a voice and a movement of our own that deals with issues of deeper, multilayered oppression that White women can only marginally appreciate. Feminist claims about the alleged disadvantages women face in Western society are often less relevant to the lives of minority women, and this set of factors is the key in postcolonial minority feminism. Minority feminists are sometimes wary of the transgender movement because it challenges the distinctions between men and women, and between White women and women of color. White women often have more in common with White men than they do minority women, often haggling over who gets a bigger chunk of the colonial pie. We minority women, however, do not choose to be separated from our men, be they gay or straight. Rather, we desire to find a way to teach them about our oppression by them through helping them see their own oppression by White colonizers. Transgender and transsexual individuals who identify as female are excluded from some "women-only" gatherings and events and are rejected by some feminists who say that no one born male can fully understand the oppression that women face. But we minority women do not direct our militancy against our men the way White women do; rather we try help our men rise above their oppression of us by becoming aware of their oppression at the hands of the colonizers.

Throughout history, women have been relegated to subservient roles, often even abused in many different societies. In the traditional world, in particular, women have been oppressed for centuries by their fathers, brothers, and husbands. I have tried to study how this has occurred in my own culture through the onerous practices of arranged marriage and dowry. Women in my traditional homeland were seen as child-bearers, homemakers, and caregivers. These women had to watch their children, perform household chores, and cook and care for their husbands. Many men did not consider women to be capable of working outside the home in our past, which is part of the reason why the term *weaker sex* was coined. In traditional Nepali society, women living at those times had to act according to male-dominated social standards. They were not seen in a good way if they spoke to men they did not know. Meanwhile, prostitution was legal in many areas in our society, and men were not criticized but rather seen as heroic, even if they had several girlfriends when they were married. Women, on the other hand, were relegated to the roles of dutiful wife, dutiful daughter-in-law, and dedicated mother.

Motherhood is a social construction, and as such most permutations of motherhood should be possible. Standard socially constructed forms of motherhood for Nepali women, like many other traditional minority women, are: 1) women should stay at home during children's early or formative years; and 2) paid employment is less important, or "secondary," to their domestic duties; in other words, as a social construction, our identity rests on an assumption that women's biological abilities to bear and suckle children are "natural" and fundamental to women's "fulfillment." What is not stated, however, is that this position fails to recognize that some minority women, like myself, are liberated, and this is demonstrated by the fact that I have chosen my own husband who is a friend that has supported me in making my own life choices, such as choosing motherhood over career for the time being. And all feminists should respect this choice since each woman has her own identity whose meanings can vary and whose life path is subject to its own vagaries and changes over time.

The fact is that the realities of motherhood often contradict White feminist social ideology, and many of us liberated minority women have chosen motherhood over ideology (children are often far more fun to hug and kiss than one's ideals). And the facts do not lie: 1) over half of all women with children work for wages, many not by choice; 2) traditional gender role expectations are changing, as there is greater acceptance of women working outside the home, but many women are still unhappy and do not feel liberated; 3) there is a good deal of literature on the "ambivalence" and "guilt" mothers feel when they work outside the home; and 4) some minority women, like myself, happily choose to stay at home with our families. The only kinds of fulfillment for a liberated woman are not just career and money. This should be a given but apparently some people need to be reminded that changes in expectations are still needed and it should never go uncontested that the only way to be liberated is to follow White feminist ideals.

Nowhere does it say that the only legitimate daughters of our Great Mother are White feminists. And while our White feminist sisters' voices are salient, all women are her children and thus every permutation of Her creation is above reproach. It is "She" who set the limits, not majority females. The feminist movement and feminism have been useful and edifying means to celebrate the aforementioned reality but when feminism has been co-opted by women in the dominant majority it has become as much a means of the oppression of minority women as our history of interacting with the foolish male-dominated institutions in our traditional societies. Our liberation as minority women is about the freedom to choose and the freedom to be who we are and not to have that dictated to us by anyone, male or female, straight or lesbian.

Gender Roles in Hindu Society

Today, in Hindu society, men and women perform distinctly different roles that are based on nothing more than their gender—social differentiation. Although these roles do not hold true for each individual, the majority of people live out their lives in accordance with these extremely pervasive roles. In general, the roles prevalent in modern Hindu society prescribe that men should be domineering, aggressive, and superior at math and the sciences; they should become successful in their careers and be the breadwinners; and they should control and suppress their feelings. Women, on the other hand, should be submissive, nurturing, gentle; better at languages and the humanities; emotional; and desirous of nothing more than being controlled and told what to do by their husbands and their male elders. Women are expected to watch Hindi movies and accept traditional and popular cultural expectations uncritically while caring for the home and their children. She should do her part to make a happy family, supporting a husband who provides for her while she remains at home and tends the house.

A male-dominated family system provides very little scope for the female to assert her identity in Hindu society. Women are often marginalized from economic and social opportunities due to illiteracy, poverty, and conservative social taboos (Manandhar 2004). Also, their standing in society is mostly contingent on their husband and parents' social and economic positions. They have limited access to markets, productive services, education, health care, and local government. Malnutrition and poverty hit women hardest. Unfortunately, female children usually are given less food than male children, especially when the family has experienced food shortages. Women in working families usually work harder and longer than men. By contrast, women from high-caste families have maids to take care of most household chores and other tedious work and thus work far less than men or women in lower socioeconomic groups.

From time immemorial, before the dawn of written history, female energy was an important part of people's lives in Hindu culture. Clans venerated wise mother goddesses, dark destroyer goddesses, and cyclical fertility goddesses, of which women were the natural embodiment. But as politics evolved, these goddesses were forgotten or relegated to positions as wives or concubines, and their energy was lost to time. But, as some people are discovering, contemporary people need the guidance of the goddess more than ever. The goddess movement seeks to recapture that energy and to bring civilization back into touch with its history of feminine power (Gibson 1998, 57).

Shaktism is a denomination of Hinduism that worships *Shakti* or *Devi Mata,* the Hindu name for the Great Divine Mother. In pure Shaktism, the Great Goddess, or Devi, is worshipped as nothing less than the higher divinity, supreme Brahman itself, with all other forms of Divinity, female or male, considered to be merely her diverse manifestations.

Dedicating dancing girls to temples in the service of God was not peculiar to India. Although ancient texts like the Vedas and Upanishads do not mention *Devadasis* (servants of God), institutionalized worship of idols in temples during the early centuries of the Christian era led to the practice of dedicating women to temples as laid down in the *puranas.* Over a period of time all the "pampered family deities" of kings and nobles started getting pretty and talented servants for different rituals performed for the deity (befitting a great king or deity) like bathing, dressing, offering flowers, and creating music and dance. Their main job was to dance and sing, also playing musical instruments while the priests of the temple offered sixteen kinds of services (Banerjeee 1996, 311).

Devadasi is a religious practice in parts of southern India, including Andhra Pradesh, whereby parents arrange a marriage between their daughter and a deity in a temple—a truly unique kind of forced arranged marriage. The marriage usually occurs before the girl reaches puberty and requires the girl to become a prostitute for upper-caste community members. Such girls are known as *jogini*. They are forbidden to enter into a real marriage, and they continue to be custodians of fine arts after their ritual marriage. In the past they studied the classics, in particular Sanskrit and regional languages and they set to music lyrics, and they played and taught various musical instruments. It was they who kept the tradition of *Bharatanatyam* or Indian classical dance alive, and no social stigma was attached to their profession.

It is especially important for women to learn more about the language of symbols in their traditions because many common religious symbols were stolen from ancient woman-centered systems and reinterpreted in the contexts of patriarchy. As women struggle out from under centuries of patriarchal oppression, they find it necessary to reclaim their symbols and reapply them to feminine interests (Walker 1988, 165). So when we consider the roles of women we must also consider the symbolism embodied in some of these roles, even though from a post-modern perspective they might seem oppressive.

For example, *Teej* is the fasting festival for women. It takes place in August or early September. The festival is a three-day long celebration that combines sumptuous feasts as well as rigid fasting. Through this religious fasting, Hindu women pray for marital bliss, as well as the wellbeing of their spouse and children and the purification of their own body and soul. Traditionally, the ritual of Teej is obligatory for all Hindu married women and girls who have reached puberty. Exception is made for the ones who are ill or physically unfit. In such circumstances a priest performs the rites.

According to the holy books, the Goddess Parbati (wife of the god Shiva) fasted and prayed fervently for the great Lord Shiva to become her spouse. Touched by her devotion, he took her for his wife. Goddess Parbati, in gratitude sent her emissary to preach and continue this religious fasting among mortal women, promising prosperity and longevity for the families of the women who did so. On this day the women, both married and unmarried, assemble at one place, in their finest attire and start dancing and singing devotional songs. After the completion of the previous day's *puja* (prayer), women pay homage to various deities and bathe with red mud found on the roots of the sacred *Datiwan* bush (medicinal plant), along with its leaves. This act of purification is the final ritual of Teej, after which women are considered absolved from all sins.

The preceding example is used as a metaphor to demonstrate how Hindu women have historically been expected to sacrifice all for the good of the family, even to the point of *suttee* (committing suicide by casting oneself on the funeral pyre of one's deceased husband) if necessary. They are to accept an arranged marriage and the accompanying oppression without question. And even though there is a great emphasis on goddesses in the Hindu religion, they are almost always secondary and subservient to male deities—Kali, the Destroyer, being one of the only exceptions.

Feminist Perspective on Hindu Religion and Gender Roles

Arguably, the divine identity in classical theism and atheism is unmistakably male. "This supreme, ruling, judging, and loving male God is envisioned as a single, absolute subject, is named Father, and is conceived as standing in a relation of hierarchical dominion over the world" (Menski 1998, 74–81). In ways both implicit and explicit, this construct tends in turn to justify various social and political structures of patriarchy that exalt solitary human patriarchs at the head of pyramids of power.

According to the maxim, however, no bird can ever fly on only one of its wings. Women being the *other-wing* of the society, it is important to discuss their roles in any society. And while actual practice does not always reflect a society's ideals, ideals constitute the highest aspirations of a people, what we might call their heart and soul. But they also often reveal the inherent contradictions between idealism and practice. Hence a real in-depth understanding of the Hindu tradition concerning womanhood would essentially begin by exploring its ideals, and then looking for contradictions between stated ideals and actual practice.

Further, Hinduism considers *Moksha* or spiritual freedom as the ultimate happiness of life, whether for man or for woman. But this seems a bit ironic in a tradition that oppresses both women and members of some castes. The worship of God in the form of Mother is a unique feature of Hinduism. Through the ages, the doctrine of the Motherhood of God has established a firm root in Hinduism. Today, Hindus worship the Divine Mother in many popular forms such as *Durga, Kali, Lakshrni, Saraswati, Ambika,* and *Uma.* By worshipping God as the Divine Mother, a Hindu can more easily attribute Motherly traits to the Lord, such as tenderness and compassion and forgivingness. In this light the natural love between a mother and her child is the best expression of the Lord's unconditional love for us as children of God.

In the most representative Hindu view, the universe is the manifestation of the creative power (Shakti) of Brahman, whose essence is absolute existence, consciousness, and bliss. Since all created forms proceed from the womb of the mother, the creative power (Shakti) of God is recognized by Hindus as the female principle—the motherly aspect of nature. In this sense we are all children of the Divine Mother. We are contained by Her before our manifestation and nourished by Her throughout our existence. To a Hindu, the motherly aspect of God in nature is full of beauty, gentleness, kindness, and tenderness. When we look upon all the glorious and beautiful things in nature and experience a feeling of tenderness within us, we feel the motherly instinct of God. The worship of God in the form of Mother is seen in the embodiment of the Hindu child. When a devotee worships God as Divine Mother, he or she appeals to Her tenderness and unconditional love. Such love unites the devotee with God, like a child with its mother. Just as a child feels safe and secure in the lap of its mother, a devotee feels safe and secure in the presence of the Divine Mother. *Pararnaharnsa Sri Ramakrishna,* one of the greatest Indian sages of modern times, worshipped the Divine Mother Kali during his entire life. He established a personal relationship with "Her" and was always conscious of Her presence by his side (Neumann 1972, 97).

In Hinduism, the Divine Mother is the first manifestation of Divine Energy. Thus, with the name of Divine Mother comes the idea of energy, omnipotence, omnipresence, love, intelligence, and wisdom. Just as a child believes its mother to be all-powerful and capable of doing anything for the child, a devotee believes the Divine Mother to be all merciful, all-powerful, and eternally guiding and protecting him with her invisible arms. The worship of God as Mother has thus had a significant impact on Hinduism. The position of women in the Hindu religion is therefore dignified as an ideal because each woman is considered a manifestation of the Divine Mother. Hindus view man and woman as the two wings of the same bird, or two wheels of the same cart. Thus, a man is considered incomplete without a woman. As a Hindu woman, I am proud to say that though praxis (practice) does not always reflect the ideal, it is through the worship of God in the form of Mother that Hinduism offers the possibility for a unique reverence towards womanhood.

The status of women in any civilization reveals the level of sophistication and tolerance for all human beings in a particular society. The treatment of women is thus a bit of a litmus test for the level and kind of civilization a society envisions itself as being, and the term *status* includes not only personal and proprietary rights and freedoms but also duties and obligations. And this cuts both ways. In the case of a Nepali woman, it means her personal rights, proprietary rights, and her freedoms, as well as her duties and obligations in relation to the society and her family members. Too often, the emphasis is on her duties and obligations without acknowledging or respecting her rights and her freedom. And this is where the rub occurs. Our tradition is full of idealized forms and expressions of woman—divine, earthy, loving, creating, destroying, and nurturing. Yet in practice our society often does not reflect this ideal. The reality is that men (and women) often do not do what they say in our society, and in this way we are really no different from any other people. In fact, this reflects a human universal—ethnocentric hypocrisy. The truth is men cannot long survive without women and women cannot long survive without men so we must learn to overcome our stereotypes and idealizations of one another and engage in pragmatic discourse, action, and praxis that allows us to work out our differences in constructive ways that serve us all.

It is an aphorism in my country (and India) that men and women are like two wheels of a cart. Without one the cart is functionless. Looking back at the history of my society, however, I see that women have always had lower status than men, thereby being given a smaller wheel on the societal cart. Yet, we are still expected to keep up. But one must keep in mind that Nepal, like almost every other society, is not homogeneous (neither is India) and the extent of the gap between the sexes within Nepal varies across subcultures, castes, families, and time (for example, we have thirty-six legally recognized ethnic groups in Nepal and five major castes). Traditionally, women's lives have usually been described in terms of motherhood while men's lives have usually been characterized as heads of household or breadwinners (wage earners in modern society).

Thus, even though things are slowly changing, progressive women in Nepal must continuously combat traditional stereotypes of women's roles in society and in the home. I remember while growing up that my grandmother's work centered on the home. Moreover, women like her were also traditionally engaged in spinning, weaving, and other home industries, as well as in manual labor, to help supplement family income. The economic role of women is thus an important consideration because social status in Nepal is measured by both caste and economic standing. Land ownership is both a measure of status and a source of income, as are men's professions. And while women occupy a secondary position in business and the civil service, the constitution of our country guarantees equality between men and women. But this is an ideal not always realized.

In more rural Nepali tribal communities, communal customs dictate women's lesser role in a strict caste hierarchy that structures the society. In such instances women's status relative to men differs from one ethnic group to another in Nepal and is, in fact, usually determined by caste. Across the cultural diversity spectrum in Nepal, the majority of communities are rigidly patriarchal—a woman's life is strongly influenced by her father and husband, as reflected in the practice of patrilocal residence, patriarchal descent, and by inheritance systems and family relations that favor males. It is thus the particular localized culture in question, with its rigid hierarchical structure of caste and gender roles, which then promotes and shapes hierarchical values that reinforce caste and gender roles based upon rigid social constructs and habituated practices in Nepal.

Another important common factor in Nepali is respect for elders, wherein the senior female member plays a commanding role within the family by controlling resources, making crucial planting and harvesting decisions, and determining the expenses and budget allocations. Yet women's lives have until recently remained centered on their traditional roles; that is, raising children, taking care of most household chores, fetching water and animal fodder, and doing farm work.

My personal observations as a traditional Nepali woman who emigrated to America are indeed unique. I married a Métis man after completing my education at university, I have children with him, I participate in powwows and traditional Native culture while maintaining my own identity, and I see distinctive similarities between both our peoples and situations. I see that the power of women in both Nepali and Native American societies was slowly eroded due to contact with male-dominated colonizing nations that imposed a sexist hierarchy on the colonized peoples. Even within her own culture in both contexts, a woman had become a possession of her husband, often with no say in the matter or in her own life. Where autonomy within a collective identity used to be important to all tribe members in South Asia and Native America, the invading Aryan and European way (ironically the same people) had taken over and equality was eroded; individuality with a dominance hierarchy became dominant.

Another, more recent, set of events has also contributed to women's loss of status in both contexts. This has to do with education. Traditionally, women were nurturers, educators, and providers of and for the children, but with the advent of formal, government-sanctioned schools (residential schools in the case of Natives and British-style boarding schools in Nepal) came the loss of the children to a system of alien indoctrination. Nepali girls were historically denied education, promoting a sexist educational system that has kept women in a subservient role in our society. Young Native girls (and boys) were taken to live in residential schools against the will of their families. There, they were indoctrinated into an alien set of values that denied them participation in their own society when they returned, as well as mainstream society due to racism. When their children were taken, Native mothers lost their role as nurturer and educator. Thus, both of these seemingly divergent factors in forced colonial education systems—lack of education for girls in Nepal and forced education (indoctrination) for Indian girls in America—were a harsh blow to the status, roles, and power both Nepali and Native women originally had (Bataille 1987, 41).

In Nepal, things are changing. Marriage—this is to say, arranged marriage—has historically been of overwhelming importance in determining a Nepali woman's identity. The event of an arranged marriage determines almost all of her options and subsequent livelihood. The socioculturally constructed preference for a son has historically combined with an onerous dowry system to reinforce women's lower standing in Nepal. In fact, the dowry system, whose original intentions were good because it represented an investment in daughters at marriage, has created many serious barriers for women; and not just women, but for their families as well. Many young women are now mentally and physically tortured after marriage by their husbands, their in-laws, and others in the husband's extended family. At the same time, the perception that a dowry is not adequate frequently causes a woman's family to be publicly shamed and her father (and sometimes mother) to commit suicide.

Marriage in all societies always involves an exchange of gifts, and there are accounts of exchanging gifts during marriage ceremonies in most societies, where sometimes-disgruntled members of the bride's or groom's family have occasionally engaged in disputes over the gift-giving. But this is most often due to a lack of an exchange of bride price gifts from the groom's family, not an insufficient dowry from the bride's family. In Nepal and India, the wife is occasionally hurt or killed in disputes over dowry (or in some instances her family members as well, which can set off family feuds and revenge cycles in my country). Thus, Nepali women bear a great burden as far as social expectations are concerned. Nepali women are often seen as representing family honor, and their input is often ignored in marital decisions.

CONCLUSION

Women's experiences in traditional societies, and their relationship to natural and cultural artifacts, depend on several factors, including mythology, sacred landscapes, gender relations, and gender-specific roles. But nowadays, women face a unique set of problems that can only be understood in terms of acculturation and survival in the face of colonization, whether internal (in the case of Nepal) or external (in the case of Native women). In both instances the uniting factor is the colonizing impact of modernity and globalization. The maintenance of traditional Native and Nepali societies through oral tradition and artistic forms continues to nurture spirituality and a common bond with the land, even in the face of the overwhelming forces of modernity. As traditional societies have changed over the last few centuries, so have the nature of women's roles and their productivity.

As Bataille and Sands say, "The property of the oral tradition is derived from a concern for communal welfare, the subordination of the individual to the collective needs of the tribe (1987, 4)." So in both instances, Native and Nepali, both men and women are subservient to the greater communal good. It is just that in Nepal women's status and roles were designated more as property due to the agrarian nature of subsistence and its associated rigid caste and gender hierarchy of property ownership; whereas in Native societies, where there were less rigid notions of property ownership and nonexistent notions of caste, women were seen less as property themselves and more often as active agents with greater self-determination.

Today, the roles of women in both Nepali and Native American societies are changing. Many women in both societies are getting post-secondary education and then, in turn, are teaching or helping their people and their families. Women are actively setting up groups and associations to help those who cannot help themselves. The voices of grandmothers who are wise and willing to teach the youth about their cultures and tell the stories that teach pride in self are once again being listened to. Woman is the provider, nurturer, mother, counselor, and she is the spiritual and medical healer to her people. And in this there may lay answers and solutions for all people, not just women.

Despite a significantly altered socio-political scenario, much of the media continue to present women in gender-stereotyped roles in both my country and Native America. In my country many women are still confined to household work while men are viewed as individuals with potential, specific expertise, and professional skills. It seems like there is an obvious hesitation in introducing new role models for women in Nepal. As Chhetri (2002) states, "Women's limited participation in media is considered a major obstacle to a positive and inspiring portrayal of women."

Women of color in U.S society seek to offer alternative interpretations of the social world. People of color, both men and women, have encountered severe economic and social dislocations from the time of the arrival of Europeans in the Americas until the present. Today, women of color on average receive the lowest wages, hold the worst jobs, and are more likely to be unemployed. Social location—this is to say, racial or ethnic proximity or distance—in the labor market means that opportunities are often influenced by people who are either near or distant. Factors like male or female, White, Black, Latina, American Indian, or Asian, rich or poor, straight or gay, are often more significant than what a person's skills and abilities are.

Minority women are more likely to live in poverty and to be single mothers than their White counterparts. They are subordinated in this way because patterns of hierarchy, domination, and oppression based on race, class, gender, and sexual orientation are built into the structure of our society. In spite of these obstacles, women of color like Nepali and Native American women have shaped their lives and those of their families through acts of quiet dignity and firm determination. Their actions today have included quiet revolt and rebellion, creative conflict and social change, and adaptation and accommodation. Identity politics addresses the need to change the behavior, attitudes, norms, and values that define and influence identity issues such as gender roles in society, and this is why identity politics is so important. Family, friends, education, training, the media, arts, cultural values, and science and technology all influence a person's identity. How they do so and the identity we subscribe to, as well as that imposed on us by others, impact the way we perceive changes in male and female roles. How people are reacting to these social changes thus depends upon many overlapping and interacting circumstances. When we are in the middle of this dynamic we often wonder if changes in our identities and roles are good, as well as whether the overall social structure is supporting these changes.

In the eyes of most people today the allowance of women and men into jobs that used to be gender-defined by the mainstream and traditionally accepted as such has meant that gender identity is now already changed drastically. Some religions look upon these changes as an abomination and some people still personally believe that women belong at home and a man belongs in the workplace. While some, either for personal or religious reasons, negatively look upon these changes, overall these changes have been accepted. Such changes in the occupational roles of males and females in this modern age have also called for a change in the clothing, attitudes, and lifestyle choices provided for men and women.

The following are some words from different scholars that speak for themselves:

WORDS OF WISDOM

"The history of all times and of today especially, teaches that...
women will be forgotten if they forget to think about themselves."

—Louise Otto (Luise Otto-Peters), German feminist, 1849

Aparna Basu, Professor of History at the University of Delhi, India, says:

"History is no longer just a chronicle of kings and statesmen, of people who wielded power, but of ordinary women and men engaged in manifold tasks. Women's history is an assertion that women have a history."

"If it is true that men are better than women because they are stronger, why aren't our sumo wrestlers in the government?"

—Kishida Toshiko, nineteenth-century Japanese Feminist

There are some organizations in Nepal, like "Tewa," where they fight for equal rights opportunities for women by resisting the cultural assumptions involved in arranged marriage. But there are some other pro-woman rights activists in Nepal that I am aware of who have never raised the issue of arranged marriage or dowry seriously. They have asked for equality in the division of parent's property but not about the abolishment of the dowry system. Why are they so silent on this issue? It is not because there is no foreign aid for it. Certainly, they should have at least raised the issue. There are thousands of literacy classes, and many other *bikas* (progress) interventions targeted for educating women in Nepal today. But to me, a woman born and raised Nepali, it seems like they are barely getting started and have a long way to go. Many of these programs in fact isolate women into discrete groups embedded in particular places and social classes and castes rather than engage them as free, living beings like men. Identity for everyone is mediated by a multiplicity of relationships at home, in the community, and with the state, and thus for any real change to occur in women's identities requires structural change that is extremely difficult to effect. In other words, unless there is significant structural change, these programs with remain imprisoned within structural disparities loaded up with all kinds of implicit assumptions. A consciousness-raising paradigm that does not address fundamental issues of oppression in the preexisting structures and institutions of our society will therefore not in the end serve the cause of the women's movement in Nepal.

There is a saying in my religion, Hinduism, where we believe that all life is sacred, to be loved and revered. Therefore, we promote the practice of *ahimsa,* or nonviolence. All life is sacred because all creatures are manifestations of the Supreme Being, which is neither male nor female but the progenitor of both. Therefore, we have to come to terms with our histories of racist and sexist oppression, and then reconcile with one another afterwards by agreeing to share opportunities and power.

The implications are profound for those of us women who have emigrated to America from other countries to further our studies. We are often the product of our traditional societies having created an environment of sexist discrimination, where in one way or another our grandmothers, mothers, aunts, sisters, nieces, cousins, or other female relatives have been mistreated by a system that our people might have changed a long time ago had we but listened to our own traditional ideals. Acknowledging and respecting the traditional cultural practices and beliefs in our Asian societies that honor women, I think puts us, or at least our generation, in a position to begin demanding a balance between respect for our traditions with the insights afforded through the critical-thinking skills obtained in our modern education. I think it also raises the question of universal human rights in the face of parochial cultural traditions that may have outlived their time. In order to combat violence against women, it is imperative that people work toward a global understanding where women are viewed as equal and valuable partners in their society, not just as the property of men to be bought, sold, married, or killed for the sake of cultural tradition, family honor, or financial convenience. And if we can do so, our traditional ideals will then converge with our modern action and our practice, and we just might then all begin to live as complete human beings by standing in the circle of humanity as equals.

REFERENCES

Acharya, M., & P. Acharya. (1997). *Gender Equality and Empowerment of Women,* A Status Report. UNFPA, Kathmandu.

Alcaron, N. (2003). "Anzaldura's *Frontera:* Inscribing gynetics." In *Chicana Feminisms,* eds. G. F. Arredondo et al. Durham: Duke University Press.

Allen, W. E., & K. Darboe. (2010). *Introduction to Ethnic Studies: A New Approach.* Dubuque, IA: Kendall Hunt.

Asthana, A., & J. Revill. (2008). 3,000 women a year forced into marriage in UK, study finds (guardian.co.uk)

Banerjee, S. (1996). The *Feminization of Violence in Bombay.* Muktal, New Delhi: Muktal Press.

Bataille, G. M., & K. M. Sands. (1987). *American Indian Women: Telling their Lives.* University of Nebraska Press.

Benokraitis, N. J. (2002). *Contemporary Ethnic Families in the United States: Characteristics, Variations, and Dynamics.* Upper Saddle River, NJ: Prentice Hall.

Bonvillain, N. (2001). *Native Nations: Cultures and Histories of Native America.* Upper Saddle River, NJ: Prentice Hall.

Brown, D. E. (1991). *Human Universals.* New York: McGraw-Hill, Inc.

Buffalohead, P. K. (1983). *Farmers Warriors Traders: A Fresh Look at Ojibway Women.* (Document No. 28). In *Minnesota History; the Quarterly of the Minnesota Historical Society* 48 (6) Saint Paul: Minnesota Historical Society, 1983. pp. 236–244. (HRAF Public Information: New Haven, Conn.: HRAF 2000. computer file).

Castillo, A. (1994). *Massacre of the Dreamers: Essays on Xicanisma.* New York: Plume.

Chhetri, A. (2002). *Mainstream Media and Women Participation.* Kathmandu, Nepal: Patrakaritama Mahila Prashna, Nepal Press Institute.

Divorce Rate in India: divorce rate in India (http://www.divorcerate.org/divorce-rate-in-india.html)

Estes, C. P. (1995). *Women Who Run With the Wolves; Myths and Stories of the Wild Woman Archetype.* Ballantine Books: New York.

Fisk, J. (1990). "Native Women in reserve politics: Strategies and struggles." *Journal of legal pluralism* 30 (2): 121–137.

Fox, T., & D. Long. (2000). Struggles within the circle: Violence, healing and health on a First Nations reserve. In *Visions of the Heart,* eds. D. Long and O. Dickason. Harcourt Canada Ltd., pp. 271–297.

Gibson, C. (1998). *Symbols of the Goddess.* Saraband, Scotland: Ziga Design.

Huerta, J. (2000). *Chicano Drama: Performance, Society and Myth.* Cambridge: Cambridge University Press.

Kehoe, A. B. (1995). Blackfoot persons. In *Women And Power in Native North America,* eds. L. F. Klein & L. A. Ackerman. Norman, OK: University of Oklahoma Press, pp. 113–125.

Knaster, M. (1977). *Women in Spanish America: An Annotated Bibliography from the Pre Conquest to Contemporary Times,* Boston: G.K. Hall.

Levine, N. E. (1989). *The Dynamics of Polyandry: Kinship, Domesticity, and Population on the Tibetan Border.* Chicago: University of Chicago Press.

Melwani, L. (2004). Bharatnatyam in jeans. *Little India* 14 (7): 18–26.

Mohammed, S. *On Marriage in Islam. www.jannah.org*

Namesake (http://imdb.com/title/tt0433416/)

Niethammer, C. (1977). *Daughters of the Earth: The Lives and Legends of American Indian Women.* New York: Collier Books.

Paudel, G. S. (2007). *Gender, Technology and Development.* 11 (2): 199–233.

Popick, J. (2005). "Native American Women: Past, Present, Future." *Studies in Popular Culture* 13 (2): 33–38.

Radha Krishnan, S. (1972). *The Religion and Philosophy of the Veda and Upanishads.* Calcutta, India: Ratna Pustak Press.

Stopforcedmarriages.com

Voyageur, C. J. (2002). *Contemporary Aboriginal women in Canada: Visions of the Heart; Canadian Aboriginal Issues.* Nelson; Thompson Canada, pp. 81–106.

Walker, B. (1988). The *Woman's Dictionary of Symbols and Sacred Objects.* San Francisco: Harper & Row, Publishers.

Jean-Marie Le Pen and the National Front: The Rising Tide of Anti-immigration in France

Miho Chisaki

The National Front is a far right political group that was founded on October 5, 1972, in France.[1] Its leader has been the charismatic Jean-Marie Le Pen, who is conservative and nationalist. The National Front is the most distinguished conservative political group in France and has been vocal for the last three decades. He and his party have focused on issues of unemployment and immigration, and they have been gaining support since the beginning of their establishment.[2] One of their most significant appearances was in the late 1970s and early 1980s when the French economy experienced a major decline. The main targets of the National Front's conservative rhetoric and attacks were Muslim immigrants from North African countries and their French-born children.[3] It was considered one of "the most significant developments of French politics" in recent years, and it connected immigration issues and nationalism by focusing on unemployment and Islamic immigrants.[4]

Many scholars have criticized the National Front's attitudes towards North African immigrants and the xenophobic strategies of Jean-Marie Le Pen. Since the effects of globalism and multiculturalism have occurred all over the world, the main aims of French scholarship criticizing this movement have been limited to discouraging their possible policies and emphasizing the importance of maintaining human rights. However, many French see it is also important to preserve their own culture and language in the racial and ethnic melting pot of globalization. In this light, then, it has been deemed necessary by many in France to discuss the restrictive immigration policy proposals of the National Front. Such proposals will become even more salient if Jean-Marie Le Pen becomes a prime minister or a president of France.

Scholars have primarily criticized Jean-Marie Le Pen because of what appears to be the National Front's policy of attacking immigrants. However, scholars have also looked at how Jean-Marie Le Pen and his party's policies have contributed to maintaining French tradition, language, and culture. It is important to analyze some of the questions they raise in order to understand if they are really extreme nativist fear mongers or simply trying to protect France from the influx of foreign influences.

Although some of his party's political attitudes are considered extreme, some of his principles of preserving the traditional language and culture of one's country are considered by many to be valid. A majority of previous scholars only focused on criticizing all or almost all of his party's policies for the nation. It is important, however, to analyze and dig out critical policy positions from what some might consider extreme policies. In order to make a valid and accurate analysis, we have to be careful not to be convinced by all the criticisms from the left that discourage Jean-Marie Le Pen and the National Front's policies. It is necessary to see if positive and effective changes will happen as a result of these policies if and when their party comes into power. Also, it is important to understand how their policies will contribute to a better society and better life for French people. Will they have to sacrifice some freedoms in order to preserve their identity as French people and maintain their language and culture in the face of globalization and immigration? It will only be after an appropriate analysis of his policies that we can finally answer the question whether Le Pen and the National Front are extreme.

Immigration and racism have been major debates in French politics for many years. France has accepted immigrants and refugees since the Second World War until now, and like countries with all immigration trends, the characteristics of immigrants have changed over time. For example, "in the 1950s, 80 percent [of immigrants in France] were European, coming mainly from Italy, Poland, and Spain."[5] In 1992, the number of European immigrants began declining, and immigrants from Algeria, Tunisia, and Morocco became much more visible. This created conflicts because, unlike European immigrants, these immigrant groups are different from most Europeans in ethnicity, religion, and culture.[6] The fact that this trend started after decolonization of those countries also contributed to anti-immigrant attitude in France.[7] Because of its predominantly White and Catholic culture, it was seen as a challenge to turn "into a multicultural nation whose second religion is Islam."[8] In fact, many began to question France's immigration policies and assumptions about just whom **Liberté, égalité, fraternité** were for. The growing number of North African immigrants increased due to family reunification and, by the late 1960s, this began to catch the attention of French citizens. Citizens wondered if these groups could be assimilated into mainstream French language and culture, or if they would create conflict within their country.

One of the most common criticisms of the National Front is that Jean-Marie Le Pen and his followers use immigration and unemployment issues only for obtaining votes for the elections. The main arguments are usually concentrated on how much he and his followers exploit immigration and unemployment issues to gain support while the condition of working class people is not actually his main concern. He utilized this method to derive "the ability first to attract and then hold voters, and second from its ability to influence the priorities of voters who support other political parties."[9] This strategy is also effective for catching the attention of voters of other political parties of the Left and abstainers.[10] This is because most of the Left party supporters are concerned about unemployment and are from working-class backgrounds.[11] Therefore, it is easy for the National Front to present "employment issues" as their main political focus in order to attract as many as voters as possible. ". . . [T]he party succeeded in altering the spatial distribution of party voting in a way that touched almost every circumscription in the country, but far more in areas of high immigrant concentrations."[12]

The most well-known example of this strategy was the election in the city of Dreux. The National Front saw the situation in Dreux as a great opportunity to catch voters' attention.[13] The town was experiencing the influx of mass immigration and unemployment during that time, and yet was in need of cheap labor. The National Front successfully obtained votes by focusing on nationalism and blaming immigrants for taking "their jobs."[14] After the case of Dreux, the party was able to gain the support of people who were racist and nativist. These individuals finally had an outlet for their nationalist, nativist political views, and this strengthened the numbers for the National Front.[15] Daniel Singer predicts that once the world economic crisis has been solved, there would be no support for Extreme Right parties in Europe.[16] But many argue this viewpoint is Pollyannaish—overly idealistic—and that it does not seriously address the problems and conflicts on the ground right now.

Although there has always been prejudice and discrimination against foreigners in France, North African immigrants have been victimized due to the rise of extreme xenophobia in France. Immigrants in France have always been marginalized by French politics and the public in general. Jean-Marie Le Pen and the National Front did a successful job of using these nativist sentiments to turn people into anti-immigrant supporters, and in turn gained votes for their political movement.[17] In politics it is an effective strategy to play on people's fears and victimize a certain group of people that appear to be threatening the status quo of the in-group. This creates a sense of unity and solidarity in political parties like the National Front.

France is predominantly White and Catholic, but there is a growing fear that "[it] has turned into a multicultural nation whose second religion is Islam," and this engenders so much xenophobia that it has influenced contemporary French politics.[18] Because of this unstable cultural situation in France, it was easy for Jean-Marie Le Pen and the National Front to describe the danger their nation faced by focusing on non-White and non-Christian culture. Even someone who does not hate immigrants had negative impressions towards the North African immigrants because they saw them as threat to French language and culture. The idea of the French culture and nation being overtaken by Islam does indeed threaten the average French citizens' traditions and culture to some degree.[19] This goes to the issue of citizenship, whether immigrants should just gain citizenship or whether they have to earn it by showing their loyalty to the nation, its history, its language, and its culture.

Although some saw what Jean-Marie Le Pen and the National Front are arguing as not extreme at all, other people overreacted to the rhetoric and saw this perspective as extreme. Because many scholars consider this ideology extreme, they feel it is a violation of human rights. But one could also argue that the National Front is just trying to protect the French cultural property and identity.[20]

Although Jean-Marie Le Pen and his National Front party have never become the dominant party, many scholars are afraid of what will happen should they come to power. It is going to be very harsh to immigrants and their French citizen children. Katrina Gorjanicyn, for example, predicts, "[if] Le Pen were President of France, non-citizens would have no right of stay and non-Europeans in particular would become the main victims of his racist ideology."[21] She is also concerned Le Pen would just exaggerate the issue of immigrants to gain more support for his party.[22] If he were in power, all the negative things he has advocated would happen to non-European immigrants, and they would simply be sent back home.[23] Jean-Marie Le Pen was asked if the immigrants had come from Germany, would he send them back or not? He answered that he would not do so because they are Europeans.[24] Scholars claim that this type of attitude is racist. However, one could also argue that he is just saying it is easier for Europeans from neighboring countries to assimilate into French society, rather than claiming he simply wants to exclude non-European immigrants.

Jean-Marie Le Pen and the National Front are also concerned about second-generation immigrants' loyalty to the French nation as well as that of the recent immigrants because they have not been in France for generations. However, scholars argue that immigrants in the second generation who were born and raised in the country are not a threat to France.[25] Schain suggests that the majority of second-generation immigrants have loyalty and faithfulness to the French nation because most of them have only lived in France. Because of this, he believes Le Pen and his party are extreme and close-minded.[26] Le Pen and his followers believe religion prevents new immigrants from becoming true citizens of France because their religion is very different from traditional French religion and culture that has been preserved over thousands of years. Hargreaves argues, "[there] is now a mass of survey evidence to show that second-generation members of immigrant families originating in Muslim countries are far less attached than their parents to Islam."[27] This is totally opposite to Le Pen's assumption that immigrants cannot assimilate into the French culture. Although I agree with Hargreaves to some degree, what Le Pen is claiming is also accurate because it cannot be demonstrated that second-generation Muslim immigrants will melt into a new culture and become no threat.

Many scholars argue that it is not fair for North African immigrants to face discrimination and victimization from the National Front, while at the same time the party accepts and welcomes immigrants from other European nations.[28] Although Le Pen and his National Front party say they are just concerned about the future of France, Lloyd and Waters completely disagree with him and defend North African immigrants.[29] The National Front party distinguishes between "easily assimilable" European immigrants and "unassimilable" immigrants principally from North African nations.[30] Le Pen and his party argue this not as discrimination but distinction, and they say they respect the differences of other ethnicities, they just do not want them swamping and overwhelming French language and culture.[31] Although Le Pen made it clear that his ideas towards immigrants are just acknowledging the differences and not representing whether they can all get along, many journalists and other political parties have criticized this attitude.[32] Le Pen and his party have nothing against family reunification, especially because it is one of the National Front's principles. However, Le Pen claims that French people should be careful when it comes to family reunification of immigrants.[33] Other scholars have criticized this attitude of the National Front as being racist and extreme while still others claim that Le Pen is simply questioning whether family members of foreign workers and immigrants can have loyalty and faithfulness to a different nation where only one or a few of their family members have been attached for a very short while.[34] This debate is valid because how can someone all of the sudden respect and love a different nation just because one of his or her family members work there. Citizens do need to be cautious if they want to preserve their own unique culture.

Finally, there are many scholarly opinions that claim that France and its citizens should not complain about immigrant issues, especially those related to unemployment, because France has benefited from cheap foreign workers.[35] Simmons' main argument against immigration policies by the National Front is that the French government should take a good care of immigrants and foreign workers because they contribute to the French society by fulfilling the lower-wage, disadvantaged occupations.[36] It also benefits business owners who are French; therefore neither citizens nor their government should object to immigrants.[37] This issue can go back to previous criticism of Jean-Marie Le Pen and the National Front in this paper that they used already existing immigration issues just to obtain votes.[38] Simmons states that immigrants and foreign workers should not be accused of taking the French citizens' jobs; instead, they have contributed to the French society and its economy.[39] It is true that not all the immigrants and foreign workers are a burden on the nation, but this fact is not enough to ignore cultural preservation. The real question is: Should Jean-Marie Le Pen and his National Front party be criticized as being extreme for wanting to maintain traditional French language, culture, and religion?

The scholarly arguments highlight that we need to be very careful when we read and analyze either criticisms of or support for Jean-Marie Le Pen and the National Front. Under the mask of globalism and multiculturalism all over the world, especially led by the United States, people are made to believe that a melting pot society should be good and work out. However, it is important to be aware of the negative aspects of globalism—one of them is losing a nation's unique identity and failing to preserve its culture and tradition. We need to examine what Le Pen and the National Front are going to achieve for the French people as a better society before assuming they are knee-jerk nationalists and conservative extremists. We need to reexamine the National Front's political policies carefully in order to understand what is actually going to happen if and when Jean-Marie Le Pen becomes a president or a prime minister of France. It is crucial to acknowledge some of the positive changes that might happen if Le Pen were to come to power. Even if some of the policies of Le Pen and the National Front seem onerous, we need to consider what the consequences might be if they did not implement their new policies about foreign workers and immigrants.

It is obvious that no one wants to experience any more major wars or conflicts because we all have all learned from history everyone gets hurt when that happens. But in order to preserve peace and harmony, people need to sacrifice something and find some alternatives. If the alternative in the case of France is Jean-Marie Le Pen and his party, we should consider the reality that their policies will bring about. Will they bring some order and perhaps even improve French society? It certainly raises important questions about the assumptions associated with rampant globalization.

Even after examining the literature more carefully, we can still cannot finally say whether Le Pen and the National Front are really extreme or if their ideology is a result of victimization by the pressure of globalism and multiculturalism. Further research should be done to explore ethnic conflicts that might have arisen due to immigrants in different nations, especially in Europe. Some of the examples would be Yugoslavia, Germany, and Britain. It is also important to examine whether there are successful examples of countries that have accepted immigrants and foreign workers both in and outside of Europe. After thoroughly examining Jean-Marie Le Pen and the National Front, accompanied by an analysis of other nations who have engaged in extreme nativist policies, we may better understand what could happen if they assume power.

ENDNOTES

1. Marcus 1995, pp. 16–18.
2. Ibid., pp. 12–25.
3. Silverman 1991, p. 37.
4. Lloyd & Waters 1991, pp. 49–65.
5. Mayer 1992, pp. 103–104.
6. Ibid., pp. 104–105.
7. Ibid., pp. 122–123.
8. Roemer, Lee, & van der Straeten 2007, p. 237.
9. Schain 2002, p. 26.
10. Ibid.
11. Ibid., pp. 229–230.
12. Ibid., p. 231.
13. Singer 1991, pp. 367–381.
14. Ibid.
15. Ibid.
16. Ibid.
17. Roemer, Lee, & van der Straeten 2007, pp. 237–240.
18. Ibid., p. 237.
19. Ibid., pp. 246–248.
20. Ibid., pp. 245–246.
21. Gorjanicyn 1993, pp. 89–115.
22. Ibid.
23. Ibid., pp. 93–95.
24. Ibid., pp. 95–96.
25. Schain 1996, pp. 171–175.
26. Ibid., pp. 169–172.
27. Hargreaves 1996, p. 213.
28. Lloyd & Waters, pp. 51–52.
29. Ibid., pp. 61–64.
30. Shields 2007, pp. 172–176.
31. Ibid., pp. 186–187.
32. Ibid., pp. 183–191.
33. Ibid., p. 202.
34. Ibid., pp. 202–204.
35. Simmons 1996, pp. 143–162.
36. Ibid., pp. 152–154.
37. Ibid.
38. Ibid., pp. 157–160.
39. Ibid.

REFERENCES

Adler, Franklin Hugh. (1995). "Racism, 'difference' and the Right in France" *Modern & Contemporary France*, NS3(4): 439–451.

Bréchon, Pierre, & Kumar Mitra Subrata. 1992. "The National Front In France: The Emergence of an Extreme Right Protest Movement," *Comparative Politics* 25 (1): 63–82.

Davies, Peter. (1999). *The National Front in France Ideology, Discourse and Power.* London: Routledge.

Gorjanicyn, Katrina. (1993). "Racism in France: the image of respectability." *Melbourne Journal of Politics* 21: 89–115.

Hargreaves, Alec G. (1996). "Immigration, Ethnicity and Political Orientations in France." In *France: From the Cold War to the New World Order,* ed. Kumar Mitra. Houndmills, Basingstoke, Hampshire: Macmillan Press.

Hester, Robert James. (2009). "Co-opting the immigration issue within the French right." *French Politics* 7 (1): 19–30.

Levy, Deborah R. (1989). "Women of the French National Front." *Parliamentary Affairs* 42 (1): 102–111.

Lloyd, Cathie, & Hazel Waters. (1991). "France: one culture, one people?" *Race & Class* 32(3): 49–65.

Marcus, Jonathan. (1995). *The National Front and French Politics: The Resistible Rise of Jean-Marie Le Pen.* Washington Square, N.Y.: New York University Press.

Mayer, Nonna. (1992). "Presence of Immigrants and National Front Vote: The Case of Paris, 1984–1990." *National Political Science Review* 3: 103–126.

Pryce-Jones, David. (1992). "The Holocaust and its Consequences in France." *British Journal of Holocaust Education* 1 (2): 156–170.

Roemer, John E., Woojin Lee, & Karine van der Straeten. (2007). *Racism, Xenophobia, and Distribution: Multi-Issue Politics in Advanced Democracies.* New York: Russell Sage Foundation.

Schain, Martin A. (1996). "The Immigration Debate and the National Front." In *Chirac's Challenge: Liberalization, Europeanization, and Malaise in France,* ed. John T. S. Keeler. New York: St. Martin's Press.

Schain, Martin A. (2006). "The Extreme-Right and Immigration Policy-Making: Measuring Direct and Indirect Effects." *West European Politics* 29 (2): 270–289.

Schain, Martin, Aristide R. Zolberg, & Patrick Hossay. (2002). *Shadows Over Europe: The Development and Impact of the Extreme Right in Western Europe.* New York, Palgrave MacMillan.

Shields, James G. (1996). "Nationalism and Europeanism: Reconciling Opposites on the French Far Right." *European Legacy* 1 (2): 586–594.

Shields, James. (2007). *The Extreme Right in France: From Pétain to Le Pen.* London: Routledge.

Silverman, Maxim. (1991). "Citizenship and the nation-state in France," *Ethnic & Racial Studies* 14 (3): 333–349.

Simmons, Harvey G. (1996). *The French National Front: The Extremist Challenge to Democracy.* Boulder, CO: Westview Press.

Singer, Daniel. (1991). "The resistible rise of Jean-Marie Le Pen." *Ethnic & Racial Studies* 14 (3): 368–381.

Wihtol de Wenden, Catherine. (1991). "Immigration policy and the issue of nationality." *Ethnic & Racial Studies* 14 (3): 319–332.

Korea's Struggle to Decide Whether to Be a Monoethnic or Multiethnic Nation: The Reality of Multicultural Children in School

Nayoung Heo

The Nation of Pureblood

Few Korean people question the statement that Korea is a nation of one-single-ethnicity. The notion of the nation being a one-single-ethnicity (or ethnically homogeneous) country is repeatedly shown in textbooks for elementary schools under the pretext of exposing students to Korean nationalism and strengthening their pride for being Korean. However, people in Korea who advocate the concept of the one-single-ethnicity do not really pay attention to the fact that the term *danilminjok,* "monoethnic nation," had not been used until the beginning of twentieth century (Kim 2007; Park 2009). Kim (2007) and Park (2009) analyzed the fact that nationalist leaders started to adopt the term *danilminjok* to instill the idea that Koreans are one and should fight against foreign powers to be the independent people of the Joseon Dynasty, the last dynasty on the Korean peninsula. At that time, Japanese imperialism reached Korea to annihilate Korean subjecthood and install a dependency under Japanese control. During this period, nationalism, along with the idea of a homogeneous, pure ethnicity, was a necessary strategy for the people of Korea to stand strong in the face of the turmoil of Japanese imperialism.

As Korea went through the Korean War in 1950s when American soldiers came into Korea to support the South against the North, the notion of pureblood was shared by the general public, which often led to a deep sense of revulsion at the young Korean women who were raped by or sold sex to American soldiers. To the general public, those women were considered to bring disgrace to their family and even the whole Korean society, because they had a *Twigi*—a "half-breed" baby. Those women and babies were often expelled from the family and the community (Choe 2009). In the thinking of Korean people who were educated and learned from others that Koreans always had been and always would be one-single-ethnicity without any taint from other peoples, accepting different people was not a choice, and anyone who tainted the pure-blood-ethnicity was a betrayer.

105

Multicultural Families

The term *multicultural family* was officially adopted by the Ministry of Education of Korea in 2006 to refer to the children from a different ethnic or cultural background. This occurred after a civil association first suggested using the word (United International Immigration 2010). Although the term *multicultural family* is still debated for its use because it technically fails to include couples who are both foreign workers from the same country and their children, it is highly encouraged to use it rather than other terms, such as *Hon-hyul*, "mixed-blood," *Twi-Gi* (Choe 2009, 12), "half-breed," or *Kosian*, a compound word for Korean and Asian, which is not correct because Koreans are also categorized as Asian (Cho, Lee, Kwon, Seo, & Lee 2007). According to the National Assembly Research Service (2011), there are two types of multicultural children. The first type is a child or children of an internationally married couple, including one Korean spouse. For example, a Korean male in the farming area and Vietnamese female immigrating to Korea for marriage and economic reasons can marry and have a child. The second type is a child or children of a couple who both emigrated to Korea from the same country to work temporarily. These workers' nationalities are diverse.

Currently, issues related to multicultural families or children are a topic that is highly discussed at the national level more than ever, due to the growing number of multicultural families in Korea. However, difficulties that multicultural children confront are often difficult, as they have to fight against not only prejudice and discrimination but also the "myth" of pureblood or being a one-single-ethnicity nation prevalent among Korean people. This literature review will focus on understanding the reality that multicultural students are going through in Korean education. To understand the current situation, this paper will first explore political, economic, religious, and social factors related to the growing number of international marriages in Korea to understand how the pattern of international relationships/marriages and family types have evolved. Brief demographics of multicultural children and their adjustment issues in educational institutions will be discussed next, with a glance at relevant national policies. Finally, similarities and differences that Korea has with the United States will be examined for future implications.

International Marriage/Relationship in Korea

Since the end of 1980s, unfamiliar scenes began to surprise Korea after a mass wedding ceremony hosted by the Unification Church in 1988. Six thousand five hundred couples that were all Korean men and Japanese women married at the same place on the same day (Jo 2005). This wedding was the beginning of a new marriage pattern in Korea. Mass wedding ceremonies have happened continuously under that same religious institution, and the most recent ceremony, in which 7,200 couples from all over the world married, was held in 2010.

Along with the religious factor, a political factor also accelerated the change of the marriage pattern in Korea. According to Korean Social Trends (The Statistical Research Institute, The Korea Social Science Data Archive, & The Institute for Social Development and Policy Research 2009), the number of ethnic Korean women emigrating to Korea from China to marry a Korean man had greatly increased, after Korea established a diplomatic relationship with China in 1992. Those women had Chinese citizenship, and mostly married an older Korean man who could not marry because he was engaged in agriculture in a rural area.

As globalization has accelerated, nationalities of women who go to Korea to marry a Korean man have been diversifying, and now they include the Chinese, Vietnamese, Filipinas, Japanese, Cambodian, Thai, and Mongolian, who are all, except for the Japanese, from less-developed countries. However, Korean women's international spouses display the opposite economic characteristic, as the statistics showed Korean women tended to marry a man from a more developed country, such as Japan, the United States, Canada, Australia, Britain, and Germany (The Statistical Research Institute et al. 2009). It seems that more Korean females want to live in a metropolitan area, while many of the people who decide to return to farming are male, which makes it hard for the men in the rural area to find a Korean woman. The Statistical Research Institute et al. (2009) pointed out that the unbalanced sex ratio was also one of the reasons why more Korean men married a foreign woman.

The number of married couples composed of one Korean and one foreigner had increased from 4,710 in 1990 to 35,098 in 2010, with the highest being 42,356 in 2005 (The Statistical Research Institute et al. 2009; Statistics Korea 2011). Interestingly, among the couples in 2010, Korean-born men consisted of 74.6 percent of the total number of males, and foreign women accounted for 74.9 percent of the total females. In other words, most international marriages were between a Korean-born male and foreign female, and the relatively small percentage of foreign males, 22.7 percent, married a Korean female (Statistics Korea 2011). As briefly mentioned earlier, this result is not unrelated to the unbalanced sex-ratio and different migration patterns depending on the sex. In addition, according to Statistics Korea (2011), the number of international marriages accounted for 10.8 percent of the entire marriages in Korea as of 2010. Twenty thousand three hundred twelve babies were born to internationally married couples in 2010, making up 4.3 percent of the total births in that year (Statistics Korea 2011). The number of babies born to an internationally married couple had steadily increased since 2008.

Multicultural Children and Their Education

In this section, children who were born to an internationally married couple (one Korean spouse and one foreign spouse) will be referred to as multicultural children. However, a child or children of a couple that are both foreign workers will be also included in the category of multicultural children, following the definition used by the Korean government, although strictly speaking, some of them are not "multicultural" (both parents are likely from the same country and were already married before going to Korea). Also, this literature review will use the statistics related to students only, due to the difficulty of figuring out the number of the multicultural children who are not enrolled in school or do not have legal status.

The Ministry of Education, Science, and Technology of Korea stated that there were 38,890 multicultural students as of April 2011 (as cited in National Assembly research Service 2011, 30). Most of them were children of internationally married couples, while only 2,214 were from foreign worker families (The National Assembly Research Service 2011). Considering the fact that the number of all students was about 7,000 in 2010 (The Center of Educational Statistics and Information 2010), it is assumed that multicultural students made up about 0.5 percent of the total number. Although this figure might not seem significant, the number of multicultural students has been steadily growing since 2007, while the number of all students has been decreasing (The National Assembly Research Service 2011).

There are four institutions that multicultural children can choose to go to for their education: regular schools, alternative schools, multicultural education centers in college, and local centers for children, as the National Assembly Research Service (2011) categorizes them. In regular schools, multicultural students are assigned in a regular class, as well as a special class if there are enough multicultural students, where they can learn difficult subjects, such as Korean, social studies, and math, separately from their Korean classmates. If there is no special class, they will study in the same classroom with their Korean classmates. Second, an alternative school is another option if they are not able to adjust in a regular school. Currently, there are three alternative schools commissioned by the local government, and they provide courses from the pre-school to high school level. Third, education centers in universities were founded to support students, parents, and the teachers for a better understanding of what they need to know in school. Finally, local centers offer multicultural children comprehensive care from protection to education. However, the ultimate goal of all of these institutions except regular schools is to prepare multicultural students for and send them to their original school. It implies the government already acknowledges that separating multicultural children is not the answer, even though some time might be needed for the students to adjust in a different institution.

The reasons multicultural students are led to move to a different institution or quit school can be inferred based on the research conducted by the Korean Women's Development Institute and the National Youth Policy Institute (2007). According to the authors, a survey of 70 multicultural students going to a regular or alternative school in 2006 revealed that about 30 percent of respondents wanted to quit school because 1) they did not enjoy studying (10.1%); 2) they were discriminated against or treated unfairly (5.8%); or 3) they did not like the teachers and classmates (5.8%) (The Korean Women's Development Institute et al. 2007). Kim and Yang (2012) adds to this telling fact that some of the multicultural students ended up leaving school or lost interest in studying due to the lack of Korean skills to communicate and understand, economic support, or a lack of interest in difficult subjects. Similar arguments are found in news articles dealing with multicultural children's difficulties. For example, in 2010, the National Human Rights Commission (as cited in Kim and Yang 2012, para. 4) concluded that 37 percent of the multicultural students surveyed had been bullied or shunned because of their accent, origin, bad rumor, skin color, or status. However, it does not seem that Korean students' attitudes toward multicultural students are all identical. In detail, Korean students tend to judge multicultural students according to their parents' origin or their skin color. If a multicultural student's parents are from a country considered a developed or White-dominated country, the student is likely to be welcomed and easily approached by Korean students. This point is supported by Sim's (2010) survey of 718 Korean-born elementary school students. In the section of Korean students' ethnic preferences, Russian-descent students were scored highly compared to other student categories. Similarly, Jeong (2010) conducted a survey of 138 middle and 138 high school students on their ethnic preferences, and pointed out that the students preferred White Europeans (the mainstream culture) to African/African American or Southeast Asians.

Policies for Multicultural Children and a Comparison with the U.S.'s Case

The National Assembly Research Service (2009) stated that the Korean government had not paid serious attention to issues related to multicultural families until 2006. Although there is not any provision in the constitution guaranteeing the Koreans' coexistence with other ethnicities but accentuating nationalist values, laws, or rules relevant to multicultural families and students began to be established since 2007 (The National Assembly Research Service 2011). Detailed programs are designed and implemented mostly by five ministries of the government, but there is not a single ministry specifically in charge of general service and policies for multicultural families and children (The National Assembly Research Service 2011). Possible problems could originate from the lack of the ministries' cooperation with each other, competition between them on similar programs, inefficient implementation of policies and outcomes, confusion among multicultural families and students regarding which service they should utilize or where they locate the service, and so forth.

Programs established by the ministries are focusing on improving multicultural families' Korean skills, assisting them to adjust in society, providing financial support for multicultural students' education, and multicultural education for Korean students, with local governments supporting them (The National Assembly Research Service 2011). However, it is questionable if these programs will be applicable to all multicultural children whose economic status, legal status, and parents' ethnicities are all different. In addition, one of the most important issues for multicultural children is to move up to a higher grade school, while school principals have a right to deny multicultural children even before the students can have a chance to utilize those programs provided by the government. According to a news article (hljxinwen.cn 2012) in an ethnic Korean newspaper, children who were raised in another country and went to Korea were frequently denied in the school admission process due to their lack of Korean skills.

It is somewhat understandable that there is not yet a congruent, stable policy for multicultural children, considering that the large influx of various peoples was a fairly recent happening in Korea. Many people in Korea still believe in the homogeneity of the country, have an aversion for foreigners neglecting the changing international environment, and consider looking differently as a wrong thing. Nevertheless, because of the demographic changes currently happening, it is not a thing that can be stopped or fade away. One must, therefore, refer to another country with a longer history of foreign immigration, which could assist Korea to compare, contrast, and establish a model that suits it most.

The U.S. model for multicultural education changed from the assimilation model to the cultural pluralism model in the 1960s, in which the Civil Rights Movement occurred. Because American education policy before was focused on producing people who were perfectly assimilated to the mainstream White American society, anger and dissatisfaction from minority people were greatly expressed during the period. The U.S. education policy now has set the goal of protecting the right to learn and achieve, fostering understanding of various backgrounds, and building rightful relationships (The National Assembly Research Service 2011). Although a lot of conflicts, prejudices, and discrimination are still observed between different ethnicities, and biased class materials are oftentimes used in class, programs for multicultural education are more established and institutionalized than in Korea, and more people are used to multicultural education due to the presence of different ethnicities in school, along with well-established programs. The National Assembly Research Service (2011) provided two programs of the United States as examples: the counseling program in school for immigrant students and the ESL program for immigrant students for learning English before they can be assigned to a regular class.

These two programs have great implications for Korea's multicultural education. First, because there are few counselors who can take care of multicultural children's issues in Korean schools, teachers are expected to be in charge of it. However, it can be an additional burden to teachers as they are already supposed to teach, guide, contact parents, and counsel students. Teachers now should worry about how to communicate with multicultural children's parents, which is part of the reason some multicultural children are not admitted to school. Trained counselors could lessen this burden and perform more efficiently (The National Assembly Research Service 2011). Moreover, the growing number of multicultural children annually tells that investing in these kind of programs is inevitable to avoid greater confusion as well as both Korean-born and multicultural students' maladjustment. Also, the ESL program can be a model for establishing consistent Korean language classes in schools for students with too few Korean skills to be in class with Korean classmates.

CONCLUSION

The frequency of contacting multicultural children might be the key in fostering multicultural education for all students. However, Korean students' more frequent contact with multicultural children should go a long way towards recognizing each other without prejudging. According to Sim (2010) in his survey, students who had multicultural friends or had been abroad expressed more positive feelings toward multicultural students. The establishment of adjustment programs in school will be more efficient with efforts to grow awareness about other peoples. For example, opportunities in class to talk about each other's lives and listen to each other talk about where they are from will help students recognize each other and empathize. For another example, having a culture day regularly and giving students an assignment to find an interesting thing about a foreign country could expose students to different countries a little more. In this sense, the period for multicultural students to adjust in a special class or alternative school should be minimized so that they can interact with students in a regular school.

Considering the growing number of multicultural students, who might account for 20 percent of the total number of students in Korea in about ten years (Jeong 2011), the "separate but equal" principle is not an answer, just as it was not in the United States. Korea should avoid the segregation of the multicultural population from the whole population, even if people who want to protect their mythical monoethnic nation advocate to do so in the near future.

REFERENCES

The Center of Educational Statistics and Information. (2010). *Statistics Publication* 1-1-3. 학생현황. Retrieved from *http://cesi.kedi.re.kr/index.jsp*

Choe, S. (2009). South Koreans struggle with race. *The New York Times*, November 1. Retrieved from *http://www.nytimes.com/2009/11/02/world/asia/02race.html?pagewanted=all*

Jeong, S. (2010). 다문화 시대 한국 청소년의 인종에 대한 명시적 및 암묵적 태도 발달. Retrieved from RISS database, Korea (http://www.riss.kr/index.do)

Jeong, Y. (2011). 10년뒤엔 청소년 20%가 다문화 가정 출신. *The Kyunghyang Shinmun* (April 25).

Jo, H. (2005). *A study for the survey on the Korean life of the international blessed family and educational program: Centering on the blessed Japanese housewives*. Retrieved from National Assembly Library database.

Jo, H., C. Lee, S. Kwon, D. Seo, & E. Lee. (2007).다문화가족 자녀의 학교생활실태와 교사·학생의 수용성 연구.

Kim, Y., & M. Yang, M. (2012).다문화 가정 자녀 37%가 왕따... "엄마, 학교엔 제발 오지마". *The Chosunilbo*, January 10.

The Korean Women's Development Institute, & The National Youth Policy Institute. (2007).다문화가족 자녀의 학교생활실태와 교사·학생의 수용성 연구. Retrieved from *http://www.bokjiro.go.kr/data/bookView.do?board_sid =295&data_sid=180515*

Lee, J. (2010). 통일교 아산서 7200쌍 국제합동결혼식. NEWSis, October 10. Retrieved from *http://news.naver.com/ main/read.nhn?mode=LSD&mid=sec&sid1=102&oid=003&aid=0003476257.*

The National Assembly Research Service. (2009). [정책보고서] 다문화정책의 추진실태와 개선방향. Retrieved from http://www.nars.go.kr/publication/

The National Assembly Research Service. (2011). 다문화교육의 현황과 과제. Retrieved from *http://www.nars .go.kr/publication/boardView?currentPage=1&invest_id=000000014906&div=10&type=05&baseURL=%2F publication%2Fboard%3Fdiv%3D10%26type%3D05&dept_cd=&team_cd=&charge_id=&searchOpt=all& searchText=*

Our Documents. (n.d.). *Brown v. Board of Education (1954)*. Retrieved from *http://www.ourdocuments.gov/ doc.php?flash=true&doc=87*

Park, D. (2009). "민족"이라는 단어의 등장은 '1897년'. *PRESSian*, June 11.

Sim, W. (2010). 초등학생의 다문화 아동에 대한 인식과 태도. *The Journal of Elementary Education, 23*(4), 43–63.

Statistics Korea. (2011). 다문화인구동태통계. Retrieved from *http://kostat.go.kr/portal/korea/kor_nw/2/2/3/ index.board?bmode=read&bSeq=&aSeq=251920&pageNo=1&rowNum=10&navCount=10&currPg=&sTarget=title &sTxt=*

The Statistical Research Institute, Korea Social Science Data Archive, & The Institute for Social Development and Policy Research. (2009). *Korean Social Trends*. Retrieved from *http://kostat.go.kr/edu/sri_kor/2/1/index .action?bmode=read&p_idx=187&pageNo=2&search_mode=&keyword*

United International Immigration. (2010). 다문화 가정 자녀를 위한 교육. Retrieved from *http://www.uiim.org/ ?mid=Education&sort_index=readed_count&order_type=asc&page=2&document_srl=1133*

흑룡강신문. (2012, January 16). 한국 다문화가정 자녀 초중교 입학 거부 많다. 흑룡강신문.

A Review of Citizenship Theories

Kebba Darboe

What Is Citizenship?

Citizenship is one consequence of immigration. Citizenship means participating in a direct democracy. Therefore, a citizen is a member of a political community, one who enjoys the civil, political, and social rights and assumes the duties and responsibilities of membership (Joppke 1999). Citizenship was originally exclusionary and discriminated on the basis of race, class, and gender. There are three main dimensions of citizenship: legal, political, and identity (Cohen 1999; Kymlicka & Norman 2000; Carens 2000). This study applies citizenship theories to four countries, which are identified as destination places for many immigrants: France, Germany, Great Britain, and the United States.

Arguably, there are two models of citizenship: republican and liberal. The republican model pointed out that citizenship is political because individuals are free citizens and not subjects; therefore, they can, at free will, participate in their community—governance by citizens (civic self-rule). This model originated from the Greeks and was influenced by writings of Aristotle and Rousseau (Barker 1959; Rousseau 1762).

By contrast, the liberal tradition characterized citizenship as a legal status; therefore, a relationship exists between the individual citizen and state. For instance, the state provides citizen's access to certain privileges and protections; in return, the citizen is obligated to follow laws, pay taxes, or serve in the military (Dunn 1969). This model originated from the Roman Empire, and influenced the writings of the seventeenth century English liberal philosopher John Locke, and the eighteenth century French writer Montesquieu. Further, in the Baron of Montesquieu text, *The Spirit of the Laws,* he argued for the separation of powers—the three-branch type of government: executive, legislative, and judicial, which was later adopted by the framers of the constitution of the United States of America (Montesquieu, Cohler, Miller & Stone 1989). The liberal model of citizenship dominates contemporary constitutional democracies.

According to Marshall (1950), the fulfillment of citizenship depended on a person's access to civil, political, and social rights. First, civil rights are individual freedoms; for example, freedom of speech and religion. Second, political rights allow citizens to vote and seek political office in free elections. Third, social rights are economic welfare and security.

The end of empires—for example, the Roman—and signing of the Westphalia Treaty in 1647 led to the formation of nation states during the sixteenth and seventeenth centuries in Western Europe, and now the world over (Solsten 1996). Additionally, the democratic nation-state was created by the French Revolution in 1848 (Censer & Hunt 2001). A nation-state is a country organized by either race or cultural background with defined borders and territory. Immigration and the rise of the nation-state as an organizing form of governance across the world have produced differentiated explanations of citizenship into three theoretical perspectives.

Traditionalism Theory

Brubaker (1992) advanced citizenship traditionalism theory when he compared France and Germany. The French law of 1889 and the German law of 1913 established the principles of citizenship. Brubaker pointed out that France employs a model of territorial inclusion and assimilative citizenship that is citizenship by place of birth (*jus soli*—law of land). However, the French assimilationist (integration) model was challenged through acts of violence by North African people—Algerians, Moroccans, and Tunisians—who felt that they were never really treated as French (Haddad & Balz 2006). President Nicolas Sarkozy of France, in 2007, responded to urban violence with more restrictive immigration and citizenship policies and populist statements that have further increased ethnic tensions (Koff & Duprez 2009).

By contrast, Germany applies ethnic origin as the criterion for equal citizenship; therefore, citizenship is awarded on hereditary grounds or exclusionary bloodline (*jus sanguinis*—law of blood) (Joppke 1999). The idea of the true German has historically guided German citizenship from the Prussian era to today. As a result, German ethnicity became equated with citizenship. The German citizenship law dates back to 1913, and therefore even to pre-Weimar Republic times. According to the law, the father's nationality is used as the basis for determining the child's citizenship because women did not receive citizenship rights until in 1953 (Brinkmann 2004).

According to McFarlane (2009), the 1999 State Citizenship Law reformed the 1913 law, and was implemented on January 1, 2000, to deal with the issues of dual citizenship and naturalization. Following this reform, it is now possible for migrants, who have a permanent residence permit and who have lived in Germany for at least eight years and no criminal record, to take on German citizenship. A further revision of the law in 2007 has made passing of a naturalization test obligatory. These reforms have brought German citizenship law more in line with countries in which citizenship is decided by place of birth—*jus soli*. However, the 1999 reform has refused to grant dual citizenship and naturalization to Turks (the largest ethnic minority), thereby discouraging Turkish integration into German society (McFarlane 2009).

Historically, according to Brubaker, in Europe few states were completely organized politically, geographically, and institutionally on the French model. For example, the Kurdish nation's geographical surface extends onto the territory of Turkey, Iraq, and Syria, but it is a nation without a state. On the other hand, the Basques, the Quebecois, the Flemish, and the Catalans are formed or declared nations, though none have their own state (Brubaker 1992). Therefore, a nation is seen as a voluntary construction of a democratic state; and when there is symbiosis, or a relationship of mutual benefit, between cultural and political identity, the nation-state is established; for example, Germany, France, and Japan.

Post-national Citizenship Theory

Migration of individuals or groups between countries contributes to the formation of post-national identities and beliefs. Post-nationalism is linked to the expansion of international human rights laws and norms, which regard individual "personhood," not just their citizenship (Soysal 1994). Consequently, individuals are judged on universal laws not particularistic criteria such as ethnic origin. However, in the 1990s, the debate on universalism and particularism began to diminish because of the rise in post-nationalism (Joppke 1999). It is in this context, that Soysal (1994) advanced post-national citizenship theory and argued that the discourse on human rights has put pressure on nation-states to extend citizenship to non-citizens, especially "guest workers" in France and Germany. Furthermore, "personhood" is beginning to replace citizenship status and the territorial borders that Brubaker stresses to be important are becoming less important (Soysal 1994, 3). As a result, both post-national and transnational conceptions of citizenship capture the meaning of citizenship by highlighting ways in which people belong to more than one state.

Post-national citizenship does not refer to an identity or a unitary legal status. In essence, it is an analytical construct, which narrates changes of rights and identity in the institutions. Post-national rights are results of struggles and negotiations, which are subject to challenges. As a result, the principles of human rights that foster post-national forms of citizenship and the principles of nation-state sovereignty and agency are reified by the same transnational discourses and institutions. Thus, as the source and legitimacy of rights increasingly move to the transnational level, rights and membership of individuals remain organized within nation-states (Soysal 1994). Arguably, transnationalism and globalization have weakened the geographic borders that separated nation-states, thus raising questions about citizenship. The geographic borders that once marked boundaries between nations have been replaced by political borders, which make distinctions between citizens and non-citizens living in the same nation-state (Soysal 1994). However, full political membership in a nation-state is usually obtained through citizenship status.

Multicultural Citizenship Theory

Kymlicka (1995) advanced "multicultural citizenship" theory and argued that the modern nation-state is multinational because it consists of more than one group—for example, Canada. Further, Will Kymlicka observed that liberal states are not assimilating their immigrants but rather respecting and protecting their ethnic identities. Kymlicka's work provides a framework for fair treatment of minority groups, which he divides into two basic categories: polyethnic or immigrant groups, and national minorities such as the Canadian French-speaking Québécois or the Maori of New Zealand. However, Miller (2000) defended the nation-state and pointed out that nationality and citizenship complement one another. For, without a common national identity, there is nothing to hold citizens together, no reason for extending the role just to these people and not to others.

Further, the theoretical explanations and immigration factors are putting pressure on nation-states to make changes to citizenship requirements. In regard to immigration, citizenship has two different meanings: legal and identity. As a legal status it denotes formal state membership—nationality, for example, in Germany.

In the United States, the discourse surrounding citizenship is limited to the legal status. The American constitution makes personhood and residence rather than citizenship protected categories. For instance, a formal citizenship and equality before the law was only introduced and granted through the Fourteenth Amendment in 1868 for freed slaves—that is, African Americans (Sullivan 2005). The basis of the constitutional claim of birthright citizenship is the Citizenship Clause of the Fourteenth Amendment, which states: "All persons born or naturalized in the United States, and subject to the jurisdiction thereof, are citizens of the United States and of the State wherein they reside," (Graglia 2009, 5). Therefore, not everyone born in the United States is automatically a citizen, but only those "subject to the jurisdiction" of the United States. Further, some of the citizenship requirements are tests and oath taken based on the United States Constitution. Many European countries have now adopted this process.

Citizenship, as an identity in the United States, refers to the shared understandings and practices that constitute a political community. The 1965 Immigration and Nationality Act, which eliminated nationality-based quotas, opened the United States to a new wave of immigration from Africa, Asia, Caribbean Islands, Middle East, and Latin America (Schaefer 2012). The primary objective of the 1965 Act was to make the immigration law consistent with modern civil rights legislation, so that immigrants would not be discriminated against on the basis of ethnicity or nationality. As a consequence, citizenship based on race or identity is challenged in the United States by the aforementioned immigrants, who are classified as "racial minorities." In this context, the institutional pillars of the American race paradigm, unlike the European ethnicity, are affirmative action and multiculturalism in education (Glazer 1997). These programs attempt to compensate the victims of American nation building, for example, African Americans. Additionally, the civil rights laws have put pressure on federal courts and administrations to change the color-blind policy of equal opportunity or fair play to equal result or fair share (Shapiro 2004). As a result, through administrative fiat, state agencies identified four racial minorities: African Americans, American Indians, Asians, and Hispanics (Lowry 1982). These groups have suffered discrimination in the process of American nation building; for instance, African Americans are victims of slavery; American Indians are victims of genocide, for example, at the Trail of Tears and Wounded-Knee; Asian immigrants are victims of racial exclusion during the Chinese Exclusion Act of 1882 and the internment of Japanese during World War Two; and the Hispanics were conquered and segregated after the Mexican-American War and signing of the 1848 Treaty of Guadalupe Hidalgo, which ceded the southwest region to the United States (Schaefer 2012).

Contemporary debate regarding United States citizenship centers on the Development, Relief and Education for Alien Minors Act (The "DREAM Act") (Senator Durbin 2011). The purpose of the DREAM Act is to provide millions of immigrant children, who came at the age of fifteen or younger and graduated from United States High Schools, the opportunity to receive residency (a "Green Card"). However, the Dream Act failed in the Senate in 2009, 2010, and 2011, and opponents noted that it is a path to amnesty for illegal immigrants. However, through executive fiat by President Obama, the Dream Act is de facto law (Kirkwood 2011).

Historically, British citizenship tradition is more complex and hierarchical because of its multinational character and imperial status. So the dichotomy of citizenship traditionalism (Brubaker 1992) and membership post-nationalism (Soysal 1994) is inappropriate. Great Britain has a concept of *subjectship* that is allegiance to the Crown—that is, the Queen. However, in response to the Canadian government's decision to enact its own citizenship law in 1946, the Commonwealth Heads of Government decided in 1948 to change the law of nationality throughout the Commonwealth; as a result, the formal institutionalization of citizenship in 1949 emerged in Great Britain (Hansen 1999). Subsequently, in 1981 British Nationality Act, Commonwealth immigrants introduced the British citizen category; prior to this Great Britain had no citizenship. The Act also repealed most of the provisions of the 1948 Act; for example, it ceased to recognize Commonwealth citizens as British subjects. Therefore, the British Nationality Act of 1981 marked a shift away from the *jus soli* principle toward the *jus sanguinis* principle of ethnic descent. Today, it ethnicized citizenship the opposite of Germany.

Since the terrorist attacks on September 11, 2001, Great Britain, France, and Germany passed anti-terror legislations by making a link between migration, terrorism, and security (Diez & Squire 2008). As a consequence, the theory of securitization was introduced to examine different ways in which free movement of certain groups and individuals could be monitored and assessed, and possibly controlled. For example, "Muslim immigrants" is constructed as existential security threats; therefore, justifying extraordinary or "emergency" measures (Hampshire & Saggar 2006). This theory of securitization is associated with the so-called Copenhagen School and does not make objectivist claims as to whether or not particular groups or individuals serve as a security threat (Stritzel 2007). The processes of securitization include introduction of identification cards, border controls, airline searches, and biometric technologies. Given the heightened concerns regarding the dynamics of immigration, security, and terrorism, the United States Congress passed and President Bush signed on October 26, 2001, into law the Patriot Act (Uniting and Strengthening America by Providing Appropriate Tools Required to Intercept and Obstruct Terrorism Act of 2001), which gives the federal government broad powers to indefinitely detain suspected terrorists (Congressional Digest 2004).

CONCLUSION

In summary, a tradition of civic nationalism remains evident in contemporary British citizenship legislation, while a tradition of ethnic nationalism remains evident in the strict rules governing naturalization in the German case (Joppke 1999). Citizenship is an historically contested and continually evolving social construct. However, the general trend in Western Europe is towards liberalized citizenship regimes. Today, arguably, the path to full citizenship in many nation-states require access to civil, political, and social rights.

REFERENCES

Barker, E. (1959). *The Political thought of Plato and Aristotle.* New York: Dover Publications, Inc.

Brinkmann, T. (2004). "The Politics of Citizenship in Germany: Ethnicity, Utility and Nationalism" (Book). *German Politics & Society* 22 (2): 65–69.

Brubaker, Rogers. (1992). "Civic and ethnic nations in France and Germany." In *Ethnicity,* ed. John Hutchinson & Anthony Smith. Oxford – New York: Oxford University Press, pp. 168–173.

Carens, J. H. (2000). *Culture, Citizenship, and Community. A Contextual Exploration of Justice as Evenhandedness.* Oxford: Oxford University Press.

Censer, Jack, & Lynn Hunt. (2001). *Liberty, Equality, Fraternity: Exploring the French Revolution.* Pennsylvania: Pennsylvania State University Press.

Diez, T., & V. Squire. (2008). "Traditions of citizenship and the securitisation of migration in Germany and Britain." *Citizenship Studies* 12 (6): 565–581. doi:10.1080/136210208024506

Dunn, J. M. (1969). *The political thought of John Locke: an historical account of the argument of the 'Two treatises of government.'* London: Cambridge U.P.

Glazer, N. (1997). *We are all multiculturalists now.* Cambridge, MA: Harvard University Press.

Graglia, L. A. (2009). "Birthright Citizenship for Children of Illegal Aliens: An Irrational Public Policy." *Texas Review of Law & Politics* 14 (1): 1–14.

Haddad, Y., & M. J. Balz. (2006). "The October Riots in France: A Failed Immigration Policy or the Empire Strikes Back?" *International Migration* 44 (2): 23–34. doi:10.1111/j.1468-2435.2006.00362.x

Hampshire, J., & S. Saggar. (2006). "Migration, integration and security in the UK since July 7" [online]. *Migration Information Source.* Available from: *http://www.migrationinformation.org* [Accessed February 2012].

Hansen, Randall. (1999). "The Politics of Citizenship in 1940s Britain: The British Nationality Act." *Twentieth Century British History* 10 (1): 67–95.

Joppke, C. (1999). *Immigration and the Nation-State: The United States, Germany and Great Britain.* Oxford: Oxford University Press.

Joppke, C. (1999). "How immigration is changing citizenship: a comparative view." *Ethnic & Racial Studies* 22 (4): 629–652. doi:10.1080/014198799329323

Kirkwood, Cort R. (2011). "Napolitano: Dream Act Is Now De Facto Law." *New American.* Retrieved on February 15, 2012 from: *www.thenewamerican.com/usnews/?immigration/...dream-act-is*

Koff, H., & D. Duprez. (2009). "The 2005 Riots in France: The International Impact of Domestic Violence." *Journal of Ethnic & Migration Studies* 35 (5): 713–730. doi:10.1080/13691830902826111

Kymlicka, Will, & Wayne Norman. (2000). *Citizenship in diverse societies.* Oxford University Press.

Lowry, Ira S. (1982). "The Science and Politics of Ethnic Enumeration." In *Ethnicity and Public Policy,* ed. Winston A. Van Horne. University of Wisconsin System, American Ethnic Studies Vol. 1.

Marshall, T. H. (1950). *Citizenship and Social Class and Other Essays.* Cambridge: Cambridge University Press.

McFarlane, Elaine. (2009). "From Guest Workers to Permanent Foreigners: German History, Citizenship Reform and Germany's Turkish Immigrant Population." *Interdisciplinary Undergraduate Law Journal,* pp. 53–89.

Miller, David. (2000). *Citizenship and national identity.* Stafford BC, Australia: Polity Press.

Montesquieu, C. de Secondat., A. M. Cohler, B. Carolyn Miller, & H. Samuel Stone. (1989). *The spirit of the laws.* Cambridge: Cambridge University Press.

Rousseau, J.-J. (1762). *On the Social Contract with Geneva Manuscript and Political Economy.* ed. R. D. Masters, trans. J. R. Masters (1978). New York: St. Martin's Press.

Schaefer, Richard T. (2012). *Racial and Ethnic Groups,* 13th ed. Boston: Pearson.

Senator Durbin, Richard [IL]. (2011). The `Development, Relief, and Education for Alien Minors Act of 2011' or the `DREAM Act of 2011' (112TH CONGRESS 1ST SESSION: S. 952). Library of Congress.

Shapiro, Thomas M. (2004). *Great Divides: Readings in Social Inequality in the United States,* 3rd ed. New York: McGraw-Hill.

Solsten, E. (1996). *Germany: a country study,* 3rd ed. Washington, DC: Federal Research Division, Library of Congress.

Soysal, Y. N. (1994). *Limits of Citizenship. Migrants and Postnational Membership in Europe.* Chicago and London: University of Chicago Press.

Sullivan, Harold J. (2005). *Civil Rights and Liberties: Provocative Questions & Evolving Answers,* 2nd ed. Prentice Hall.

Stritzel, Holger. (2007). "Towards a Theory of Securitization: Copenhagen and Beyond." *European Journal of International Relations* 13 (3): 357–383 DOI: 10.1177/1354066107080128

Using the PATRIOT Act to Fight Terrorism. (2004). *Congressional Digest* 83 (9): 266–268.

SECTION
Four

INDIGENOUS STRUGGLES

RACIAL AND CULTURAL GENOCIDE IN AMERICA

Jamie Erickson

Anyone who is the least bit educated knows genocide really did occur against American Indians in the United States of America. In fact, it is the most egregious case of genocide in the history of the world. But is it still going on? When looking at this subject one will have to look deep into certain beliefs and biases about America. There will not be clear answers that will satisfy everyone's idea of what is considered genocide, and the domination of Native populations that has been indoctrinated into mainstream society's way of thinking about these remarkable people raises that ubiquitous obstacle of bias in most non-Indian Americans when one engages in this discussion. I am not an Indian, but I am a veteran who has served in war and loves his country, and many Indians have also served and love this country, too—one of the men raising the flag at Iwo Jima was an Indian.

American Indians consist of many diverse peoples, not just in the United States but also in the rest of the Americas, North and South. While they all share some cultural similarities, each American Indian society is as different from one another as Germans are to French or Swedish people are to Albanians.

There are 557 separate American Indian tribes that are recognized by the U.S. government.[1] In addition, there are dozens of other American tribes that are recognized by the individual states that make up the United States, and many more "unrecognized" American Indians that are seeking federal recognition for their people in the United States.

The term *American Indians* also includes the Indian people of Canada, Mexico, Central, and South America. There are over 600 American Indian tribes in Canada, where they are usually called First Nations instead of tribes.[2] Dozens more American Indian tribes live in Mexico, and there are thousands of American Indians who belong to hundreds of American Indian tribes in Central America and South America.

After 1492, European exploration of the Americas revolutionized how the Old and New Worlds perceived themselves. One of the first major contacts occurred when conquistador Juan Ponce de León landed in Florida on April 1513.[3] Ponce de León was later followed by other Spanish explorers, such as Pánfilo de Narváez in 1528 and Hernando de Soto in 1539.[4]

From the sixteenth through the nineteenth centuries, the population of Native Americans declined due to epidemic diseases brought from Europe, but also due to genocide and warfare at the hands of European explorers and colonists, displacement from their lands, internal warfare, enslavement, and a high rate of intermarriage.[5] Most scholars believe that among the various contributing factors, epidemic disease was the overwhelming cause of the population decline of the American natives because of their lack of immunity to new diseases brought from Europe.[6] With the rapid declines of some populations and continuing rivalries among their own nations, Native Americans sometimes reorganized to form new cultural groups, such as the Seminoles of Florida. Although enslavement was tried it was not considered cost efficient after the African slaves were introduced because the American Indian would escape and was not good for forced labor.

When forming our nation, some of our founding fathers have been said to have visited some American Indian tribes to get ideas on how to run the country. The Iroquois nations' political confederacy and democratic government have been credited as major influences on the Articles of Confederation and the United States Constitution.[7] Historians debate how much the colonists borrowed from existing Native American governmental models, but it is known several founding fathers had contact with Native American leaders and had learned about their styles of government. Prominent figures such as Thomas Jefferson and Benjamin Franklin were involved with leaders of the Iroquois Confederacy, based in New York, while John Rutledge of South Carolina is said to have read lengthy tracts of Iroquoian law to the other framers, beginning with the words, "We, the people, to form a union, to establish peace, equity, and order . . ."[8]

Is this not ironic that we form our nation around wording from people that the United States considers "savages" and tried to exterminate in many instances? What would have happened to our nation if we had adhered to what George Washington thought of Natives and their rights? Here is what he wanted to lay out, but only after they were "civilized" into modern culture.

1. Impartial justice toward Native Americans
2. Regulated buying of Native American lands
3. Promotion of commerce
4. Promotion of experiments to civilize or improve Native American society
5. Presidential authority to give presents
6. Punishing those who violated Native American rights[9]

Another area we must look at is the implementation of an oppressive education system that was forced upon the tribes of Native Americans as a form of cultural genocide. Through mass indoctrination of their youth in boarding schools, the U.S. government, in collusion with churches, tried to systematically exterminate Indian cultures. We have made reparations to the Japanese internment camp survivors. Then why have we done nothing about this? And the sad irony is that this is still going on today. Unfortunately, it is an extension of the cultural destruction of Native Americans begun back in 1611. This method was one of forced culture change through indoctrination in the form of education. Methods included the forced removal of children from their cultures, then enrolling them into "educational programs" that were intended to instill European beliefs and values.

The most incriminating evidence against the United States concerning this issue comes from events after 1948, the year of the Convention on Genocide, which the United States had signed, making such practices illegal anywhere in the world. Yet, one must ask if we are still doing it in the twenty-first century right here in our own country? Let us go back and then come forward through time by tracking the evidence, and then you tell me.

Beginning in 1778, the United States Board of War, a product of the Continental Congress, appropriated grants for the purpose of "the maintenance of Indian students at Dartmouth College and the College of New Jersey . . . The young Indian people who had returned from these schools described their teachers and fellow students as ignorant of not knowing how to live in the Woods, unable to handle Cold or Hunger, did not know how to build a Cabin, take a Deer, or kill an Enemy, they spoke our language wrong, and were neither fit for hunters, warriors, nor counselors; they were totally good for nothing."[10]

In 1820, the United States colluded with mainstream Christian churches and made plans for a large-scale system of boarding and day schools. These schools were given the mission to "instruct its students in letters, labor, mechanical arts, and morals and Christianity, training many Indian leaders."[11] In the case of boarding schools, Native American children would be forcibly stripped from their homes as early as five years old. They would then live separate from their families and cultures until the age of seventeen or eighteen, and usually a long way from their homeland so they would not try to escape and get back home. Conditions in these boarding schools were horrible for the children in many instances, being made to suffer extreme corporal punishment and deprivation. In fact, many of the children died.

In 1886, it was decided by the United States federal government that Native American tribal groups would no longer be treated as sovereign nations, even though the U.S. had signed treaties with them saying they were. The decision was made not by Native American tribes and Congress entering into treaties but by the power of the United States legal system. This self-ordained power allowed Congress to legally marginalize Indian nations, eliminating their sovereignty by simple fiat. Congress then passed a variety of other laws directed towards assimilating Native Americans so that they would become a part of "mainstream White America."[12]

By this time, the United States government had been funding over a dozen distinct agencies to provide mandatory education to all native children aged six through sixteen. Enrollment was enforced through leverage given by the 1887 General Allotment Act, which made Natives dependent on the government for annuities and rations.[13] The practice of students' indigenous religions was prohibited, hypocritically depriving Indians of religious freedom, one of the fundamental rights every American worth his or her salt would stand up and fight for. Students were compelled to undergo daily instruction—indoctrination—in Christianity. In addition, only the use of English was accepted within these schools. If they used their native language they were beaten and the little food they did get was used against them. The food was not sufficiently nourishing, health supervision was generally neglected, and an effort was made to develop the type of school that would destroy tribal ways. While being held captive at these schools, the students were forced to learn a set of ideals, values, and practices completely foreign to them. They would study world history, which had no significance to their own beliefs. The students must have felt as if they were in another world.

To compound the torture, the students at these schools were forced to work as maintainers and farmers in order to provide for the continued existence of the very schools that were destroying them. In the summer they were farmed out as forced labor to earn their room and board for the following year. In fact, that is where the expression "farming something out" comes from. The problem with this practice, however, was the mortality rate—50 percent of these students never came back at the end of the summer, and it was not because they ran away. "The methods of forced labor were considered by the educators to be a means of developing the native character and as a way of financing further expansion of the system itself."[14] The military style enforced by the schools amounted not just to assimilation, but to cultural annihilation of the Native Americans culture as well. "The students began to not only think white but also to work white."[15]

To this point, I have provided enough evidence to point out the hypocrisy of the United States and its practices towards Indians. It is my intent to demonstrate that, in its treatment of Indians, the United States has actually engaged in criminal acts under International Law. I will do so by describing genocidal acts committed well after the time of the international convention on genocide (1948). Until the 1990s, there were many boarding schools still operating. This alone is against the international convention. Until as recently as 2007, there were seven boarding schools still operating in the boundaries of the United States, again totally against the convention. The convention says the following:

> . . . any of the following acts committed with intent to destroy, in whole or in part, a national, ethnical, racial or religious group, as such:
>
> (a) Killing members of the group;
> (b) Causing serious bodily or mental harm to members of the group;
> (c) Deliberately inflicting on the group conditions of life calculated to bring about its physical destruction in whole or in part;

(d) Imposing measures intended to prevent births within the group;

(e) Forcibly transferring children of the group to another group.

—*Convention on the Prevention and Punishment of the Crime of Genocide, Article 2*

Our government was not satisfied with only educating the Native American youth; they desired to brainwash them with our ideals. They fractured the cultural infrastructure of their people in every way possible. An insidious example of this strategy is clearly delineated in The Indian Self-Determination and Educational Assistance Act of 1975. In this act, the United States government declared that educated Native Americans should be used to staff the "various programs aimed at them by federal policy makers."[16] These are the same programs that the government has always viewed as the ideal means by which to condition Native Americans to accept its values, and thus reinforce the domination of Euro-America. This was in 1975. You would think this would be back in the 1800s. Through the implementation of this act, nothing really changed in the curriculum taught in Indian schools. It remained exactly the same, reaching exactly the same conclusions, indoctrinating children with exactly the same values as when the schools were staffed entirely by White people. The government attempted to mask the face of colonialism with familiar faces—those of Indians who were surrogates in their compulsory education programs.

These were violent acts—yes, forced education was an act of violence—that have not ended even with the international convention on genocide. The United States is guilty of committing a crime, violating a law that it has promised not only to abide by, but also to help enforce. Does this represent the mainstream American culture we so want to instill into the minds of Native Americans or the rest of the world? We should begin taking a look at our own culture and worrying about its problems before we start thinking about trying to solve our worlds' problems. If it was not bad enough that we would take the American Indians' way of life, we would do something even sneakier, far worse because it had been done without the knowledge of the individuals involved. Our government would take away the ability of women to make life, and they would do it through forced sterilization!!!!!

A young American Indian woman entered Dr. Connie Pinkerton-Uri's Los Angeles office on a November day in 1972. The twenty-six-year-old woman asked Dr. Pinkerton-Uri for a "womb transplant" because she and her husband wished to start a family. An Indian Health Service (IHS) physician had given the woman a complete hysterectomy when she was having problems with alcoholism six years earlier. Dr. Pinkerton-Uri had to tell the young woman that there was no such thing as a "womb transplant" despite the IHS physician having told her that the surgery to remove her womb was reversible. The woman left Dr. Pinkerton-Uri's office in tears.[17]

Two young women entered an IHS hospital in Montana to undergo appendectomies and received tubal ligations, a form of sterilization, as an added benefit. Bertha Medicine Bull, a member of the Northern Cheyenne tribe, related how the "two girls had been sterilized at age fifteen before they had any children. Both were having appendectomies when the doctors sterilized them without their knowledge or consent." Their parents were not informed either. Two fifteen-year-old girls would never be able to have children of their own.[18]

What happened to these three females was a common occurrence during the 1960s and 1970s. Native Americans accused the Indian Health Service (HIS) of sterilizing at least 25 percent of Native American women who were between the ages of fifteen and forty-four during the 1970s.[19] The allegations included: failure to provide women with necessary information regarding sterilization, use of coercion to get signatures on the consent forms, improper consent forms, and lack of an appropriate waiting period (at least seventy-two hours) between the signing of a consent form and the surgical procedure. Does the United States government have the right to do these procedures without consent?

Court rulings have played an important role in federal family planning policies that have an influence on IHS family planning programs. The Supreme Court, and lesser courts, set legal precedents regarding informed consent, family planning, and sterilization between 1914 and 1973.

Schloendorff v. Society of New York Hospital in 1914 concerned a surgeon who performed an operation that left a man partially paralyzed. The court stated that any person who physically touches another individual without that person's consent commits battery. Justice Benjamin Cardoza spoke for the court when he stated that "every human being of adult years and sound mind has a right to determine what shall be done with his own body; and a surgeon who performs an operation without his patient's consent commits an assault."[20]

In 1942, the Supreme Court heard the case of *Skinner v. Oklahoma.* Jack Skinner was incarcerated in an Oklahoma prison following his third offense for armed robbery. Oklahoma had passed legislation that allowed habitual criminals to be sterilized. During this time period many states believed that sterilization laws were valid because the eugenics movement advocated sterilization for those deemed "unfit." The Court recognized "the right to have offspring as a fundamental right but did not declare compulsory sterilization laws totally invalid." Justice William Douglas wrote the majority ruling stating that Skinner's crime did not merit sterilization, declared that the Oklahoma sterilization law was unconstitutional under the Fourteenth Amendment, and expressed concern over the possibility of sterilization abuse arising from such legislation. He stated that "the power to sterilize, if exercised, may have far-reaching and devastating effects . . . [and in] evil hands it can cause races or types which are inimical to the dominant group to wither and disappear."[21] Looking at these two court rulings, one would assume that an American Indian would have the same rights and, in the case of Jack Skinner, the rights that all laws would be applied equally. When it comes to American Indians, it seems that all laws are only applied when the government deems it fit to apply them.

Various studies revealed that the Indian Health Service sterilized between 25 and 50 percent of Native American women between 1970 and 1976.[22] Dr. Connie Pinkerton-Uri conducted a study that revealed that IHS physicians sterilized at least 25 percent of American Indian women between the ages of fifteen and forty-four. Cheyenne Tribal Judge Marie Sanchez questioned fifty Cheyenne women and discovered that IHS doctors had sterilized twenty-six of them. She announced her belief that the number of women that reportedly were sterilized was too low and that the percentage was much higher than 25 percent. Mary Ann Bear Comes Out, a member of the Northern Cheyenne tribe, conducted a survey on the Northern Cheyenne Reservation and Labre Mission grounds. She found that in a three-year period, the IHS sterilized fifty-six out of 165 women between the ages of thirty and forty-four in the survey area.[23] She wrote that "the data indicate that the same rate of sterilizations would reduce births among this group by more than half over a five-year period."[24]

The sterilization of Indian women affected their families and friends resulting in many marriages that ended in divorce, and numerous friendships became estranged or dissolved completely. The women had to deal with higher rates of marital problems, alcoholism, drug abuse, psychological difficulties, shame, and guilt. Sterilization abuse affected all Indian communities in the United States. American Indians already have to contend with all of these issues without adding forced sterilization to the list of problems that are commonplace on the reservations.

The encounter at Wounded Knee in 1890 must be seen in the context of the Ghost Dance religion, a movement that a year earlier had caused a great excitement among Indians in the area and that was interpreted by Whites as a general call to war. While an encampment of Dakota was being searched for arms, a few young men created an incident and the soldiers, thinking they were trying to start something, opened fire on the Indian encampment. This encampment consisted mainly of elders, women, and children. More than 300 American Indians lost their lives while there were twenty-five Army casualties and thirty-nine wounded. Most, if not all, of the Americans killed and wounded were considered friendly fire.

Wounded Knee has been called the best-known case of genocide directed against North American Indians. Although we could list many, many more incidents, this is the best known. On January 15, 1891, the last Dakota Warriors surrendered and apart from clashes here and there the America Indian Wars had ended. But the new silent war had just begun for the majority of Indians across the United States.

In exploring the idea of genocide in America we came across things that have happened and still are happening to American Indians. In our society we must right the wrongs that we have forced upon differing peoples and their cultures. By doing these inconceivable acts to these people, we have, perhaps, lost medicines that could have helped us today; maybe we have killed someone that could have become President or become a winner of the Congressional Medal of Honor; or someone who had knowledge that could have saved someone's life or gave the world a new invention. What this statement means is if just one of these people who may have made a difference were never born due to the forced sterilization, even if it was just being a great grandfather or mother, it was one too many. And if all of this, my friends, is not a violation of the international convention on genocide, then what is?

ENDNOTES

1. Mander, Jerry. (1992.) *In the Absence of the Sacred: The Failure of Technology and the Survival of the Indian Nations,* San Francisco: Sierra Club Books, 349.

2. Mankiller, Wilma & M. Wallis. (1993). *A Chief and Her People.* New York: St. Martin's Press, 8.

3. Memi, Albert. (1965). *The Colonizer and the Colonized,* Boston: Beacon Press, 151.

4. Ibid.

5. Susan Brill, Bradley U. (brill@bradley.edu). Discussion group regarding the genocide of Native peoples.

6. *http://www.igc.apc.org/toxic/; http://conbio.bio.uci.edu/nae/knudsen.html;* Federal Indian Policy *http://mercury.sfsu.edu.cypher.genocide.html.#children*

7. The Reader's Digest Association, Inc. (1995). *Through Indian Eyes,* Pleasantville, New York/Montreal, 338.

8. Olson, James & R. Wilson. (1988.) Native American, *In the Twentieth Century. University Press,* 11.

9. Trail of Tears *http://ngeorgia.com/history/nghisttt.html*

10. Adam David Wallace. *Education of Extinction: American Indians and the Boarding Schools.*

11. Ibid.

12. Ibid.

14. Adam David Wallace. *Education of Extinction: American Indians and the Boarding Schools.*

15. Ibid.

16. Federal Indian Policy *http://mercury.sfsu.edu.cypher.genocide.html.#children*

17. Ibid.

18. Ibid.

19. Olson, James, & R. Wilson. (1988). *Native American, In the Twentieth Century* University Press, 11.

20. Federal Indian Policy *http://mercury.sfsu.edu.cypher.genocide.html.#children*

21. Susan Brill, Bradley U. (brill@bradley.edu). Discussion group regarding the genocide of Native peoples.

22. Federal Indian Policy *http://mercury.sfsu.edu.cypher.genocide.html.#children*

23. Susan Brill, Bradley U. (brill@bradley.edu). Discussion group regarding the genocide of Native peoples.

24. Ibid.

REFERENCES

Adams, David Wallace. (1995). *Education for Extinction: American Indians and the Boarding School Experience 1875–1928.* University Press of Kansas.

Bierhorst, John. (1979). *A Cry from the Earth: Music of North American Indians.* Washington, DC: Smithsonian Center for Folklife and Cultural Heritage.

Electronic Code of Federal Regulations (e-CFR), Title 50: Wildlife and Fisheries Part 22-Eagle permits.

Hirschfelder, Arlene B., Mary G. Byler, & Michael Dorrisl. (1983). *Guide to research on North American Indians.* American Library Association.

Johnston, Eric F. (2003). *The Life of the Native American.* Atlanta, GA: Tradewinds Press.

Johnston, Eric. F. *The Life of the Native.* Philadelphia, PA: E.C. Biddle, etc. 1836–44. University of Georgia Library.

Jones, Peter N. (2005). *Respect for the Ancestors: American Indian Cultural Affiliation in the American West.* Boulder, CO: Bauu Press.

Krech, Shepard. (1999). *The Ecological Indian: Myth and History.* New York: W.W. Norton, 352.

Kroeber, Alfred L. (1938). "Cultural and Natural Areas of Native North America." *University of California Publications in American Archaeology and Ethnology,* 38.

Nichols, Roger L. (1998). *Indians in the United States & Canada, A Comparative History.* University of Nebraska Press.

Pohl, Frances K. (2002). "Framing of America." In *A Social History of American Art,* pp. 54–56, 105–106 & 110–111. New York: Thames & Hudson.

Shohat, Ella, & Robert Stam. (1994). *Unthinking Eurocentrism: Multiculturalism and the Media.* New York: Routledge.

Sletcher, Michael. (2005). "North American Indians." In *Britain and the Americas: Culture, Politics, and History,* eds. Will Kaufman and Heidi Macpherson. New York: Oxford University Press, 2 vols.

Snipp, C. M. (1989). *American Indians: The first of this land.* New York: Russell Sage Foundation.

Sturtevant, William C. (Ed.). *Handbook of North American Indians* (Vol. 1–20). Washington, DC: Smithsonian Institution. (Vols. 1–3, 16, 18–20 not yet published), (1978–present).

Tiller, Veronica E. (Ed.). (1992). *Discover Indian Reservations USA: A Visitors' Welcome Guide.* (Foreword by Ben Knighthorse.) Denver, CO: Council Publications.

Vine, Delora. 1969. *Custer Died for Your Sins: an Indian Manifesto.* New York: Macmillan.

A Lakota Oral Teaching on Learning about Self and Other

Sebastian "Bronco" C. LeBeau II

There is a mantra of mine that I used to begin classes with each semester when I was a professor at Minnesota State University, Mankato:

Before you can learn about others, you must first learn about yourself. Before you can understand others, you must first understand yourself. When you learn about others, you learn about yourself.

When we set out to learn about people belonging to ethnic minority populations we do so through a process of observation. Watching the *other* perform a cultural activity, demonstrating culturally prescribed behaviors, we attempt to interpret the meaningfulness of the activity in order to understand how and why it is significant to the people performing it. Once we believe we understand what we've seen, we then have to explain our findings and conclusions about the cultural meaningfulness and the significance of the activity. When we present our findings and conclusions we should do so in a manner that demonstrates not only our comprehension of our understanding of the activity, but also our appreciation of what we have learned.

So what are the kinds of things people wish to learn about ethnic minority populations here in the United States? They are things like ethnic identity, gender and gender roles, religious beliefs, rites of passage, child rearing, age set rituals, dating within an ethnic population group(s), interracial dating, marriage, dress, sex and sexuality, craft working, language, and politics—the list is endless when you think about it. So if you wish to learn about contemporary minority populations within the United States, then be cognizant of the fact that your basis for understanding ethnic population groups are based on your own understanding of your own population group's beliefs concerning the very same things you wish to learn about ethnic minority populations. For example, if you wish to learn about Native American religion, your basis for understanding their religious beliefs is based on your own understanding of your own religious beliefs. But let me state it this way as well. If you are looking for God in Native Americans then you better know God within yourself. If you don't, then how will you recognize God in them?

One thing you must do in order to learn about others is you must first know about your own culture, and know your own belief systems, and know your own ways of doing things. You must learn to realize just how you as an observer and learner create the foundation(s) for the meaningfulness and significance of things that you experience in your life. And, yes, I do mean here your personal life because, although we are taught in school to believe that as researchers we must always remain impartial and objective in making observations and interpreting the meaningfulness and significance of activities or the behaviors of others, only a fool believes they are capable of being completely objective. No one is completely objective, including me. The reason for this is because we can only perceive things from our own cultural perspective.

You see, in every ethnic cultural group its members possess within them a schema-driven sense-making rationale. "Schemas serve as mental maps which enable individuals to traverse and orient themselves within their experiential terrain (Louis 1980; Weick 1979) and guide interpretations of the past and present and expectations for the future" (Harris 1994, 310). Essentially, schemas allow people to structure impressions, interpret information, and create frameworks for problem solving and they do affect how people perceive and interpret external stimuli (LeBeau 2009, 14). For instance, people who come from diverse cultural and ethnic backgrounds interpret the meaningfulness of things differently because they are taught by their unique cultural differences and experiences to encode information along their own prescribed cultural norm. As a Lakota, I possess a different set of sense-making structures and thought processes apart from non-Lakotas due to my cultural background. Basically what this means is I see and perceive things outside myself differently than, say, an African American, a Hispanic, an Asian American, and yes, a Euro-American, because I'm subscribing to Lakota thought patterns about my relationship to my surroundings and environment. The foundations for how I create the meaningfulness and significance of my personal experiences is rooted upon how I think, and so are yours my reader, so are yours.

As a result of this fact, we create understanding in terms of our own environment and do so by ordering and structuring our own environment into safe comfortable frames. We order what we see, and what we create, in terms of what makes us comfortable especially when it comes to creating our perceived image of what minority ethnic populations look like to us on our own personal level, and what they represent to us on our own personal level. This is framing. Yet, at the same time, this framing process is also the comforting process because when we order and structure like this we are also creating a distinction for ourselves in which we separate things into two consistent fundamental categories: Self and Other.

Self is you. Self is comforting. But Self is also imposing. By this, I mean we impose what we believe is Self onto Other and we do this in order to frame Other in a manner that will allow our Self to understand Other from our own perspective so that we can then interpret Other and the meaningfulness of Other to our Self. That is a bit wordy and perhaps overly philosophical sounding, but that is the process we go through when we order and frame our environment into a comfortable structure. A structure that then allows us to make our observations of Others performing activities and demonstrating behaviors, upon which Self can then interpret the meaningfulness of those activities and behaviors by using analogous comparisons to what Self says is normal or abnormal. However; realize that these conclusions are based on what Self believes in pertaining to what is considered normal or abnormal behavior, and not necessarily what Other believes is normal or abnormal behavior.

What I want to share with you and expose you to as you read through this written lecture is information that is not specifically about the history of Ethnic Studies as an interdisciplinary study of racialized people here in the United States. I don't want to visit with you about racial theories of why or how ethnic population groups interact with the dominant majority population of this country or with other ethnic minority populations. Nor do I want to discuss any of the academic studies previously done on ethnic minority populations. You are going to get enough of that by simply reading this book. No. What I want to share with you and visit with you about is learning about Other and what it is about you as a person that affects your construction of Self and Other. I want to visit with you like this because I want to challenge you; to challenge you to think critically, to think analytically, but also to think creatively, and to think convergently about Self and Other. Why? So you can learn to recognize how you as a person, an individual, identifies your own foundations that you use to create your own understanding of the meaningfulness and significance of your learning experiences. Only then can you honestly open yourself up to learning about Other and not talk about them from your perspective but talk about them from their perspective.

Over the course of our visit, I want to discuss with you just how truly important it is that you become aware of what I mean concerning my mantra. I will use it for what it is, a Lakota teaching tool, and show you during our visit that before you look outward for knowledge and understanding it's even more important for you to first look inward. Inward so you can realize the type of personal relationship you create to what you learn because that relationship affects positively and negatively how you learn about yourself and others.

To begin our visit, let's return to something I've stated previously, and that is the issue concerning the kinds of things people wish to learn about regarding ethnic minority populations here in the United States. Remember, I said they are things like ethnic identity, gender and gender roles, religious beliefs, rites of passage, child rearing, age set rituals, dating within an ethnic population group(s), interracial dating, marriage, dress, sex and sexuality, craft working, language, and politics that people wish and desire to learn about. With that being said, let's recognize something important about learning, which is the central theme of this written lecture that you are reading.

As students, each of you has academic strengths and weakness concerning your topics of study. To be blunt, though, some of you taking this introductory course are doing so because it's required, while others of you are doing so because you really are interested in learning about Ethnic Studies. However, let me point out that for all of you reading this lecture, that what you will learn in this introductory course that actually stays with you as you complete the semester and go on with your studies is that one topic reviewed in this course that most captured your interest. That is, what interests you and motivates you to learn. With your interests you invest something of yourself into your learning process. As a result of the investment you personalize the meaningfulness of the subject matter because the information becomes a part of you emotionally. That's why you will remember that one topic you were exposed to in this course. That is the wonderful thing about learning with regards to college. In college, we actually get to explore our interests and take those course studies that teach us what we wish to know, and what we desire to know, about any given subject we are interested in, and that includes learning about Others.

Let's do a couple of things before we move on to the next phase of our visit. First, take a moment and honestly identify a specific ethnic group of people living here in the United States that you really honestly want to learn about. Next, now that you've identified a specific group, what is it about that group that you really want to learn about? Be honest here and don't hesitate over the subject matter. Follow your interests and just honestly say to yourself I want to know about [you fill in the blank]. Okay, now that you have identified your group and the subject matter you wish to learn about concerning this group, it's time to move to the next phase of our visit.

Before you can learn about others, you must first learn about yourself.

Do you know what bias is? Bias means a tendency or inclination, especially one that prevents unprejudiced consideration of a question. In short, bias is a prejudice, and it is a learned trait each of us acquires in life as we grow up. Every individual possesses a bias. There is no such thing as an unbiased person, and frankly our bias tendencies do reflect how we have learned and what we have learned about ourselves and about others. It is important that you learn to recognize your own biases, especially if you wish to learn about a different ethnic cultural group of people. It is easy to say "learn to recognize your own biases," but in reality it is very difficult to do because our biases are rooted in our emotions and in our personal beliefs. Consciously and unconsciously they are a part of us as human beings and they help shape who we are as we express ourselves to others. This is why it's hard to recognize them and harder still to rid ourselves of them, if ridding ourselves of our own bias is even possible. A personal bias means you feel positive or negative towards someone or something for some reason. Frankly the only way you can lose a bias is to do it from an emotional level. But for the purposes of our visit I'm not asking you to attempt doing that. What is important to know about bias is that we have them, and we must learn to recognize them in order to guard against them negatively influencing our perception of other people belonging to a different ethnic cultural group.

The first thing you must realize concerning our little exercise is that your American education is how you learned about the world and the environment you live in, and it has actually helped create within you a cultural bias and an ethnocentric bias, which affects how you learn about people from another cultural group. A cultural bias is basically interpreting and judging phenomena by the standards of one's own culture. An ethnocentric bias is the tendency to interpret human behaviour from the viewpoint of your own ethnic, social, or other group.

One example of a cultural and ethnocentric bias is stereotyping. A stereotype is nothing more than a popular belief held by a group of people about specific types of individuals or other groups. Stereotypes are standardized, oversimplified conceptions, often exaggerating the physical attributes of individuals or other groups that are based on some prior assumptions that people use to distinguish that differences exist between them. Those differences can be based on things like race, ethnicity, culture, religion, sexual orientation, or physical appearances. Stereotypes can be both negative and positive, but they do focus on and exaggerate differences between groups. Stereotypes are also messaging tools that often become self-perpetuating even in the face of evidence proving a stereotype is inaccurate. The harmful thing about stereotyping is that people tend to use them as an initial rudimentary basis for framing the Other into a representative category that they believe gives them a truthful personal understanding of Other. This, of course, isn't true. Stereotypes actually hinder our capability to learn about Other because stereotypes inhibit our ability to understand the true nature of Other both as an individual and as an ethnic cultural group. Let's look at one ethnic population group here in the United States that is possibly the least understood of all minority groups, Native Americans. I'll demonstrate how stereotypes of Native American people affect how non-native people unconsciously create a stereotypical mental image for themselves of what a Native American looks like. Keep in mind the ethnic group you identified earlier because as we visit about Native Americans the points I will make about them are the same points you must apply to learning about your chosen group.

No other ethnic population in the United States has been as studied and written about as Native Americans have been. And no other ethnic group in this country has been so variously categorized and stereotyped to such a degree that it has become extremely difficult for non-natives to construct within themselves an accurate mental image of what Native American people actually look like. When I taught Perspectives on American Indians, ETHN 202W, at MSU, Mankato, I began the course with a class exercise. What I did was ask my students to write down what they thought an Indian looks like and told them to make a list; a list of attributes that they believe describe an Indian. I did this to drive home a point that non-native people, regardless of their ethnicity, actually possess stereotypical images of Native American people that they use as a tool to identify Native Americans. The responses I would get as I went around the classroom pointing at my students individually to name one thing from their list they said describes Indians always made me smile. The responses always included the following things—long hair, buckskins, feathers, braids, dark skin, teepees, tall, paint, big nose, breech-cloth, a warrior, moccasins, bow and arrow, canoe, a squaw, tomahawk. The attributes were extensive but very descriptive and perfect for illustrating what I wanted to get them to realize, not about Indians, but about themselves.

Once we completed the exercise I would inform my students that the class presentations for the semester would revolve around how we learn about Indians at home and in school by using the various ways Indians have been negatively stereotyped through history by non-Indians. I said to them that, as a result of this negative stereotyping, it has become quite difficult for non-native people to construct within themselves an accurate mental image of what an Indian actually looks like, even when one is standing right in front of them. You see, no student ever described me, their Lakota teacher in this exercise. My students came to my class knowing I was an Indian, perhaps not knowing I was a Lakota, but they knew I was an Indian. Yet no student during this exercise ever listed mustache, light skin, glasses, cotton shirt, vest, blue jeans, boots, teacher. The attributes they used to describe an Indian were always constructed by using certain kinds of identifying physical characteristics associated with various historical, representational, and cultural symbols they believed represented Indians. To them, Indians were a thing of the past, and not because they believed that Indians no longer existed. The reason they automatically contextualized their image of an Indian into a historic image was because of how they had learned about Indians. To explain this to them,

I told them that most of what they had learned about Indians during their formative years as children and young adolescents had been presented to them only from a historical perspective. At home, they learned about Indians from several sources such as the television, movies, books, and comics and cartoons, and from these sources the depictions of Indians they were most often exposed to was a historical one. Consequently, it was only reasonable they had internalized what they were exposed to as being illustratively correct. It was always at this point that I would begin to see my students start nodding their heads in agreement with my explanation. As I moved on I told them that the historical image of Indians that they got at home was mirrored and reinforced in school as well. In school, I said, while they were taught about the history of the United States of America in those lessons, Indian participation in that history was only discussed in terms of the past, never the present. As a result of this, this kind of learning is what had helped shape their present preconceived image of what an Indian looks like. In other words, they were taught that Indians were of the past and so it was only natural for them to view them as belonging in the past. As non-Indians, my students had simply absorbed what was presented to them as children and as young adults, and without realizing they were doing it they had invested something of themselves in the learning process. They had personalized their image of Indians based on what was presented to them and their imagined image of an Indian became a part of their emotional frame for Indians. This, I said to them was an example of a bias—one based on a historical stereotype reflecting a prior assumption. Their stereotypical assumption was that to identify a real Indian one does so using preconceived notions of what they believe are representative identifying physical characteristics Indians possess such as long hair, braids, dark skin, tall, big nose; as well as historical representational cultural symbols such as buckskins, feathers, teepees, paint, breech-cloth, moccasins, etc.

Before you can understand others you must first understand yourself.

As students, one of the research methods you are being exposed to in this course is a method called comparativism. Comparativism is simply the search for similarities and differences between and among human beings (Lassiter 2009, 40). Remember that what interests you motivates you to learn, and one of the reasons why we want to learn about Other is we oftentimes mistakenly believe that Other possesses real cool kinds of cultural things that we believe our own culture doesn't have. For instance, a rite of passage like a ritual or ceremony one participates in signifying an event in a person's life that is indicative of experiencing a transition from one stage of life to another such as a girl becoming a woman or a boy becoming a man.

However, structured events, rites of passage, marking stages in life do in fact exist in American culture. In religion, Baptism, Confirmation, Bar Mitzvah, the Hajj, are rites of passage; going through puberty is a rite of passage, as is sweet sixteen, hazing, and graduation. What is important for you to realize is that rites of passage are not often recognized as such in the culture they occur in. One reason for this is because we become blind to them due to their commonness within our own cultural environment. It's because we can't see what is right in front of us that we so easily see what is apart from us. And because we mistakenly believe that what is apart from us doesn't exist within us, we become interested in Other in order to satisfy our personal desire to learn why they have something as cool as a rite of passage in their culture and we don't have one in ours. Since rite of passage is our current topic, for our visit's sake let's pretend that this is the subject matter that you wanted to know about within the minority group you identified earlier. Know that there are three phases to a rite of passage—separation, transition, and reincorporation (see also Van Gennep 1909). The first phase is separation, performing a symbolic behavior signifying one's separation from their previous group. The second phase is transition—the short interval occurring after the first phase during which the person has left one stage but hasn't yet entered the next. The third phase is reincorporation, meaning passage is achieved by the person and they are welcomed into their new stage.

What I want you to do now is think of yourself as Group A, and you are observing Group B the minority group you identified. Perhaps the hardest challenge you will face when you make cross-cultural comparisons between Self and Other is learning how to describe what you observe so your descriptions communicate understanding about Group B to Group A. The issue of description goes to the matter of context, and properly contextualizing observations can be hard to accomplish even for seasoned, experienced researchers. Realize that in trying to interpret the meaningfulness and significance of behaviors, in this case a rite of passage, the only means you have of communicating understanding to Group A why the behavior observed in Group B is considered meaningful and significant is through a process of analogy. Analogy means you are making a comparison between two things that are similar in some way in order to help explain something or make that something easier to understand. You are relating what you see to what you know, or at least to what you think you know. Essentially, this means you have to cast around within your own group for a similar kind of behavior that helps you explain to the people of Group A why the behavior you've observed within in Group B is considered meaningful and significant to THEM. However, what we don't often realize is that as we ascribe that meaningfulness and the significance of the behavior we observed within Group B, we are doing so from an influenced position. I will demonstrate what I mean by this in this final part of our visit.

In the sequence of events that follow I will discuss learning, behaviors, meaningfulness, significance, cultural perspectives, schemas, frames, creating relationships to learning, personal biases, cultural and ethnocentric biases, analogies, context, and influenced positions, all of which are factors you should account for when you try to learn about and explain a rite of passage. But I'm going to present all this to you in a manner you probably don't expect. Instead of reviewing Other to communicate the meaningfulness and significance of what I'm trying to share with you, I'm going to turn things around and give you an example of comparative contextualization based on an American cultural behavior. Read carefully and keep in mind that I am challenging you to think critically, to think analytically, but also to think creatively, and to think convergently about Self and Other. If you do these four things and apply them to the list of factors provided, then you will be able to realize what you have actually learned in our visit.

When you learn about others you learn about yourself.

The American educational system teaches its attending students to value making scientific, objectified observations of the world and the environment. As a result of our education, we have been taught to ascribe meaningfulness to things from a very narrow perspective. In short, we describe and interpret what we see in terms of logical rationale or perhaps better stated, cause and effect. For example, let's talk about a cultural behavior that is commonly performed on a seasonal basis here in the United States. This will be a simple scientific, objectified observation of a cultural behavior we call, mowing the lawn.

We mow our lawns because of cause. Meaning the grass is tall and it needs to be cut so we need to shorten it. We interpret the meaningfulness of this behavior based on effect. The effect of shortening the grass makes our lawn look pretty. For us, even if we were or were not consciously aware of it the significance of mowing our lawn is interpreted by us from a cause-and-effect position. However, when we describe the behavior to Other it is described meaningfully from our own cultural basis as being a chore. Yet mowing the lawn is a common cultural behavior we can also identify as a rite of passage of sorts that is primarily for American boys to experience. We can do this because we can contextualize it according to our American cultural beliefs about the meaningfulness and significance of mowing the lawn.

When a boy reaches a certain age in their life, when they have grown physically large enough to manipulate a lawn mower in a safe manner, they are given the responsibility of mowing the lawn. Once the boy completes this task the beaming parent(s) of the boy proudly declare to him that mowing the lawn is an accomplishment in his life, an important accomplishment that is often defined as a part of growing up. And frankly that is all a rite of passage is. It is an event a person experiences in their life as they move from one stage to another. In this case the boy is becoming a man. He is growing up and his mowing of the lawn demonstrates this. So where is the ritual or ceremony?

Ask the boy.

Listen to him describe to you the emotion and sense of awareness he experienced when his parent(s) took him outside and spoke to him about what he was going to do. Let him describe the meaningfulness and significance of mowing the lawn as he interprets it in relationship to his accomplishment. Then you decide and demonstrate as a part of this American cultural group, Group A, how something as mundane as a lawn chore can be a ritual or a ceremony.

Can you do it?

If you have listened to the boy tell you what it meant to him to mow the lawn, then you can describe the behavior in terms of being a ritual or a ceremony of sorts. But it isn't for me to accomplish this for you. You have to accomplish this on your own. You have to trust yourself to take what I've shared with you so far and apply it to this task. What I can and will do though is point out things for you to consider that will help you contextualize this event so it can be considered a ritual or ceremonial rite of passage for American boys.

Understand that you have a bias affecting your thought process now. The bias is how you view mowing the lawn and its connected to how you have been taught to describe the cultural meaningfulness of the behavior, which is simply thought of as being a chore. But you are also looking at in terms of being a full grown adult right now, not as a young boy mowing the lawn for the first time. You see over time your personal understanding of what it means to mow the lawn has changed. More likely than not, as an adult you see the behavior as work, and not fun work. If, like me, you grew up mowing grass and did so when all you really wanted to do was go play with your friends, then the meaningfulness of mowing the lawn gets changed and you yourself changed it. You see cutting grass for the first time does give young boys a personal sense of accomplishment. They do feel like they have attained something important, something that imparts to them a sense of feeling special because they are big boys now. They are becoming men. Unfortunately, mowing the lawn gets real old real fast. Once you do it every weekend from May through October, cutting grass isn't making you feel so special anymore. Now can you see the importance of me telling you to "Ask the boy"? Look at the objective cause-and-effect rationale that we visited about earlier. Apply it to this matter of asking the boy about mowing the lawn. Then go ask an adult male about mowing the lawn. Ask each in order to help you recognize and understand how the meaningfulness and significance of mowing the lawn got changed, who changed it, and why it changed.

Here is something else to consider when it comes to identifying rites of passage. We want to think of a rite of passage as a one-time event in life. An activity one takes part in only once. As far as performing a structured ritual or ceremonial activity is concerned one can argue that the ritual or ceremony really is a one-time event. But a rite of passage is an event in life revolving around a behavior that is continuously demonstrated and performed throughout the rest of a person's life. Pertaining to mowing the lawn, which aspect of mowing the lawn is considered the most meaningful: the activity part, the experience part, or the behavior part?

With these things I've shared with you, you should be able now to take the information and use it to contextualize and explain how a mundane lawn chore can be described as a rite of passage for American boys. More importantly, you should by now have realized that what you are seeking to learn about in Group B does exist within your own group, Group A. Remember, it's easy to recognize in any ethnic minority group what we believe is apart from us. The challenge in learning about Other is in learning about ourselves and understanding ourselves first. Only then can we see Other not as we think we see them, but as how they see themselves. Now, hopefully, you appreciate what my mantra means:

Before you can learn about others you must first learn about yourself. Before you can understand others you must first understand yourself. When you learn about others you learn about yourself.

It's time for our visit to come to an end now. Together, we have been on a learning experience from the moment you began reading my words. I've been teaching you in this class lecture presented in the form of a written presentation very much like I used to teach students in my classes at MSU, Mankato. I'm a Lakota, and I teach like a Lakota. So for many of you, I may have come across as unconventional and possibly hard to follow and understand. But I have been true to my own cultural normal, and I've visited with you from within my own cultural context. I've spoken as best I can in this written form directly to you, the reader, and I've constructed our visit exactly as I would have done had we been face-to-face in a classroom. Believe it or not by simply reading my words you have all gotten to experience Other. Now it is up to each of you to determine what you have learned and decide upon the value of that learning.

Hecatu Yelo (Enough Said)

REFERENCES

Harris, Stanley G. (1994). "Organizational Culture and Individual Sensemaking: A Schema-Based Perspective." *Organization Science* 3: 309–321.

Lassiter, Luke E. (2006). *Invitation to Anthropology.* AltaMira Press, Lanham, p. 40.

LeBeau, Sebastian C. II. (2009). "Reconstructing Lakota Ritual in the Landscape: The Identification and Typing System for Traditional Cultural Property Sites," p. 14. Unpublished Ph.D. Dissertation, Department of Anthropology, University of Minnesota, Minneapolis.

Louis, M. R. (1980). "Organizations as Cultural-bearing Milieux." In *Organizational Symbolism,* eds. L. R. Pondy, P. J. Frost, G. Morgan, & T. C. Dandridge. pp. 39–45, JAI Press: Greenwhich.

Van Gennep, Arnold. (2010). *The Rites of Passage.* New York: Routledge Publishing.

Weick, K. E. (1979). "Cognitive Processes in Organizations." In *Research in Organization Behavior,* ed. B. M. Staw, pp. 41–74. JAI Press, Greenwhich.

The Métis: The Ethnogenesis of a People through Racial, Ethnic, and Cultural Mixing in America

Wayne E. Allen

The *Métis* people, and their name, have ancient roots in North American history. The words by which they named themselves, their collective actions over the centuries, and the sweeping tide of European colonization came to define them as a nation. The word, Métis, is French for "mixed," and the French-Catholic priests of early Canada and the U.S. used it as a descriptive term for French-Canadians (in this chapter referred to as *Canadiens*) of Native-American background. The early American Colonists had a similar word, *mustee*, by which to call English and Dutch "mixed bloods," but the English colonists soon replaced this with the derisive "breed."

—"A New Nation in Their Hearts, The Historical Evolution of the Métis People,"
by Richard Kees. In *Gone to Croatan,* eds. Ron Sakolsky
and James Koehnline, 1993, p. 283. Brooklyn, N.Y.: Autonomedia.

Introduction

Most Americans today are descended from a mixed cultural, ethnic, and racial background. After all, the mixing of a multitude of peoples into one nation—*e pluribus unum*—is what America is really all about. Yet, everyday in this society one is confronted with an immediate yet unspoken identity dilemma. It would seem that in practice most Americans are incapable of counting or considering identity categories that go beyond the standard binary oppositions of us versus them, red versus white, black versus white, brown versus white, or yellow versus white, where being white (specifically WASP) is unconsciously considered the normative factor in any identity calculation in America.

My people, the Métis, embody the difficulty of this dilemma because we are neither European nor Indian, but both/and. We do not easily fit into the standard historical narrative of Europeans confronting frontiers and Indians defending homelands. We are the Halfbreeds, the mixed-bloods, the half-castes who stood, and continue to stand, between both worlds. We are the embodiment of an historical intersect that creates cognitive dissonance in the American identity narrative. As a consequence, we are either portrayed as the bad guys in the historical narrative—neither the Noble Savages nor the civilized Man conquering the frontier while promoting progress and civilization—or, even worse, we are wiped out of the historical narrative entirely and altogether conveniently forgotten. But the truth is that it was our people who bridged the colonial dilemma and defined what it is to be truly American in a global context. In fact, our current president is the living embodiment of the dilemma surrounding what it is to be Métis. And this can be seen by the fact that his legitimacy as an American is constantly brought into question simply because he is of mixed ancestry.

We Métis look like all the members of all the other racial, ethnic, and cultural categories because we are a mixture of them all—that has never been a problem for our people from our perspective, but it is for outsiders with an agenda. We end up being labeled by all others by our physical appearance, where there is an implicit assumption that because we do not fit neatly into mainstream social categories that this is somehow a shortcoming. Some of us look Indian (like my Métis brother, Pat Burke, in northern Canada), others look European (like myself), while still others look African (like President Obama) or Asian (like his sister), so it is assumed we have to be members of the categories outsiders impose on us. And this has gone so far, and has gone on so long, many of us no longer remember or acknowledge who we really are. It is exceedingly difficult to prove your pedigree when you are Métis and do not look it, whatever that means. Records were often not kept when individuals were the product of miscegenation because the very act of mixing—*metisage*—was considered immoral. So those of us who were the product of metisage, the *métis, mestizos,* and *mulattos,* were like a stick in the eye. We were a racial, ethnic, and cultural sliver that just kept rankling the raw nerve of intercultural interaction and intermixing that has, in fact, defined American life since the first Europeans set foot on the islands in the Caribbean.

The following article is an attempt to briefly describe the history of our people and the roots of this dilemma, as well as briefly resurrect and discuss some of the facts about our role in American life, past and present. Its purpose is also to remind the reader that if you live in America, you are in fact Métis on one level or another whether you like it or accept it or not.

The Ethnogenesis of the Métis People

One cannot discuss the history and ethnogenesis of the Métis people without briefly discussing the history of colonialism and the fur trade in North America. Were we to do this discussion justice, however, it would require multiple voluminous tomes. We would have to point out the intersection between exploration, imperialism, and colonialism; notions of frontier and the delegitimization of pre-existing indigenous peoples' land claims and intellectual and cultural property rights—in a word, their identity; and the commoditization of nature accompanied by the loss of traditional language and culture as the price that is paid to participate in a global economy; as well as the miscegenation that is part and parcel of colonialism, whether the colonizers will admit it or not. We cannot, however, do that in this article. Instead, we will briefly touch on some of these topics in an attempt to introduce the reader to the flavor of the issues that surround issues of Métis identity in America.[1]

In 1600, a French trader named Pierre Chauvin established the first trading post in what would be called New France in northeastern North America. This began over four centuries of trade between Indians and European colonizers that would be characterized by cultural and economic contact, as well as intermixing, that is still going on today. Economic and social ties, often established, reinforced, and maintained through the marriage of our Indian mothers with our French fathers, were the means whereby the genesis of our people arose. It could be said of us in our creation narrative that we are the children of powerful yet seemingly irreconcilable historical forces that will either end up welding the fabric of America together into a single tapestry—rather like hydrogen and oxygen that are seemingly irreconcilable, highly volatile, and explosive gasses, but can combine to make the Water of Life—or these forces will rip America apart in an explosion of irreconcilable ethnic conflict. And this has ever been our dilemma here in America—to conflict and separate, or to reconcile and unify and grow.

The import of this ethnic, racial, and cultural mixing has been the ethnogenesis of a people— our people—who are still struggling in the U.S. for some small degree of recognition and acceptance. I am a professor at a university who teaches Ethnic Studies, and I still have colleagues of many diverse backgrounds across our campus that cannot or will not accept my mixed ethnic and cultural Métis identity even and especially when they pretend to be champions of diversity. And it often seems these are the folks who crow loudest about their own identity and that of "their group of people" being recognized and honored while they disregard and disrespect our Métis identity and heritage. I look White and I have long hair and teach Indian Studies so I am often viewed as a "wannabe" hippie, one who is overcompensating for a lack of ethnic and cultural identity by adopting the ways of ethnic others like Indians. But the fact is, I was born on my Indian uncle's birthday and raised between White and Indian cultures, growing up with my relatives on either side of that line. I, like most other Métis, have lived that intersect, having to engage in a constant daily identity struggle with myself, let alone with the judgment of others who are uncomfortable with my failure to meet their expectations of what I should look like or be in their eyes and, therefore, project their rationalized and justified none-too-subtle discrimination upon me and my people.

A Yankee American observer in St. Paul, Minnesota, our state capitol, summed up this dilemma best in 1859 when he said of our people:

> One hardly knew whether to be surprised at the odd uniformity of their costume of coarse blue cloth, richly ornate with brass buttons, their showy belts of red flannel, and their small jaunty caps, or at the remarkable diversity of their figures and complexions, including as it did, the fair skin and light brown curls of the Saxon, and the swarthy hue and straight black hair of the Indian, with every intermediate shade that amalgamation could produce.[2]

CONCLUSION

The observation discussed here reveals the inherent ethnocentrism and racism projected upon our people because we do not fit into the assumed categories, then and now. Our phenotypes are a mixture, as are our clothing, our food, our language and lifeways, our land and resource use patterns, and our aspirations. We do not want to be like anyone else; we want to be ourselves and to have that right treated with the same dignity and respect of every other ethnic population in America deserves. We want to be heard and listened to, and we want our contributions acknowledged. We have played a significant role in the history of Minnesota (and many other states in the union) for the last few hundred years, and we are still here contributing. Most of the French names in our state are Métis in origin. When the settlers began arriving in the mid-nineteenth century, the U.S. military began evicting our people from their lands. We were called squatters because we held our lands in longitudinal plots along rivers (we are river and lake people) rather than in gridded squares like Thomas Jefferson advocated, and labeling us as such was a way to delegitimize our land claims. We ". . . were hated by the Americans for [our] many-hued skins, our French language, and [our] overwhelming support for the British in the War of 1812."[3] The 1849 and 1850 censuses indicated a population in Minnesota of about 19,000 people, 66 percent of whom were Dakota, Winnebago, and Ojibway; 18 percent of whom were Métis; and 16 percent of whom were newly arrived Yankee American settlers. During the census our people were identified with an "H," indicating "Half-breed."

By 1885, our people had been involved in a failed rebellion, our leaders were rounded up and imprisoned, Louis Riel had been hung, and our people were scattered as refugees across northwestern Minnesota, North Dakota and Montana, and southern Canada in the plains provinces. The half-century that followed was a bleak time for the Métis people. Both governments in Canada and the U.S. disavowed our people as a distinct ethnic or nationalist group, our land base eroded, we experienced social isolation and poverty, and both countries wrote us out of the history books.

Then, in the 1970s, our people began to regain their voice due to gains brought about by the Civil Rights Movement, the American Indian Movement, and the Canadian Indian Brotherhood

Movement. On September 23, 2003, the Supreme Court of Canada ruled that Métis are in fact a distinct people with significant rights. The Supreme Court of Canada outlined three broad factors to identify Métis rights-holders:

- self-identification as a Métis individual;
- ancestral connection to an historic Métis community; and
- acceptance by a Métis community.

All three factors must be present for an individual to qualify under the legal definition of Métis, but there is still a great deal of ambiguity. Whether or not Métis have Treaty Rights is an explosive issue in the Canadian Aboriginal community today. Some say that only First Nations could legitimately sign treaties so, by definition, Métis have no Treaty rights.

Today, we are a distinct, legally recognized aboriginal group in Canada, with formal recognition equal to that of the Inuit and First Nations peoples. The statistics that follow tell the tale:

Total Population
As of 2006, 389,780 Métis
1.25% of the Canadian population

Regions with Significant Populations
Canada, United States

Languages
English, Métis French,
Gaelic, Michif, Bungee

Religion
Predominantly
Roman Catholic, Protestant; mixed with
Traditional Beliefs

Related Ethnic Groups
French, Cree, Ojibwa, Dakota,
Acadians, Cajuns, Scots
English, Irish, Anglo-Métis[4]

Métis people continue to live throughout the United States, with greater or lesser community identity depending on location. A strong Prairie Métis identity exists on the northern plains. This region considered the Métis "homeland" was once known as Rupert's Land. It extends south from Canada into North Dakota west of the Red River of the North. The historic Prairie Métis homeland also includes parts of Minnesota and Wisconsin. Many Métis families continue to show up in the U.S. Census in the historical Métis settlements areas along the Detroit and St. Clair Rivers, Mackinac Island, and Sault Ste. Marie in Michigan, as well as Green Bay in Wisconsin. Métis settlements existed all along the Allegheny and Ohio rivers and their tributaries. This is revealed by the French names of the many towns and villages in these areas.

Many of the descendants of the Métis ceased to exist as a distinct people with the arrival of the English-speaking settlers. Initially, the light-haired Métis, and later with the arrival of immigrants from southern Europe, the dark-haired Métis, intermarried with these new immigrants. Today, most are unaware of their Métis heritage, and the descendants of the Métis in the areas of western Pennsylvania, Ohio, Kentucky, Indiana, and Illinois assume they are descended from the more recent immigrants from Europe when, in fact, their European heritage can be traced back hundreds of years.

An estimated 10,000 self-identified Métis live in North Dakota, mostly in Pembina County, North Dakota, although their cultural status is not as pronounced as that of their northern brethren in Manitoba, Canada. Many of the members of the Turtle Mountain Band of Chippewa Indians, which is a federally recognized Tribe, consider themselves to be Métis. In the Northeastern United States there is an active Métis movement. The Métis Eastern Tribal Indian Society, often referred to as the Métis of Maine, seeks to teach and carry on its mixed ethnic and cultural heritage. They emphasize their North Eastern Woodland Native American heritage by holding cultural events that honor the "mixed blood" members of the band. At their Cultural Center located in Dayton, Maine, Métis band elders teach traditional Eastern Woodland Native spiritual and social culture in the Medicine Wheel way, which teaches harmony and respect between the cultures. Membership in this Métis band does not preclude tribal membership in other bands.

In North America today, millions of people could, and many thousands do, claim Métis heritage. We are the direct descendants of our European and Native American ancestors. Many of our people of mixed heritage are not aware of our Métis identity, as well as our movement for recognition and respect within the United States. But through consciousness raising and legal action, our identity is once again gaining credence and recognition. Aho!

ENDNOTES

1. For thorough, well-written introduction and overview see: Kees, Richard. 1993. "A New Nation in Their Hearts: The Historical Evolution of the Métis People." In *Gone to Croatan,* eds. Ron Sakolsky and James Koehnline. Brooklyn, NY: Autonomedia.

2. *Collections of the Minnesota Historical Society,* Volume 7, p. 343. [St. Paul: **The Society**], 1872–1920 (St. Paul: Ramaley, Chaney & Co., printers).

3. Kees, Richard. 1993. "A New Nation in Their Hearts: The Historical Evolution of the Métis People." In *Gone to Croatan,* eds. Ron Sakolsky and James Koehnline, pp. 304–305. Brooklyn, NY: Autonomedia.

4. Wikipedia, 2012.

Reclaiming the Indigenous: Origins, Development, and Future of the Taino "Revival" Movement among Caribbean Latinos

Francisco J. González

Introduction

Issues of race, ethnicity, and group identity have permeated the history of the peoples of what we now call Latin America since the arrival of the Spanish in 1492, and the ensuing sudden, violent, and profound changes that it brought to the lives of the indigenous peoples of the Western Hemisphere.

In the Caribbean islands of Hispaniola, Puerto Rico, and Cuba, Spanish settlers and enslaved Africans co-existed with the local Native Americans that were eventually incorporated into the European colonial system. While contributing to the racial and cultural heritage of the modern inhabitants of these islands, the indigenous peoples were thought to have become extinct as a separate and distinct community. Beginning in the nineteenth century, Cubans, Dominicans, and Puerto Ricans struggling to achieve political self-determination and develop a national identity out of diverse racial and social groups, a single unifying concept of who was a *cubano, dominicano,* or *puertorriqueño,* developed based on the premise a common culture shared by all the inhabitants of each of the islands.[1]

With their arrival to the mainland United States in successive mass migrations during the twentieth century, islanders were pressed to adapt to this nation's particular system of race classification and power politics, which introduced an additional layer of ethnic and racial criteria to the self-identity of these diaspora communities. In the post-civil rights era, many Latinos gravitated towards the study, promotion, and preservation of their traditional cultures and languages.[2] For many in the Cuban, Puerto Rican, and Dominican communities, a growing interest in their shared indigenous roots also led to the eventual self-identification of many individuals with the Taíno—the Native American ethnic groups found across most of the Caribbean at the moment of the European arrival.

In addition to the internal sociopolitical dynamics in the United States, the later part of the twentieth century also saw the reaffirmation of national, ethnic, and cultural consciousness among minority peoples as diverse as the Ukrainians in the former Soviet Union and the Maya in the Mexican state of Chiapas. A convergence of different and even unrelated geopolitical events (collapse of multiethnic states like the Soviet Union and Yugoslavia and the signing of the North American Free Trade Agreement, for example), historical celebrations (such as the 500th anniversary of Columbus

138

"discovery" of the New World), and technological developments (such as the exponential increase in the ability to communicate and exchange information facilitated by the Internet) contributed to this phenomena.

This article will explore the historical origins of the cultural, political, and social initiatives to reassert their identification with the Taino among Latinos from the Spanish-speaking Caribbean and related diasporic communities in the United States, in the context of evolving concepts of race and ethnicity, and the trends for future development of this indigenous identity.

A final note on the terminology: among many self-identified Taíno, terms like *revival, neo-Taino, tribe, nation,* and *organization* have multiple and sometimes conflicting meanings. Some individuals object to the term *revival* because it implies that the Taino were at some point extinct. Others deny that they form an organization, preferring to use the term *tribe* as better representing their position that they are a distinct ethnic and cultural entity along the lines of formally government recognized tribes in the United States and Canada. For purposes of consistency in this paper, I will use the term *organization* to refer generically to formal, organized bodies of self-identified Taino.

The Setting: Taino Origins

The modern-day Taino organizations invariably trace their origins to the indigenous peoples of the Caribbean, who were the first Native Americans encountered by Christopher Columbus during his voyage in 1492. Columbus described them as ". . . very well made, with very handsome bodies, and very good countenances. Their hair is short and coarse . . . down to the eyebrows, except a few locks behind, which they wear long and never cut. Some paint themselves white, others red, and others of what color they find. Some paint their faces, others the whole body, some only round the eyes, others only on the nose."[3] These people, the Taino, inhabited the islands of the western Caribbean, including Cuba, Hispaniola (the island shared by Haiti and the Dominican Republic), Jamaica, the Bahamans, and Puerto Rico. The Taino language (related to Arawak) originated in northern South America.[4]

The Taino, however, were not the first humans to settle in the Caribbean. Archaeological records and historical accounts indicate that there were other people from different cultural and ethno-linguistic characteristics that predated and even co-existed with the later South American arrivals.[5] Recent scholarship and archaeological data appear to indicate that these so-called Archaic populations (perhaps originating in the southeastern United States) had a greater influence in the formation of the Taino societies and their specific variability as observed by the Spanish.[6]

There are even indications of trade networks that facilitated the exchange of products between the Taino of Cuba and other Native American cultural areas.[7] The pre-Hispanic Caribbean, far from being an isolated backwater, was a dynamic center of cultural exchange that led to the creation of a distinct Taino culture.

Society, Economic Life, Customs, and Religion[8]

Estimates of the population of the pre-Columbian Caribbean vary considerably, but some sources indicate that the population of Hispaniola alone may have been as high as seven or eight million.[9]

The Taino lived in village groupings called *yukayekes,* comprised of palm-thatched dwellings (*bohios*) close to ceremonial open spaces (*batey*) and farmland where root crops like yucca (cassava) as well as corn, beans, and other useful plants were cultivated. Fishing was also an important activity, but due to the absence of large land animal species, hunting was a secondary activity.

Social structure was divided in three principal strata: local chieftains or *caciques,* wielding power over each individual yukayeke, although there is evidence that in parts of Hispaniola (cacique Guaironex) and Puerto Rico (cacique Agueybana) a paramount chief was rendered deference by other cacikes. The *nitainos* constituted the middle strata, or nobility, and the commoners, or *naborias,* constituted the bulk of the population.

Taino religion included a pantheon of deities identified with forces of nature (the term *hurricane* comes from the Taino god identified with storms, Urakán) as well as lesser spirits that served as protectors and intermediaries between humans and the gods. The cemi or three-pointed carved stones commonly associated with Taino spirituality were venerated as a physical presentation of these protective forces.

The Taino produced fine woven cotton textiles, colorful and well-decorated ceramics, and gold alloy ornaments mostly for symbolic insignia of cacikes and to decorate religious artifacts.

The Arrival of the *Maboya*[10]

The world of the Indigenous Caribbean was forever changed with the arrival of the Europeans. Columbus established the first Spanish settlements on the island of Hispaniola, La Navidad, in 1492. Subsequent settlements were made in other parts of this island. Initially, the Taino sought to accommodate the Spanish presence and even collaborated with the Spanish.[11]

The Spanish eventually implemented a *repartimento* or *encomienda* system, the allotment to Spanish settlers of the labor and tribute of yukayekes or individual Taino.[12] The resulting working conditions led to increased indigenous resistance and open warfare, which caused deaths and disrupted the Taino economic life. However, a far deadlier result of the forced contact with the Europeans was the spread of imported contagious diseases. The resulting mortality devastated the Taino. Spanish records indicate that, by 1509, there were only 60,000 indigenous people left in Hispaniola.[13] The encomienda system was extended to subsequent Spanish settlements across the Caribbean and elsewhere, with similar catastrophic results for the native populations.

In Cuba, Puerto Rico, and Jamaica the same cycle of initial accommodation, conflict, and massive population loss occurred. By the end of the sixteenth century, the pre-Columbian Taíno social and economic organization, was replaced by *encomiendas* and *repartimientos,* the Taino religion suppressed, and the Taino language largely supplanted by Castilian. However, by forming into scattered enclaves or assimilating into the multiethnic populations of the Spanish settlements, the Taino endured.

Survival 1600 to 1900

The traditional consensus among historian archaeologists proclaimed that, by 1600, the Taino had become extinct in the Caribbean, and while some cultural and genetic traits remained, these became amalgamated with the Spanish and African populations to form the "three roots" of the modern-day peoples of Cuba, Dominican Republic, and Puerto Rico. The resulting national culture became more than the sum of its parts and became instead a new entity.[14]

Furthermore, the Taíno contribution to the ethnic and cultural ancestry of the post-colonial peoples was deemed to be small due to their rapid disappearance. Dr. Ricardo Alegría, the father of modern Puerto Rican archaeology, articulated this view in an interview shortly before his passing in 2011:

> "Very few Indians were left after 50 years," said Ricardo Alegría, a Puerto Rican historian and anthropologist . . . "Their culture was interrupted by disease, marriage with Spanish and Africans, and so forth, but the main reason the Indians were exterminated as a group was sickness. . . . by 1519, a third of the aboriginal population [of Puerto Rico] had died because of smallpox. You find documents very soon after that, in the 1530s, in which the question came from Spain to the governor. 'How many Indians are there? Who are the chiefs?' The answer was none. They are gone."[15]

On the other hand, historical records, ethno-cultural studies, and even genetic testing have revealed that indigenous traits remain imbedded in the fabric of the modern Spanish-speaking Caribbean. The indigenous mortality of the first years of the conquest, and the fact that the Spanish preferred to settle in the richer colonies of Mexico and Peru, resulted in vast tracks of lands in the interior of these islands, which remained sparsely populated until well into the eighteenth century. This is one of the reasons why the French managed to establish themselves on the western part of the Hispaniola, which eventually became modern day Haiti. It is almost certain that communities of Taíno, now including *mestizo* (individuals of mixed indigenous and European ancestry) and Africans (either escaped slaves or freed), remained in comparative isolation.

Contemporaneous documents from the Spanish colonial authorities and church records do confirm a continuous presence of non-European individuals as part of the population, but under Spanish social construct, "race" and "ethnicity" were rather fluid concepts, and the use of terms such as *indio, mestizo,* and *pardo* to classify individuals depend rather on the specific context of the document and the interpretation of the official collecting and processing of the data.[16]

Nevertheless, there is evidence of continued Taíno presence in their ancestral Caribbean homeland well past the date of their supposed extinction.

In Hispaniola (modern day Dominican Republic and Haiti), the Spanish interacted with cohesive Taíno chiefdoms from their first permanent arrival in 1493 to the end of active Taíno armed resistance with the peace settlement with the Christianized caciques Enriquillo and Murcio in 1533 and 1545, respectively.[17]

Despite the population crash of the island, Spanish records continue to make reference to the presence of "indios" or unassimilated indigenous people. For example, as late as 1555, a Spanish patrol encountered four villages "full of Indians about whom nobody previously knew." One of these villages was close to Puerto Plata, on the Atlantic Coast; a second one was close by; a third village was on the Samaná peninsula; and a fourth one was on the northeast part of the island in Cabo San Nicolás.[18]

In the Blue Mountains region of Jamaica, conquered by the Spanish in the early sixteenth century but sparsely settled, there is evidence of continuation of Taíno cultural life, now including escaped African slaves (Maroons), well after 1655 when the English expelled the Spanish.[19]

In Puerto Rico, the census compiled by the Spanish authorities also reflected the presence of "indios" until the end of the eighteenth century. The 1771 census indicated the presence of 1,756 individuals classified as "indio (Indian)." The 1778 census revealed an increased "indio" population of 2,302 individuals.[20] Ethnological researchers during the twentieth century continued to observe individuals with superficial physical traits consistent with indigenous ancestry, as well as the prevalence of certain cultural practices among the inhabitants of the more isolated, mountainous central part of the island.[21]

By far the best documented extant Taíno community can be found in eastern Cuba, among the inhabitants of the region around the towns of Yáteras and Caridad de Los Indios in the province of Guantánamo. Jose Barreiro, currently at the Smithsonian National Museum of the American Indian, has done intensive fieldwork with this community and documented its preservation of Taíno religious and cultural practices.[22] The continued survival of this distinct Taíno population was recognized in Cuban government documents as recently as the mid-nineteenth century. During the 1895–1898 war, the pro-independence insurgents organized the Hatuey Regiment (named after a cacique that had first resisted the Spanish conquest) from the "Indian" inhabitants of the region.[23]

Additional evidence of the survival of the Taíno are the several DNA studies completed since the 1990s, concluding that a significant proportion of the population of Puerto Rico carry Taíno DNA. According to geneticist Carlos Bustamante at the Stanford University School of Medicine in Stanford, California, "On average, the genomes of Puerto Ricans contain 10–15% Native American DNA, which is largely Taíno."[24] An earlier study directed by Dr. Juan Carlos Martinez Cruzado at the Mayaguez campus of the University of Puerto Rico had concluded that up to 53 percent of Puerto Ricans had Indigenous ancestry.[25] Some scholars caution against the racist undertones of focusing on genetic makeup that reinforces the colonial legacy of discrimination against blacks and mulatto,[26] but Taino leaders counter that the DNA studies are simply another piece of evidence confirming that indigenous people survived the conquest and are not extinct.[27]

This archaeological, documentary, and ethnographic evidence provides the foundation of the modern Taíno revival movement by indicating that the indigenous DNA (however attenuated) found among modern-day populations, the presence of Taino cultural traits imbedded in the Spanish-dominant creole culture, and the indigenous identity officially recognized through the centuries by the Spanish colonial authorities (albeit restricted to small, isolated communities in rural areas) and family oral histories are proof that the Taino never became extinct nor completely assimilated.

Awakening: Rise of Taino Tribes, Nations, and Organizations

The development of the modern Taino awakening, expressed in organizations whose members declared themselves to be Taino, can be found not on the Caribbean homelands but in the diaspora communities residing in the United States. The diverse social, political, and economic situations of Cuba (ruled by a socialist revolution since 1959 and immersed in Cold War politics), Dominican Republic (struggling with poverty and the aftermaths of dictatorship and civil war), and Puerto Rico (a U.S. territory still debating its future post-colonial status) did not focus on introspective issues of race or ethnicity self-identification.

In the late 1960s and 1970s the U.S. civil rights and antiwar movements divided into groups and organizations more focused on ethnic, racial, and gender politics.[28] Within the Puerto Rican community of New York, Taino symbols were already incorporated in the visual imagery of social and cultural activist groups, such as the Young Lords, El Taller Boricua, and El Museo del Barrio.[29]

This romanticized discussion of Taino cultural artifacts and indigenous resistance against Spanish colonialism, and as precursors of modern social and political struggles, sparked the interest of several individuals to, in essence, shifting the emphasis from talking about the Taino to, instead, talking about *being* Taino.

The Catalyst: Indigenous Response to the Columbus Quincentenary

The 500th anniversary of the arrival of Christopher Columbus to the Western Hemisphere, commemorated in 1992, culminated years of protests and discussions on the impact of European colonization on the lives of indigenous peoples all over the Americas.[30] In the Dominican Republic, the government and business sectors openly celebrated the event and lionized the figure of Columbus, including the building of a huge lighthouse honoring the Genoese sailor in Santo Domingo, while pointedly ignoring the catastrophic impact of colonization on the local Taino people.[31] In the U.S., however, indigenous groups such as the American Indian Movement (AIM) conducted many protests against "celebrating" the arrival of Columbus. In one of the most dramatic protests, on May 29, 1992, AIM leader Verne Bellecourt threw a pint of his blood on a replica of Columbus' ship "La Niña" temporarily on display at the Science Museum in Minneapolis, Minnesota.[32]

Issues of indigenous self-government, economic empowerment, preservation of native languages, culture, and traditional, gained worldwide interest with the granting of the Nobel Peace Prize to noted Guatemalan Maya activist Rigoberta Menchu in 1992; and by the vocal opposition by Mexican indigenous and peasants to the North American Free Trade Agreement (NAFTA) during the early part of the decade, which eventually led to the *Zapatista* uprising in Chiapas on January 1, 1994.[33]

Self-identified Taino writers and scholars, such as Jose Barreiro in the United States, were an integral part of this discussion, bringing attention to the fact that it was the Taino who first met Columbus and inevitably bore the brunt of the conquest, subjugation, and decimation later visited on the rest of the native populations.[34] It is no coincidence that many of the early Taino organizations first became formalized at this time.[35]

First Organizations

The earliest references to any type of Taino organization refers to the formation of a Taino Indian Movement in Orocovis, Puerto Rico, in 1968,[36] co-founded by Pedro *Guanikeyu* Torres, now a resident of New Jersey and an influential Taino activist and cacike.[37] Cacike *Guanikeyu* Torres went on to found the Jatibonicu Taino Tribe of Boriken (Puerto Rico) on November 18, 1970, but it appears that neither of these organizations had a formalized structure.

In 1982, Miguel *Sobaoko Koromo* Sague Jr. founded the Caney Indian Spiritual Circle (now Mother Earth Church of the Grand Caney) in Pittsburgh, Pennsylvania. *Sobao Koromo* Sague, originally from Cuba, is a *behike,* or shaman, with a religious ministry based on Taino spirituality.[38]

Another prominent leader, Rene *Cibanakán* Marcano Quiñones, residing in New York, compiled and published a handout in 1988 describing the Cheverez family in Morovis, Puerto Rico, highlighting their physical characteristics and work in ceramics and pottery using Taino designs.[39] Cacike *Cibanakán* Marcano was also one of the founders of the first formal organizations on record, La Asociación Indígena Taína, formed on December 21, 1990, in New York.[40] The organization later changed its name to Maisiti Yucayeke Ti Taino on July 1, 1993. In common with latter organizations, Maisti Ti Yukayeke limited membership to people of indigenous ancestry.[41]

Cacike *Cibanakán* Marcano departed Maisiti Ti Yukayeke and founded the Nación Taína de las Antillas—Taino UaraA Bauaken (Taino Nation of the Antilles) in New York on November 19, 1992, the 499th anniversary of the arrival of Columbus to Puerto Rico. Cacike Cibanakán, however, adopted the position that Nación Taína was not an organization but "a tribal nation encompassing all Tainos in eastern Cuba, Boriken (Puerto Rico), the U.S. diaspora or anywhere else who once again claim the right to our indigenous identity and recognize the restores nation of the Taino people."[42] Nación Taína also prepared a registry of individuals claiming Taino identity and who had demonstrated with documents that the candidate has "Taino bloodline" from one or both parents.[43]

Bronx-based historian, researcher, and storyteller Bobby Gonzalez, active in educational activities and a speaker on Taino culture as early as 1992,[44] co-founded Tainos del Norte on July 1993 as a cultural organization dedicated to the preservation of Taino history, language, and traditions.[45]

Also in 1993, Cacike Peter *Guanikeyu* Torres founded The Taino Inter-tribal Council in Millville, New Jersey. The organizational bylaws indicate that "this organization will serve as a tool to bring awareness of our Taino Native American culture to the general public by promoting the Indigenous culture of our ancestors."[46] The bylaws also stated that the members of this Tribal Council will fall under the Taino Tribe of Jatibonuco.[47] The Council published a newsletter, *The Taino Indian Land Review/Revista de la Indierra (sic) Taína,* with articles on culture, language, as well as poetry. The Taino Inter-Tribal Council, Inc. of New Jersey Organization closed in January 1, 2001,[48] but the organization remains active as the Jatibonicu Taino Tribal Nation of Boriken.[49]

The first Taino organization formed on the Caribbean homeland islands was the Consejo General de Tainos Borincanos, formally constituted in 1994 under the direction of Elba *Anaka* Lugo, Roberto *Múcaro* Borrero, and Valeriana *Abuela Shashira* Rodríguez Valentín. Peter *Guanikeyu* Torres was recognized as an Elder of the Council.[50] The Consejo had its roots in Paseo Taino, a folkloric dance group that incorporated Taino instruments and music into its performances since 1978.[51]

Roberto *Múcaro* Borrero also was instrumental in founding the United Confederation of Taino People on January 3, 1998, "dedicated to the promotion and protection of the human rights, cultural heritage, and spiritual traditions of the Taíno and other Caribbean Indigenous Peoples for our present and future generations."[52]

Since the end of the 1990s, a multitude of Taino organizations have been created in the United States, the Dominican Republic, and Puerto Rico; many of them are formally incorporated as not-for-profit cultural entities.

Development and Challenges

By the late 1990s the various organizations of the Taino movement had gained a measure of visibility and acceptance. For example, self-identified Taino have worked with members of federally recognized Native American tribes in organizing[53] traditional powwows and performing as dancers.[54] Jose *Hatuey* Barreiro, born in Cuba, is arguably the most significant Taino scholar currently active. His far-ranging body of research and long-standing collaboration with indigenous leaders and researchers are recognized both by mainstream academics and indigenous leaders from all over the Americas.[55] Equally significant is the fact that Taino organizations have gained admittance to consulting bodies related to the United Nations. Roberto *Múcaro* Borrero participated in the first session of the newly-created Permanent Forum on Indigenous Issues[56] and is the Chair of the NGO Committee on the International Decade of the World's Indigenous Peoples.[57]

Virtual *batey*

One of the most interesting aspects of the Taino movement is the key role played by the Internet and online communications in enabling the growth and development of a Taino identity, both virtual and real. Dr. Maximilian Forte's seminal examination of this phenomenon rightly points out that the Internet has not only facilitated the exchange of information but has actually helped create community bonds between individuals across the Caribbean and the diaspora in the United States.[58] According to Forte ". . . the Internet also helps to embody groups facing difficulties in gaining acceptance as 'indigenous,' whilst facilitating mutual recognition and validation between these groups thus lending further authority and authenticity to the individual groups in their own offline contexts."[59]

Fort observes that "there is an important and dynamic relationship between the offline and the online dimensions of cultural practice" and that "online practices of self-representation are a vital facet of offline politics, shaped by them and shaping them in their turn . . . While realities are being constructed and disseminated on the Internet that have not yet taken root on the ground— i.e., a sovereign Taino government—it is important to recognize the possibility of the 'real-life facts on the ground' being reshaped and informed by electronically-generated realities."[60]

The Internet became, in essence, the modern equivalent of the *batey,* the plaza or meeting grounds near their villages where pre-Columbian Taíno held their ceremonies and important events. But going beyond the exchange of information and networking, the act of interacting online with likeminded, self-identified Taino is creating the community solidarity and shared culture that are the hallmarks of a real-life ethnic group.

Controversies

The rise of the Taino reconstruction movement inevitably led to a reaction among scholars and academics that questioned the ethnological underpinnings of the claim that the Taino were not "extinct." As discussed, academics and scholars such as Dr. Ricardo Alegría and Dr. Gabriel Haslip-Viera noted that, while Taino DNA could be found in many living individuals, this did not mean that the Taino remained a viable community during the centuries of Spanish colonization, much less now, and dismissed the idea that the Taino are a distinct, divisible component of these modern Caribbean populations. For Alegría, the indigenous, the Spanish and the African elements were fused long ago into an indivisible entity, the modern Puerto Rican. Commentators in Puerto Rico also reacted with strong words, ridiculing modern Taino. Noted Puerto Rican writer Magali García Ramis compared modern day Taino with children that pretend to dress to play cowboys and Indians.[61] The author goes on to state that:

"[t]odo lo que uno querría representar de ese pueblo que cesó de existir como tal queda reducido a una payasada montada por persons ignorantes de la cultura y modo de vida de los tainos. No hay inocencia ni candidez en esa farsa, solo mal gusto en la representatividad de un legado que es de todos nosotros . . ."

(everything that one may want to represent about this people (the Taino) that ceased to exist as such is now reduced to a mockery (payasada) created by individuals ignorant of the culture and life styles of the Taino. There isn't innocence or candor in this farce, only tasteless representation of a legacy that belongs to all of us)"[62]

These conflicting sentiments among the general public towards the Taino "revivalists" were put on display during the so-called *Grito de Caguana,* or the Stand at Caguana, when a group of Tainos occupied the Caguana Ceremonial Center, a state park that includes the most important Taino archaeological site in Puerto Rico.[63] The Taino started a hunger strike and presented several demands to the local authorities, including greater protection for threatened archaeological sites, the return of Taino artifacts and remains that were sent to the United States, and more respectful handling of Taino human remains now on display in museums and at Caguana itself.[64] While the protesters received the support of some sectors of society, news articles and commentaries published in the local media continued to maintain the extinction of the Taino and questioned the motives of the hunger strikers.[65]

Future

The Taino movement continues to grow and gain acceptance among many members of the Spanish-speaking Caribbean communities in the United States and their island homelands. A recent article from CNN indicated that, since 2000, the number of Hispanics who identified themselves as Native American grew from 407,073 to 685,150, according to the 2010 census.[66] The article also spotlighted Ana María *Tekina-eirú* Maynard, a Taina educator residing in Texas, as an example of the new-found self-identification of Latinos with their indigenous roots.

The Taino "awakening" movement is coming of age at a time when several cultural, social, political, and economic currents are intersecting. Internationally, there is increased awareness of the rights and challenges of indigenous communities, which is highlighted by events such as the EZLN Maya uprising in Chiapas, Mexico, and the election of Evo Morales as Bolivia's first indigenous president. In the United States, federally-recognized Indian tribes have generally welcomed the Taino as a kindred people. In addition, growing ethnic diversity and demographic changes resulting from immigration are creating more space for Latinos to express their many diverse cultural traits, not only their "national" cultures but their specific ethnic and regional identities.

An examination of the activities and mission statements from a cross section of organized Taino communities show almost uniform agreement on areas of future work:

- preservation and dissemination of the indigenous cultural heritage of the modern-day peoples of Cuba, Puerto Rico, and the Dominican Republic
- protection of the archaeological artifacts and sacred sites
- increase ties between the different Taino communities in the Caribbean and the diaspora
- preserve the orally transmitted stories and traditions
- encourage the reconstruction and dissemination of the Taino (Arawak) language
- respect and devotion for the spiritual legacy of the Taino in the U.S. and elsewhere
- obtain sovereign rights over ancestral lands
- increase ties with other indigenous peoples, especially the related Carib and Garifuna communities in the Caribbean and Arawak and Amazonian tribes in South America
- preservation of the environment and ecosystems of the ancestral Taino lands in the Caribbean

CONCLUSION

The Taino revivalist or awakening movement is certainly here to stay. The number of Cubans, Puerto Ricans, and Dominicans that self-identify as Taino continues to increase, together with greater acceptance among the diaspora and island communities of the concept of a separate Taino identity. More than twenty years after the appearance of the first Taino organizations, there are young adults that were born and/or raised in households in which claiming to be Taino was the norm. Irrespective of whether the ancestral Taino became extinct or not during the Spanish conquest, the reality is that a distinct Taino ethnicity is coming into existence and will continue to evolve both among the diaspora communities and their island homelands of the western Caribbean.

ENDNOTES

1. Haslip-Viera, Gabriel. (2001). "Competing Identities: Taino Revivalism and other Etno-racial Identity Movements among Puerto Ricans and other Caribbean Latinos in the United States. 1980–present." In *Taíno Revival: Critical Perspectives on Puerto Rican Identity and Cultural Politics,* ed. Gabriel Haslip-Viera. Princeton: Markus Wiener, pp. 36–37.

2. Olivo, Antonio. (2001). "Movement Embraces Indigenous Past," *Los Angeles Times,* January 2. *http://articles.latimes.com/2001/jan/02/local/me-7334.*

3. First Voyage of Columbus: Meeting the Islanders (1492) *Athena Review* Vol. 1, no. 3 (1997).

4. Rouse, Irving. 1992. *The Tainos: Rise and Decline of the People who Greeted Columbus.* New Haven and London: Yale University Press, p. 5.

5. Ibid., 5–7.

6. For example, Dr. Reniel Rodriguez Ramos indicates that model of a "cultural landscape formed by multiple networks of people with different ancestries interacting with each other for extended periods of time" could better accommodate the possible linguistic and biological variability within and between the islands as well as the cultural variability evidence through time . . ." Ramos, Reniel Rodriguez. (2007). "Puerto Rican Precolonial History Etched in Stone." PhD diss., University of Florida, p. 335. *http://www.box.com/shared/gul7lzccx7*

7. Martinón-Torres, Marcos, Cooper, Jago, Valcárcel Rojas Roberto, & Rehre, Thilo. (2006). "Diversifying the picture: indigenous responses to European arrival in Cuba." *Archaeology International* 10: 38. Describing gold artifacts found in a Taino burial ground, archaeologists concluded that "[s]tylistic study, together with the chemical analysis, allowed us to suggest that these had been manufactured by skilful goldsmiths in continental South America, probably Colombia, and had been brought to Cuba through existing interaction networks."

8. Adapted from Figueroa, Loida. (1978). *Breve Historia de Puerto Rico,* vol. 1. Rio Piedras, PR: Editorial Edil, pp. 29–46.

9. Josephy, Alvin M., Jr. 1994. *500 Nations: An Illustrated History of North American Indians.* New York: Knopf, p. 116.

10. "evil spirit" in Taino Arawak. Sola, Edwin Miner. (2006). *Diccionario Taino Ilustrado.* Puerto Rico: Ediciones Servilibros, p. 29.

11. Cacike Guacanagari, who had initially met Columbus in 1492, assisted the Spanish in the repression of the first Taino uprising in the region of Higuey in 1495. Rouse, Irving. 1992. *The Tainos: Rise and Decline of the People who Greeted Columbus.* New Haven and London: Yale University Press, p. 151.

12. Ibid., 153–154.

13. Ibid., 155.

14. Duany, Jorge. (2006). "Making Indians out of Blacks: the Revitalization of Taíno Identity in Contemporary Puerto Rico." In *Indigenous Resurgence in the Contemporary Caribbean,* ed. Maximilian C. Forte. New York: Peter Lang pp. 72–73.

15. Poole, Robert M. (2011). "What became of the Taino?" *Smithsonian Magazine* (October). *http://www.smithsonianmag.com/people-places/What-Became-of-the-Taino.html*

16. Katzew, Ilona. (2004). *Casta Painting: Images of Race in Eighteenth-Century Mexico.* New Haven, CT: Yale University Press.

17. Enriquillo and Murcio rebelled against Spanish mistreatment and remained at large between 1519 and 1533; Murcio continued his resistance until 1545. Estevez, Jorge Baracutey. (2001). "A Chronology of Taíno Cultural and Biological Survival." *Caribbean Amerindian Centrelink.* *http://www.centrelink.org/EstevezCronos.html*

18. Guitar, Lynne, Ferbel-Azcarate, Pedro, & Estevez, Jorge. (2006). "Ocama-Daca Taíno (Hear me, I Am Taíno): Taíno Survival on Hispaniola, Focusing on the Dominican Republic." In *Indigenous Resurgence in the Contemporary Caribbean,* ed. Maximilian C. Forte. New York: Peter Lang, p. 51.

19. Kofi Agorsah, E. (1993). "Archaeology and Resistance History in the Caribbean." *The African Archaeological Review* 11: 187, 191.

20. Figueroa, Loida. (1978). *Breve Historia de Puerto Rico,* vol. 1. Rio Piedras, PR: Editorial Edil, p. 70.

21. Fewkes, Jesse. "The Aborigenes of Porto Rico and Neighboring Islands." In *Annual Report of the Bureau of American Ethnology for 1903–04,* no. 25, pp. 25–26.

22. Barreiro, Jose. (1996). "The Cacique's Prayer: Taíno Journal." *Native AMERICAS: Akwe:kon Journal of Indigenous Issues* 10: 38–47; Stingl, Miloslav. (1970). *Indiani cernosi a vousaci.* Prague: Albatros.

23. Barreiro, Jose. (2006). "Taíno Survivals: Cacique Panchito, Caridad de los Indios, Cuba." In *Indigenous Resurgence in the Contemporary Caribbean,* ed. Maximilian C. Forte, New York: Peter Lang, pp. 30–32.

24. Young, Susan. (2011). "Rebuilding the genome of a hidden ethnicity" *Nature* (October 14). *http://www.nature.com/news/2011/111014/full/news.2011.592.html*

25. Martinez Cruzado, Juan Carlos, et al. (2001). "Mitochondrial DNA Analysis in Puerto Rico" *Human Biology* 73: 491–511.

26. Haslip-Viera, Gabriel. (2011). "The Myth of Taíno Survival in the Spanish-Speaking Caribbean." *National Institute for Latino Policy Network Guest Commentary,* December 6. *http://archive.constantcontact.com/fs057/1101040629095/archive/1108931682221.html.*

27. *Múcaro* Borrero, Roberto. (2011). "A Taíno Response to 'The Myth of Taíno Survival in the Spanish-Speaking Caribbean'" United Confederation of Taino People Blog, December 23. *http://www.uctp.org/index.php?option=com_content&task=view&id=699&Itemid=2*

28. Romero, Mary. (2000). "Historicizing and Symbolizing a Racial Ethnic Identity: Lessons for Coalition Building with a Social Justice Agenda." *U.C. Davis Law Review* 33: 1599.

29. Dávila, Arlene. (2001). "Local/Diasporic Taínos: Towards a Cultural Politics of Memory, Reality and Imagery." In *Taíno Revival: Critical Perspectives on Puerto Rican Identity and Cultural Politics,* ed. Gabriel Haslip-Viera. Princeton: Markus Wiener, pp. 40–41.

30. Brooke, James. (1992). "Indians in Protest Against Columbus," *The New York Times,* October 13. *http://www.nytimes.com/1992/10/13/world/indians-in-protest-against-columbus.html.*

31. Ferbel, Peter J. (1995). "The Politics of Taino Indian Heritage in the Post-Quincentennial Dominican Republic: When a Canoe Means More than a Water through." PhD diss., University of Minnesota.

32. "Indian Leader Splatters Blood on Nina Replica," *The Orlando Sentinel,* June 1, 1992.

33. Vargas, Jorge A. (1994). "NAFTA, the Chiapas Rebellion and the Emergence of Mexican Ethnic Law," *California Western International Law Journal* 25: 1–22.

34. Barreiro, Jose. (1990). "A Note on Tainos: Whither Progress." *Northeast Indian Quarterly* VII: 66–77.

35. Ponce de Leon, Juana. (1992). "The Native American Response to the Columbus Quincentenary." *MultiCultural Review* 1: 20–22.

36. Peter Guanikeyu Torres' blog, accessed 01/04/2012; *http://indigenouscaribbean.ning.com/profile/DonPedro*

37. The traditional term for chieftain, *cacike* (with alternate spellings of *kacike* or *cacique*), is employed by modern Tainos to refer to respected elders or leaders. The adoption of an Arawak-language middle name is common practice among modern day Taino.

38. Mother Earth Church of the Grand Caney, *http://caneycircle.owlweb.org*.

39. Cibanakán Marcano, Rene. (1988). Indigenas Tainos de Puerto Rico: ¡Nuestros indios siguen vivos!, pp. 1–18. San Juan: University of Puerto Rico.

40. Manuscript, *Maisi Ti Yukayeke Taino* (New York, January 1994) 1–19.

41. Ibid., p. 2.

42. Cacike Cibanakán, letter to author, April 26, 1996.

43. Ibid.

44. Esters, Stephanie D. (1992). "American Indian discusses tribe at local school," *Gannett Suburban Newspapers,* October 7.

45. Taino del Norte Monthly Update (New York, July 1993).

46. By-Laws of The Taino Inter-Tribal Council, Inc., adopted November 24, 1994, and ratified January 12, 1996.

47. Ibid.

48. Letter from Peter *Guaniel* Torres, Taino Tribal Council of Jatibonuco, April 3, 2001. *http://www.taino-tribe.org/enrollment-letter.htm*.

49. The Jatibonicu Taino Tribal Nation of Borikén, *http://www.taino-tribe.org/jatiboni.html*.

50. Vicens-Anguita, Marilyn. (1995). "Una rescatadora de tainos (A rescuer of Tainos)," *El Nuevo Dia,* San Juan, Puerto Rico, June 11.

51. Consejo General de Tainos Borincanos. "Trayectoria del Consejo General de Tainos Borincanos." *http://naciontaino.blogspot.com/2005/06/trayectoria-del-consejo-general-de.html*

52. United Confederation of Taino People. "MABRIKA (Welcome) to the UCTP." *http://www.uctp.org*.

53. Kan, Michael. (2005). "Pow wow celebrates Native American culture." *The Michigan Daily,* April 3.

54. Cacibajagua Taino Cultural Society. "Ramapough Pow Wow This Weekend," May 14, 2008. *http://tainoculture.blogspot.com/2008/05/ramapough-pow-wow-this-weekend.html*.

55. Barreiro, Jose. (2006). *Indigenous Resurgence in the Contemporary Caribbean: Amerindian Survival and Revival.* Ed. Maximilian C. Forte. New York: Peter Lang, New York. *http://www.centrelink.org/resurgence/cuba.htm*.

56. The Conference of NGO's in Consultative Relationship with the United Nations. "Permanent Forum on Indigenous Issues, 13-24 May 2002, New York." *http://www.ngocongo.org/index.php?what=pag&id=207*

57. UN Permanent Forum on Indigenous Issues. "International Day of the World's Indigenous Peoples." *http://www.un.org/esa/socdev/unpfii/en/news_internationalday2011.html*

58. Forte, Maximilian. (2002). 'We are not extinct': The Revival of Carib and Taino Identities, the Internet, and the Transformation of Offline Indigenes into Online 'N-digenes.'" *Issues in Caribbean Amerindian Studies* 4. *http://www.centrelink.org/notextinct.htm*

59. Ibid.

60. Ibid.

61. Garcia Ramis, Magali. (2001). "Mami, búscame tres plumas…que me voy a vestir de india (Mom, get me three feathers…that I want to dress up as an Indian)." *El Nuevo Dia,* Revista, April 1.

62. Ibid., Author's translation.

63. Rivera, Mildred. (2005). "Citado el grupo indígena en huelga (Indigenous group on strike receives summons)." *El Nuevo Día,* July 28.

64. Stapp, Katherine. (2005). "The Taino's Last Stand." *Inter Press Service,* August 8. *http://ipsnews .net/news.asp?idnews=29818*

65. The Voice of the Taino People Online, Racist Article in El Nuevo Dia, August 31, 2005. *http://uctp.blogspot.com/2005/08/racist-article-in-el-nuevo-dia.html*

66. Gutman, Laurie. (2011). "More Latinos identify as Native America, census shows." *CNN,* September 30. *http://edition.cnn.com/2011/US/09/30/latino.native.american/index.html?npt=NP1*

The Emergence of an Independent East Timor: The Story of Permitting that "Ole World Wall Map" to be Fluid for the Sake of Ethnic Survival and Justice

Jose Javier Lopez

Introduction

The end of the Cold War era marked the beginning of a new historic period in which our world's political map experienced radical changes not ever seen since the wave of independence movements that swept Africa and Asia after World War II. Right after the end of World War II, the international community witnessed the independence of Israel and India from the United Kingdom, and Indonesia from the Netherlands; in essence, it was the beginning of the end of European supremacy overseas. Even the newest emergent global super-power at that time, the United States, was affected by this wave of post-war decolonization when it granted independence to the Philippines in 1946. In some ways, the end of the Soviet Union was a revisit to the situation of a former European "imperialist" power, in this case Russia, losing its "pseudo-colonies" in Asia and parts of Europe.

However, it is possible to identify a difference between the processes that led to the "re-drawing" of our world's map during the 1940s–1960s, which included African and Asia's secessionist era and the post-Cold War period. In essence, the new boundaries and political entities that emerged after World War II were originally the product of a decolonization period in which European powers had to relinquish voluntarily and, in some cases, involuntarily territories outside "their" Western Hemisphere "neighborhood." Basically, culturally and, in some cases, geographically distant territories conquered during the eras of European exploration and imperial expansion centuries ago. On the other hand, the reshaping of the post-Cold War era map was in a considerable number of cases the product of more localized inter-ethnic conflicts. Nevertheless, localized inter-ethnic conflicts were not completely absent during the earlier post-World War II decolonization wave. It's imperative to take into account that independence in the Indian subcontinent was not only a business of Asians cutting links with a former European power. The independence of the Indian subcontinent was also a situation in which formerly conquered and colonized entities demanded the rupture of superimposed links with other colonial subjects and communities that they considered different and not worthy of a shared citizenship due to differences in religion, customs, and language, as the cases of India, Pakistan, and Bangladesh.

In many ways, the failed attempts for a "just" partition of Palestine during the late 1940s exhibit a situation similar to that of the Indian subcontinent, but still an unresolved issue. Nevertheless, the African, Middle Eastern, and Southeast Asian independence question of the 1940s was essentially a total rejection of European presence and interference in these areas under banners such as "Africa for Africans," "Pan Arabism," and "Asia for Asians." However, this situation does not mean that localized inter-ethnic conflict or animosities were absent in those regions. The fact of the matter is that the anti-European sentiment was a priority that concealed, or perhaps kept in check, long-standing, inter-ethnic animosities.

When this post-World War II wave of independence came to an end in the 1970s, many of us saw the world map as a chart very unlikely to experience drastic changes. In essence, we view our world as a bi-polar or dialectic political reality with the background noise of a ticking time bomb, teasing us, but unlikely to explode due to the formidable might of the adversarial Eastern and Western powers. Only proxy wars in Africa, Latin America, and Asia during the 1970s and 1980s served as occasional reminders that the bomb was a real one and not a hoax. Fortunately, this bomb diffused itself when the Soviet Union came to terms with the reality that its economic system was unsustainable due to the diseconomies of scale caused by its gargantuan territorial complexities.

A casualty of the 1970s proxy wars was the former Portuguese colony of East Timor, which is the subject of this essay. While countries like the United Kingdom, France, and Netherlands realized that their days of colonial supremacy were numbered, the Portuguese during the 1960s were more reluctant to accept the unfortunate reality of being a bankrupted empire and stubbornly kept their colonies in Africa and Asia for a longer period time. The collapse of the Soviet Union is more recent case of imperial collapse.

The new era of nationalist movements after the collapse of the Soviet Union removed the veneer of apparent harmony maintained by social engineering experiments that attempted to create egalitarian societies, socialist federations, and communist unions that concealed for decades ethnic tensions between peoples with limited cultural affinity. Perhaps the only goal these peoples had in common was the desire of eradicating long-established exploitative oligarchies and monarchies. Among the most disastrous cases of a socialist federation's implosion was the collapse of Yugoslavia. Not many outside the former Yugoslavia were aware of the degree of animosity and intolerance that existed between some of the ethnic groups living in this failed Balkan federation. Religious differences were among the strongest centrifugal forces that ripped apart what many naïve political pundits perceived as a harmonious socialist experiment. Of the former members of the Yugoslav federation, Bosnia and Herzegovina served as the stage of some of the worst carnage during the federation's disintegration process. What many political commentators consider ironic is the fact that Sarajevo, the Bosnian capital, gave the international community a sense of multiethnic and intercultural harmony almost a decade earlier during the 1984 Winter Olympics.

For those who were not aware of the intense ethnic rivalries that dominated the history of the Balkans during the past six hundred years, the collapse of Yugoslavia was an unexpected event. After World War II, the political leader of the Yugoslavs, Joseph Broz Tito, astutely managed to keep in check or at least conceal multigenerational ethnic hatred. Nevertheless, after his death, the political establishment failed to come up with an effective leader that could promote centripetal political forces aimed at promoting unity in an ethnically diverse region. Even the two most akin and mutually empathetic members of Yugoslavia, Serbia and Montenegro, could not maintain unity with the latter voting for independence from the former in 2006. This dissolution took many by surprise, since Montenegro has a relatively high percent of ethnic Serbians residing within its borders. For this reason, this post-Cold War Era period of "cartographic" readjustments and world map redrawing can be considered a time in which the unlikely became more likely than what we thought. For example, the Eastern African state of Ethiopia failed to keep Eritrea as part of its territory once communist rule ended there, and more recently, and after decades of oppressive rule, Sudan hesitantly allowed Southern Sudan to become our world's newest sovereign state.

For several decades Sudan was the largest country in Africa, and its rulers had little regard for those who lived in the southern part of this state since the southerners did not practice Islam, the faith of the Sudanese political establishment. During the 1990s, the prospects of an independent Southern Sudan were perceived as almost zero since the political leaders at the Sudanese capital

Khartoum showed staunch resistance to the idea of partitioning their country, even though coexistence between diverse groups obviously was impossible. Nevertheless, we live in a new era were information flows more rapidly and effectively than even before. Our contemporary world of fast communications has helped individuals from progressive human rights movements to be aware of the existence of oppressed ethnic minorities fighting for the recognition of their territorial and political rights. Some of these ethnic minorities that have made headlines relatively recently in some of the most popular news sources available in our cyber world were unheard or unknown several decades ago, and in the worst cases little-known ethnic groups fighting for their survival were simply ignored and labeled as politically and culturally expendable. One of most outstanding cases of a small nation that fervently and against all odds fought tenaciously for its political and cultural freedom was the former Portuguese colony of East Timor. What makes the East Timor case special is that its quest for freedom was like the David versus Goliath story, since this small nation became a captive of one of the largest countries on Earth in terms of population and among the most politically corrupt and oppressive political entities in the eastern hemisphere, the Republic of Indonesia. Like the case of Sudan, Indonesia's political establishment during the 1970s, '80s, and '90s saw ethnic minorities as not worthy of serious attention since especially if these minority communities did not practice the same religion of the most influential political groups, and their cultures were labeled as inferior by the dominant society. Most of the victims of Indonesia's violent takeover of East Timor were of a different nationality and religion, with the majority of the Timorese practicing Roman Catholicism and animist traditions (Kiernan 2003, 47). Indonesia's government had a long history of repressing and discriminating against any group that differed culturally from the Javanese political establishment and among its most well-known former victims was the Chinese community living on the island of Java, Sumatra, and Borneo. During East Timor's pre-Indonesian Invasion era, many Chinese settled in the island and among the victims of Indonesia's brutal conquest of the former Portuguese territory were:

> . . . most members of the 20,000-strong ethnic Chinese minority prominent in the towns of East Timor, whom Indonesian forces singled out for destruction apparently because of their ethnicity. (Kiernan 2008, 109)

The political climate in East Timor the years before the Indonesian invasion was quite complex. While several Portuguese colonies in Africa were fighting for independence during the early 1970s, small groups of pro-independence Timorese flirted with the idea of an independent East Timor, but since this colony was so isolated, "cut off from the world, without a friendly country on their borders to act as a base, they held no hope of launching a revolutionary war" (Freney 1975, 19). Political changes in Portugal in 1974 brought political instability in East Timor as right-wing and leftist political groups were fighting for power once they realized that Portuguese administration of the territory was virtually ineffective and imploding. Practically, the East Timorese were engulfed by a brief civil war in which a popular leftist anticolonial movement, which first won in local elections, eventually prevailed in the battleground (Kiernan 2003). This leftist group is known as FRETILIN, and after prevailing in the armed conflict, they declared independence on November 28, 1975, after 450 years of Portuguese rule. However, East Timorese independence was short-lived since the United States government, under the leadership of Gerald Ford, was not willing to accept the emergence of a new independent nation lead by leftists and allowed the Indonesian government invade the former Portuguese colony on December of 1975. According to *The New York Times'* columnist Anthony Lewis (1996), the U.S. Secretary of State at the time of Indonesia's invasion of East Timor, Henry Kissinger, "suggested to aides the invasion be construed as self-defense against Communism." In essence, Saigon falling to the North Vietnamese months before gave the United States and its right-wing allies in South East Asia and Oceania the determination of not tolerating the existence of another left-wing-ruled state in the region. Liberal American journalists like Lewis (1996) strongly believe that the United States "bear a particular responsibility for the tragedy in East Timor" since Henry Kissinger and President Gerald Ford gave Indonesia's notorious dictator, Suharto, "a green light for the invasion, even though U.S. law forbade the use of American-supplied weapons for offensive purposes." Interestingly, a-year-and-a-half before the Indonesian invasion of East Timor, the Jakarta regime made the claim of adhering to the principles:

> . . . that the independence of every country is the right every nation, with no exception for the people in Timor and whoever will govern in Timor in the future after independence can be assured that the Government of Indonesia will always strive to maintain good relations. (Kohen and Taylor 1979, 17)

The Indonesian generals who supervised the repression of the East Timorese during the occupation period had little regard for the human rights and well-being of this oppressed nation. The population of East Timor in 1975 was 650,000, and approximately 150,000 people disappeared during the following four years (Kiernan 2003, 49). According to Nairn (1995), after a massacre perpetrated by the military in the capital of East Timor in 1991, General Try Sutrisno described the Timorese as "ill-bred people." The general's selection of words clearly indicated that the East Timor issue was not merely territorial politics, but also about ethnic conflict and hatred. In essence, many documents produced by Indonesia's military during that era were plagued by dehumanizing language so pervasive that instructions translated themselves into genocide. Terrorizing the East Timorese population into submission was part of Indonesia's military objective, with widespread use of detention and torture as key ingredients for social control and eradication of Timorese nationalism. According to Taylor (2003, 169), "the use of torture was officially sanctioned" throughout the occupied territory, and Army guidelines published in July 1982 included the use of drastic methods of social control in which "the severity of torture appears to have increased as the occupation developed."

The use of derogatory language to dehumanize the East Timorese was not limited to the Indonesian military. For example, Suharto who despotically ruled the vast Indonesian archipelago during that era, referred to East Timor as "a pimple on Indonesia's face" while his foreign minister, Ali Alatas, considered the oppressed Timorese nation as "gravel" in the shoes of Jakarta's political establishment (Anderson 1994). Even Henry Kissinger's language about the East Timor issue can give hints of belittlement from the American political establishment. According to Black (1999, A25), in 1995, Kissinger said that East Timor "was not a big thing on our radar screen."

According to Lewis (1996), in the first years of Indonesian occupation of East Timor "as many as 200,000 people—a third of the population—died in conflict or of starvation or disease." Even though Indonesia and East Timor share an island, the fact of the matter is that there are considerable differences between the political establishment in Jakarta and the average East Timorese. First, Indonesia is overwhelmingly Muslim, while East Timor is predominantly Roman Catholic. Second, Melanesians are the oldest ethnic group living in East Timor, and they inhabit mostly in the highlands after been forced out from the lower areas by mixed Malayo-Polynesian groups.

One of the strategies used by the government in Jakarta to consolidate their control of East Timor was to change the ethnic composition of this former Portuguese territory by encouraging Indonesians from different parts of the Republic to migrate to this forcibly taken land. In October of 1994, one of the leaders of East Timor's independence movement, who currently serves as the president of this young republic, Jose Ramos Horta, grieved that in public service jobs only 3 out of 10 were Timorese and in the streets, selling in the markets, the average estimate was one Timorese for nine Indonesians (Crossette 1994). One the main fears of those who advocated for the independence of East Timor during the Indonesian occupation era was the potential of non-Timorese outnumbering the native population in order to kill a nation. At marketplaces incidents of violence took place numerous times during the Indonesian occupation era due to the ethnic tensions between locals and traders from Indonesia. In November of 1994, riots erupted at the Timorese capital after the killing of an East Timorese man by a merchant from another part of Indonesia after a quarrel at a market, and even Indonesian officials admitted that unrest in Timor during the 1990s was caused by ethnic clashes and religious tension (Pollack 1994). According to Lewis (1996), more than 100,000 people, mostly Muslims, from different regions of Indonesia relocated to East Timor, "acquiring land and filling public jobs in a largely Roman Catholic land" during the Indonesian occupation era.

Fortunately, a combination of various political, social, and military factors saved East Timorese's aspirations for independence. These factors can be divided in two categories. The first category includes events that informed the uninformed citizens of the wealthiest countries about the existence of the Timorese, and their struggle for independence from Indonesia:

a. International news media coverage of massacres committed by the Indonesian military in East Timor during the early 1990s.
b. The selection of two Timorese human rights activists, José Ramos-Horta and Roman Catholic Bishop Carlos Filipe Ximenes Belo, for the 1996 Nobel Peace Prize for work "towards a just and peaceful solution to the conflict in East Timor."
c. Availability of critical human rights information thanks to Internet media.

The second category of factors that contributed to the independence of East Timor are related to political and military developments:

a. The resilience of the Armed Forces for the National Liberation of East Timor (FALINTIL), which included embracing the idea "to resist is to win," and recognized the fact that even though the Timorese armed resistance was no match against the Indonesians, making life very uncomfortable and dangerous for the occupying forces will have some debilitating effect.
b. Downfall of the Suharto regime in Indonesia late in 1998 and how those who succeeded the dictator underestimated the political popularity that pro-independence movements enjoyed in the East Timor, making more likely a rejection of Indonesian presence if a democratic consultation was to be offered.
c. With the end of the Cold War, the Domino Effect Theory, which predicted the emergence of new communist regimes in Southeast Asia, lost importance, and Timorese pro-Independence leaders showed no desire of turning their country into a twenty-first century Vietnam or Cuba if independence was feasible. Therefore, the United States, Australian, and United Kingdom commercial interests lost their fears of an independent East Timor as a nation difficult to deal with in the private sector, especially in the primary economic sectors of the island's and region's economy.

The history of East Timor can serve as a sign of hope for nations that have been struggling for independence for decades, perhaps centuries. During the late 1980s, many experts on the subject could not see the possibility of an independent East Timor as the government Jakarta was showing no desire of granting autonomy to the territory and closed it completely to the outside world. As detentions and torture escalated during that era, many supporters of the Timorese cause in wealthy countries were ready to give up. Nevertheless, the pride and perseverance of the East Timorese pro-independence political leadership has demonstrated that embracing the idea "to resist is to win," is far from being a futile effort. Kay Rala Xanana Gusmão was the first President of East Timor, serving from May 2002 to May 2007, and his life embodies that sentiment, which includes pride, resilience, and perseverance. If we seriously take into account the suffering of the Timorese people and Gusmão's life in the mountains of this island fighting the genocide campaigns of the Indonesian forces during the 1970s and 1980s, his capture and incarceration by the invading army during the 1990s, and his rise as a symbol of the liberation of vulnerable nations, we will be able to realize that our world map is meant to remain neither static nor unchangeable, but fluid enough to permit the survival and blossoming of endangered cultures.

REFERENCES

Anderson, Benedict R. (1994). "Imperialist Rule." *The New York Times.*

Black, Eric. (1999). "East Timor Highlights Inconsistent U.S. Policy." *Star Tribune,* June 6, 1999, p. A19.

Crossette, Barbara. (1994). "Wave of Migrations is Altering East Timor." *The New York Times,* October 30, 1994, p. 6.

Freney, Denis. (1975). *Timor: Freedom Caught Between the Powers.* Nottingham, UK: The Russell Press.

Kiernan, Ben. 2003. "Twentieth-Century Genocides: Underlying Ideological Themes from Armenia to East-Timor." In *The Specter of Genocide: Mass Murder in Historical Perspective,* eds. Gellately, Robert and Ben Kiernan. Cambridge, U.K.: Cambridge University Press.

Kiernan, Ben. (2003). *Genocide and Resistance in Southeast Asia: Documentation, Denial, and Justice in Cambodia and East Timor.* New Brunswick, N.J.: Transaction Publishers.

Kohen, Arnold, & John Taylor. (1979). *An Act of Genocide: Indonesia's Invasion of East Timor.* London UK: Tapol.

Lewis, Anthony. (1996). "No Blind Eye." *The New York Times,* November 25, 1996.

Nairn, Allan. (1995). "Free East Timor." *The New York Times,* October 26, 1995, p. A25

Pollack, Andrew. (1994). "Timorese Worry World Will Now Forget Them." *The New York Times,* November 28, 1994.

Taylor, John G. (2003). "Encirclement and Annihilation: The Indonesian Occupation of East Timor" In *The Specter of Genocide: Mass Murder in Historical Perspective,* eds. Gellately, Robert and Ben Kiernan. Cambridge, U.K.: Cambridge University Press.

The Real Root Causes of Somali Piracy

Maria Qanyare, Adam Svendsen, Abdullahi Ali, Ahmed Shiiraar,
Aish Ali, Ibrahim Alsgoor, Abdirahman Ibrahim,
Olufunsho Oguntoyinbo, and Ahmed Barkhadle

Introduction

Somali piracy is a much-misunderstood phenomenon that demands further study. A political ecology analysis reveals that environmental racism is the real root cause of Somali piracy. International overfishing and toxic waste dumping have created a situation wherein the recent spate of piracy in the waters near and about Somalia can best be explained as a reaction to powerful negative forces coming in from the outside and damaging Somalia's environment. What has been relatively ignored in much of the mainstream media is the fact that there are some simple, logical reasons for Somali piracy, and that those underlying reasons are ecological, political, economic, and social.

The evidence is clear that people living in cities and villages along the coast of Somalia have experienced economic upheaval due to illegal overfishing in their waters by the international fishing fleet as well as negative health consequences due to toxic waste dumping just off the coast. A full understanding of the convergence of factors that have led to the increase in Somali piracy begs the question: Who are the real pirates anyway? To answer that question, one needs to understand the concept of environmental racism.

Environmental racism occurs when powerful economic and political interests dispose of toxic waste in a manner that adversely affects peoples who are politically and economically disenfranchised—in this case, the Somalis after the collapse of their government in 1991. The dumping of radioactive and toxic waste along the coast of Somalia, which has been occurring since the 1980s, along with the fact that Somalia's maritime fisheries have been illegally overfished since 1991, left the members of Somalia's coastline communities with few options. Thus, marginalized when it came to the exercise of their rights, members of Somali fishing communities had no recourse but to turn to piracy when their fishing economy collapsed and they and their children were being poisoned.

The first step in addressing environmental racism, then, is raising public awareness about the facts so that, just as in other cases of racism, it is not a case where the victim gets blamed for reacting to violence that is being done to them by an oppressor or oppressors.

156

History of Piracy around the World

Piracy is the act of hijacking ships by force done by individuals or organizations for the purpose of taking the goods being transported on those ships, if not the ship itself. It is a maritime raiding strategy that goes far back in history, as far as when mankind began exploring the seas. According to the naval museum, piracy began 2000 years ago in Greece. After the start of this criminal trade, the stakes to seafaring countries were high in the absence of any military organization to protect them from the continuing attacks on their goods and ships. The peak of piracy took place in the sixteenth century and lasted all the way up to the nineteenth century. Types of piracy were divided into: privateers, buccaneers, and corsairs.

Privateers were pirates that worked under a country's auspices to raid their enemies. They had a formal allegiance to the country in question and in turn had papers—permission—from that country to commit piracy against hostile or enemy nations and strip from them goods from their ships. Privateers were usually known for working for the English (British East India Company) and the Dutch (Dutch East India Company) navies, or any other country that had a naval fleet. At the time, piracy was a crime punishable by death, and so countries issued letters that stated that the ship's crew and the captain were working under orders from a country and, therefore, could not be accused of piracy and be punished for it. It was considered an act of war so the enemy would take the privateers prisoners instead of executing them. These letters were known as "letters of Marque." The Marque letters were created to distinguish organized pirates that worked for a specific country from those who were freelancing. It was an attempt to administer some sort of control over the piracy industry.

Buccaneers were freelance pirates who attacked all sorts of ships along the Spanish coast in the Caribbean Sea in the seventeenth century. They were usually a larger crew that attacked larger cities. They used small boats to attack, often at night, and they would climb on board a ship before the watchman could ring the ship's bell as an alarm. Buccaneers had very good aim and would quickly kill anyone, especially any officers that were on the ship. Buccaneers' reputations were set as cruel pirates, and they were not protected by letters of the Marque because they did not have an allegiance to a country, unlike Corsairs. Corsairs were essentially the privateers of the French crown who pirated the Spanish coast and intercepted Spanish ships (with whom they were at war) under the auspices of letters of the Marque.

If there was one characteristic shared by these different types of pirates, it must be the sense of adventure and the dream of financial gain. Pirates of all eras have to possess a willingness to break maritime law for money, with the possibility of being killed or seriously injured. Before choosing piracy as a career in the old days, many pirates were affiliated with the sea as merchants or they served in naval ships. For many of them, the adventurous life on a pirate ship seemed more appealing. The temptation of a pirate's life included the freedom from the sea's international regulations, and it meant dignified treatment by the captain and the other crewmen. And above all, it meant an equal share of all prizes. For, you see, pirates exercise true democracy where everyone had an equal vote and an equal share. These sailors had more rights and actually had it better on their ships than did the sailors on the ships of the royal navies of the differing European countries because on those ships the captain took the lion's share of any booty, and they were virtually gods who could be brutal, vicious tyrants with no checks on their power once their ship was at sea.

Somali Piracy

Somalia has been without a functioning government since 1991, when warlords overthrew former dictator Mohamed Siad Barre. With Somali waters undefended, foreign fishing trawlers began illegally fishing in Somali waters, and ships from big companies began dumping waste off Somalia, killing nearly all the fish off the shore in Somalia's territorial waters. It was difficult for the Somali fishermen in all the cities and towns along the coast that relied on a fishing economy because their

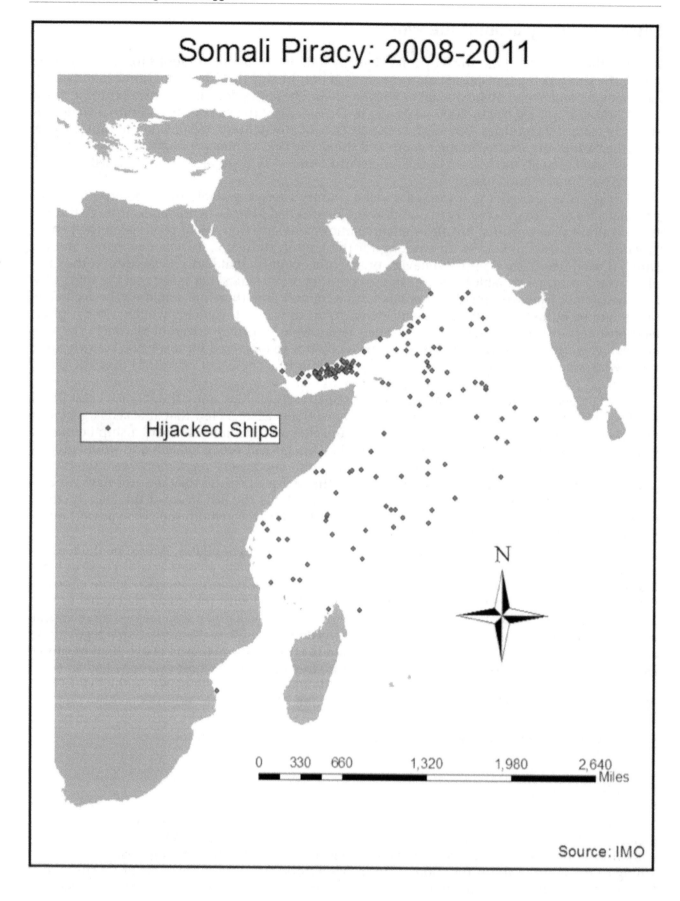

Somali Piracy: 2008-2011

• Hijacked Ships

N

0   330   660   1,320   1,980   2,640
                                             Miles

Source: IMO

only source of income was based on how many fish they caught each day. Toxic dumping and over-fishing quickly led to the loss of the fish stocks in Somali waters.

The local fishermen saw their people starving and suffering, with many people becoming sick due to the toxic waste so they started to collaborate and form groups of pirates, whose mission was to raid ships they saw as interlopers to get money while at the same time driving other ships away from their waters to protect their resources. Not only had they lost their traditional source of income, but there were other health problems that arose from the foreign ships illegally dumping massive amounts of toxic waste, including nuclear and bio-hazardous waste on their shores.

After the Somali famine in 1992, there were reports that ran in the European press of "unnamed European firms" contracting with local warlords to dump toxic waste both in Somalia and off Somalia's shores. The United Nations Environment Program was called in to investigate, and the Italian parliament issued a report later in the decade. Several European "firms"—really front companies created by the Italian mafia—sent ships containing hundreds of thousands of tons of toxic industrial waste from Europe to Somalia.

A second reason for Somali piracy was patriotism. Somali fishermen believed that the international governments would not honor their treaties, neither would they protect the interests of Somali people. Many of the pirates believed it was their responsibility to protect their resources as well as the health of their people. Some of these former fishermen, whose livelihoods were hurt by these illegal fishing fleets and waste dumping ships, organized and armed themselves, rather like the patriots in America's Revolutionary War, or even like Jean Lafitte in the War of 1812. In order to earn a living, they decided that the only possibility was for them to attack the ships in order to stop big oil companies' dumping ships and hijack them. They then held the ship hostage, demanding that these oil companies, who they suspected of destroying their lives, pay large ransoms. Once it worked, they saw the profitability in it and they continued to hijack more and more. The international governments began to pay attention to the issue after it had an effect on their economy.

According to Muammar al-Gaddafi, "It is a response to greedy Western nations, who invade and exploit Somalia's water resources illegally. It is not a piracy, it is self-defense."

Economic Implications

Somalia, now known as the Republic of Somalia, is a country found on the Horn of Africa. The countries surrounding it are Ethiopia to the west, Yemen and the Gulf of Aden to the North, the Indian Ocean to the east, Djibouti to the northwest, and Kenya to the southwest. Somalia was once a crucial trading spot for commerce with the rest of the world. Its sailors and merchants would trade various myrrh and spices with numerous ancient empires and countries.

Today, Somalia is ranked one of the poorest countries in the world. The once prominent country is in a political turmoil that continues to feed the fuel in the everlasting struggle with poverty. The colonial economy of Somalia brought stability, growth, and prosperity. Today, the political condition is viewed as open anarchy and lawlessness, with the millions of people that inhabit this proud nation suffering beyond belief.

The countries that are designated within the Horn of Africa are Eretria, Ethiopia, Djibouti, and Somalia. With the exception of Djibouti, the remaining countries are regarded as some of the poorest countries on the globe. This is due to continuous droughts, inadequate living standards, weak infrastructure, and countrywide insecurity. Rena Ravinder, a leading scholar and author of "Trends and Determinants of Poverty in the Horn of Africa: Some Implications," states the condition of the listed countries,

> The growth has been resilient; the Horn of Africa continues to face a wide range of development challenges, which undermine macroeconomic stability and the long-run growth potential, adverse weather conditions and natural disasters that generate high output volatility; poverty, infrastructure and health conditions that hold back productivity growth. (2006: 65)

The economic hardship of Somalia can be coupled with the historical roots the country comes from. A firm understanding of the tribulations faced by Somalis, both socially and politically, at the hands of colonization must be considered. The decolonization of Somalia led to immediate instability, followed by destruction from the swords of their own brothers in a period of a brutal civil war.

Knowledge of the history of Somalia is required when developing a critical overview of the different sectors of this country's economy. The different sectors that must be analyzed are agriculture, drilling and mining, total foreign investment, communications and technology, and banking/securities. The majority of the sectors have been disabled due to ongoing fighting amongst the people of Somalia, but a small degree of the sectors are in semi-productive order. Many Americans plead ignorance when viewing Somalia as a nation in dire need, and this is understandable because of the U.S. debacle in Somalia in the 1990s. But information in conjunction with initiative breeds progress, whereas information with no initiative remains and always will remain just so many words.

To better understand the different sectors of the Somali economy, one needs to understand the two main determinants of poverty. Failures in the agricultural sector, coupled with natural disasters like recurring droughts, is one determinant and lack of education, combined with unemployment, being the second. These "failures" can be regarded as the root causes, and understanding their dynamics is an essential step when trying to understand the current Somali economy. Almost determinant in nature, poverty takes on a significant "cause and effect" role in Somali life. The effects of poverty not only harm those that currently inhabit Somalia, but will also cripple the generations to come. Economists note that the effects of poverty on Somalia are numerous, entailing a lower standard of living and quality of life. Poverty's effects then go on to be the "cause" of many other dysfunctional realities in Somalia, consequently creating an economic term called *the cycle of poverty*.

The cycle of poverty is a seemingly endless progression of events that take a society further and further into poverty, eventually resulting in destitution. The moment a person or a society fall below a degree of stability, a chain of events starts to occur that have a propensity to worsen the situation (Jumah & Kunst 2005). Economists refer to a model when analyzing the different phases in which a person or a society can take a fall into the "poverty trap." This concept and model will provide insight that may be useful when trying to understand how to break the cycle of poverty. The easiest way to break this cycle is through outside intervention, thus the role of the IMF and the World Bank. But, as that is unlikely to happen, combined with the fact that Somali society does not have enough resources and means to accomplish such a thing itself, it is a dire situation where drastic measures like piracy could be seen as the only viable short-term option Somalis have. And this is especially so when one considers all of the aforementioned factors. Since the world has shown it will not put forth a humanitarian effort to ensure an established children's nutrition, health, and education system, and since starving, sick children cannot wait, one can see how something that seems so foolish, like modern-day piracy, could come about.

During the colonial era, Italy controlled southern Somalia; Britain, northern Somalia; and France, the area that became Djibouti. Under the control of the three major European powers, foreign economic investment was not sparked (USLOC). Benito Mussolini, leader of Italy, had plans to make Somalia a settlement for Italian citizens. This was a failed plan but gave birth to an ambitious outline for economic development (USLOC). British Somaliland did not put forth much means of investment towards Somalia either. Instead, the British Government did whatever they found to be profitable for themselves and their homeland.

The colonial era sparked two major economic developments: one was the formulation of a salaried official class, and the second was the establishment of plantations (USLOC). Located in the south, the Italians set a foundation for profitable export-oriented agriculture, essentially in bananas, through the making of plantations and irrigation systems (USLOC). Somali citizens became soldiers, teachers, civil workers, and small business entrepreneurs.

Somalis refused to work on farms for wage labor. This caused labor shortages in all plantation industries for the Italians. To compensate, Italian companies paid wages to agricultural families to plant and harvest export crops and allowed them to obtain privately owned gardens on some of the irrigated land (USLOC). This compensation worked with relative success, and a small workforce sprang up. Banana exports peaked at 6.4 million U.S. dollars, and cotton, at 200,000 U.S. dollars (USLOC). In 1957, exports from plantations translated into 59 percent of total exports, a tremendous input to the Somali Economy (USLOC).

There were still negative aspects of colonial rule on the Somali economy. Many Somali tribes rejected European education and scorned the development of Christian missions. Hence, as a consequence, only a small number of literate Somalis were ready to work for the British government (USLOC). Somalis in the south sent their children to colonial schools and graduates found opportunities in civil service, law enforcement, medical fields, teachers, and bookkeepers (USLOC). By 1945, there were a registered amount of 500 businesses in the Hargeysa region of Somalia (USLOC). With the north being literate in English, and the South being literate in Italian, a division in both language and politics sprang up. Opposition towards colonial rule had also emerged during this time.

Mahammad Siad Barre became the leader in 1969 and established Somalia as an independent Socialist State. He outlined a plan that stressed a higher standard of living for Somali citizens, a prosperous job market for those who sought work, and the abolishment of capitalist exploitation (USLOC). New manufacturing plants and agricultural programs were the instant results (USLOC). With the economy growing, it was during his rule that oppression towards his people occurred.

As signs of civil war sprung up in many regions, the economy of Somalia quickly crumbled in 1989 and 1990. With 80 percent of foreign currency earned coming from northern exports of livestock, there was a complete freeze (USLOC). Throughout the countryside, Somalis faced shortages in commodities such as food, medicine, fuel, and water (USLOC). The ousting of Siad Barre led to no improvement in the economic status of Somalia and left it as an impoverished country.

Today, agriculture is the most essential sector for the Somali economy. Livestock constitutes for roughly 40 percent of GDP and nearly 65 percent of export earnings (HC). Economic income mainly comes from the exportation of animal hides (HC). Preceding livestock, bananas account for a large amount of Somali exports, while sugar, maize, and sorghum are goods for the domestic market (HC). Many countries such as Saudi Arabia have prohibited imports of Somali livestock on the basis of inadequate inspection (HC). This has had a tremendous impact on the Somali economy, crippling the major sector of profit for millions of citizens.

Before the 1991 overthrow of the government, the Somali minerals sector was minimal but on the rise in terms of development. It then failed to expand in the following years due to the civil unrest causing political and economic instability (EOTN). One of the leading industries was Somalia's cement plant and oil refinery, but consequently they shut down because of the civil war (EOTN). Many natural resources such as iron, natural gas, uranium, emeralds, rubies, sapphires, and other gemstones were discovered in Somalia, but their production has been hindered due to the absence of modern equipment, destruction to the infrastructure, and civil animosity (EOTN). An EU non-governmental organization was working with the Northern Somali government (Somaliland) to establish mining of various minerals but there has only been a marginal change for the short run (EOTN).

The absence of a central government has diverted foreign investment in Somalia. There was a tremendous amount of assistance from the United Nations in helping promote a stable economy in Somalia. Foreign governments associated with the UN have contributed up to 4 billion dollars but, nonetheless, no lasting assets remained after their leaving in 1995 (EOTN). Towards the late 1990s, further foreign investment in the communications sector had also had marginal effect. The investment was to promote a communications structure in mobile phone technology and new forms of energy, but prolonged political conflicts had steered away foreign companies and governments. A reliable source, *Encyclopedia of the Nations,* stated, "For the period 1997 to 2001, annual foreign direct investment (FDI) ranged from 1.1 million in 1997 to a negative divestment of –800,000 in 1999. Across the five years, net FDI flows were barely positive, at 400,000." This shows the instability that Somalia faces, with foreign investment staying skeptical of the ongoing civil unrest the nation is enduring.

The Central Bank of Somalia is a government institution that has branches in every region of the country. The Central Bank controls the dispensing of currency and also overlooks the central banking operation of the state (EOTN). The Somali shilling as of 1996 was still mainly used throughout the country, even with the absence of a central government to back the currency (EOTN). There was a tremendous amount of counterfeit Somali shillings being distributed in 1999, which had minimized the value of the shilling in regards to the U.S. dollar from 7.5 to 10,000 (EOTN). In 2000, the exchange rate was at 2,600 to 2,000, with four different versions of the national currency being used nationwide (EOTN). There are no securities exchanges in Somalia (EOTN).

The agricultural sector is the first determinant of poverty in Somalia. A tremendous influence in the majority of Somali life is geography and climate. The level of rainfall obtained is a vital determinant in the capability for grazing and hopes of relative prosperity. Research has shown that there has been a slight increase in average temperature. The increase in temperature, with correlation to the increase in population of citizens and animals, has put an amplified strain on agriculture and water.

In early 1991, most Somali economic activity was centered around natural sources, and Somalia's economy consisted of both traditional and modern production, with a gradual shift in favor of modern industrial techniques taking root. According to the Central Bank of Somalia, about 80 percent of the population are nomadic or semi-nomadic, who keep goats, sheep, camels, and cattle. The nomads also gather resins and gums to supplement their income. Agriculture was the most important economic sector in Somalia, but Somali economic growth has been in decline since 1991.

After 1991, when the government collapsed, people lost jobs, and they no longer have workplaces/companies. The whole country fell into poverty and chaos, and poverty caused some of the worst crime rates in the world when the government collapsed. Some of the people fled to different countries to get a better life if they got the chance to do so. Education was the most needed thing that the young generation was seeking because there was no government to provide them schooling. And people who remained in Somali became some of the poorest in the world, with some of the lowest life expectancies. Civil wars and hunger were rampant everywhere, with one of the only viable local economic sectors being the fishing sector.

All many people had was the fishing along their coastline to support their families, but the Somalia coastline waters had become the site of an international "free for all," with fishing fleets from around the world illegally overfishing the waters off the coast of Somalia. The fishermen and their families could not even find enough fish for food because all the fish had gone. Then many of the Somali fishermen began gathering together and they decided to stand up and protect their coastline waters. Somalis living by the sea have been forced over the years to defend their own fishing rights and waters. Then Somali pirates began to hunt the foreign ships around the Indian Ocean, stopping them from fishing in this area. During that mission, they thought they could make some money from those ships they took hostage. And now, because of the pirates, more businesses are beginning to emerge in Somalia and the general public seems better off. There are more shops, and business is once again booming because of the influx of money from the pirates, according to the UN.

Many people around the world heard stories about Somali pirates on the news, and they began asking many questions. Many wanted to know why Somalis were becoming pirates in the Indian Ocean, whereas others seemed to believe the stereotypes about Somali people being inherently lawless. Most people in the world were ignorant of the fact that the main reason why this happened was because many countries were dumping all their bio-hazardous wastes in the waters off Somalia coast, and since there had not been a legitimate government for the last twenty years or so there was little that could be done. The common Somali people were caught in the middle of a tragedy caused by much larger global forces. According to *Time World,* a United Nations report in 2006 said that in the absence of the country's onetime serviceable coastguard, Somali waters have become the site of an international "free for all," with fishing fleets from around the world illegally plundering Somali stocks and freezing out the country's own rudimentarily equipped fishermen. In addition to this, none of the powerful countries in the world did a thing, saying nothing about what the other countries were doing in Somalia's territorial waters. This made many Somali fishermen angry to the point where they decided to stand up for themselves and fight anybody who tried to dump any more poisons and toxins in their backyard.

Personally speaking, we think Somalis were initially forced to defend their fishing expeditions and, when they did, they were called pirates. These people were not simply running around oceans trying to rob ships and kidnap innocent people, even though it eventually escalated into that after they began to be more and more successful pirates. In the meantime, the media made out these Somali pirates to be very dangerous people who were killing and robbing ships out of greed when, in fact, they were originally just trying to protect their coastlines and provide for their families.

Today's Somali economy is in a fairly ugly state. An estimated 73.4 percent of the country's population lives in general or extreme poverty, and all the average Somali earns is $600 per year. Somalia is one of the poorest countries in the world right now. The UN has said that Somali pirates have made life more expensive for ordinary people because they "pump huge amounts of U.S. dollars" into the local economy, which results in extreme fluctuations in the local exchange rate. On the other hand, pirates are putting wealth back into the local Somali economy because an estimated $1 million to $2 million is made from each captured ship. We all know that some of the impoverishment of the country due to its social, political, and economic breakdown has caused it to be seen internationally as a lawless, criminal, rogue state. Unfortunately for the common people, they have to engage in risky ventures everyday just to survive and provide a better life for their children.

Since 1991, after the Somali government collapsed, nothing has changed; people are still trying to get out of Somalia to get a better life and get to safety. Somalia's economic growth rate has been steadily getting worse; famine, malnutrition, and the spread of health problems have been increasing in East Africa, and this has affected the poor in Somalia the hardest. Yet, the international community has done little to help the country because it is viewed as a failed state.

The Wholesale Destruction of the Somali Fishing Industry

Since 1991, when a coalition of clan-based armed opposition groups ousted the nation's long-standing military government led by Mohamed Siad Barre, various factions began competing for influence in the power vacuum that followed. This precipitated an aborted UN Peacekeeping attempt in the mid-1990s. Since then, Somalia has had no functioning government that could control the people and its national territory. Today, Somalia is the best example on earth of a "failed state."

This made Somalia an easy target for foreign countries desiring to take Somali resources because of the absence of a strong, functioning government. One of the areas exploited by foreigner interlopers, who might be seen as the real pirates, is the fishing industry. Illegal, unreported, and unregulated (IUU) fishing depletes fish stocks, destroys marine habitat, distorts competition, leaves honest fishers are at unfair disadvantage, and weakens coastal communities, especially in developing countries. And it is not just Somalia where this is happening, but many other poor African countries are experiencing the problem of IUU as well. It is the same with toxic dumping in Africa; Somalia is not the only case, but it is one of the worst because of its failed state. It is estimated that IUU has led to billions of dollars of lost annual economic benefits, and it has created significant environmental damage due to unsustainable fishing practices that have also had wider consequences for the local food supply.

Illegal fishing takes place when vessels operate in violation of international maritime laws. Somali illegal fishing has been unreported or misreported to the relevant international authorities or regional organizations, in contravention of applicable laws and regulations. July 25, 2008, the UN special envoy for Somalia sounded the alarm about rampant illegal fishing and dumping of toxic waste off the coast of the lawless Somali nation by saying, "Because there is no (effective) government, there is so much irregular fishing from European and Asian countries." Ould Abdallah said the phenomenon helps fuel the endless civil war in Somalia as the illegal fishermen are paying corrupt Somali ministers or warlords for protection or to secure fake licenses. East African waters, particularly off Somalia, have huge numbers of commercial fish species, including the prized yellow tuna.

Foreign trawlers reportedly use prohibited fishing equipment, including nylon nets with very small mesh sizes and sophisticated underwater lighting systems to lure fish to their traps. "I am convinced there is dumping of solid waste, chemicals and probably nuclear (waste) . . . There is no government (control) and there are few people with high moral ground," Ould Abdallah added.[1]

The international community responded in April 2009, when Abdirahman Ibbi, who was at that time the Deputy Prime Minister and Minister of Fisheries and Marine Resources in the new Somali national unity government, said that an estimated 220 foreign-owned vessels were still engaged in unlicensed and illegal fishing in Somali waters, most of them of European origin. That same month, the European Commission said it is ready to investigate and take action against any European boats or European-owned fishing companies that fly flags of convenience to engage in illegal fishing off the coast of Somalia. The European commissioner for fisheries, Joe Borg, responded "that he had no information regarding Mr. Ibbi's allegation." And he added, "If we see that there are any European fishers or European-owned vessels that are operating illegally, there are ways and means whereby . . . we can have those vessels blacklisted as illegal, unregulated and unreported [IUU] operators if they are operating illegal fishing."[2] But since then, nothing has been done to prevent illegal fishing, which by all accounts is still going on off the Somali coast.

The international communities always make excuses by reiterating the danger of Somali piracy, whereas illegal fishing and the dumping of nuclear and other wastes are still unreported or misreported in news stories. A well-known European environmental writer named Johann Hari said while discussing this issue, "We have destroyed our own fish-stocks by over-exploitation and now we have moved on to Somali fish stocks." Continuing, he added, "More than $300m worth of tuna, shrimp, lobster, and other sea life is being stolen every year by vast trawlers illegally sailing into Somali's unprotected seas."[3]

There are many maritime laws and rules that govern both international waters as well as the territorial waters of every country in the world. Lack of proper security infrastructures in Somalia and other poor countries in Africa for policing their territorial waters becomes very challenging for these countries, making them easy targets for unscrupulous governments and multinational corporations. This has encouraged rampant IUU fishing. The alarming voices coming from Somali people are escalating day by day, and people need a quick international community response to halt the illegal fishing that has destroyed Somali's coastal economy.

Health Implications of Toxic Dumping

The rampant dumping of toxic waste in Africa, and specifically Somalia, has created serious health threats and associated issues in relation to the health of the people in Somalia. Many of the citizens that are especially close to the polluted shorelines have developed serious health problems attributable to their exposure to toxins in their water and food. It is now well-known that companies from the European countries have been, and likely still are, dumping massive amounts—millions of tons—of bio-hazardous waste along the coast. Radioactive waste does not break down for thousands of years, but unfortunately the affect it has on the local people is immediate and lasting. It also damages and has an effect on the marine life, which also regrettably results in poor sales for the local Somali fishermen who are trying to earn a living. These health issues that have occurred in the first decade of the twenty-first century post-civil war era have escalated and emerged into problems much wider than just the average cancer or illness. It has in some ways exceeded normality and has been seen to be an enormous environmental threat and a great hazard to the local communities in the region.

Generally, amongst most of the cities, there have been reports of "higher than normal cases of respiratory infections, mouth ulcers and abnormal bleedings." The United Nations Environmental Program (UNEP) published a statement whereby they spoke about the serious issues pertaining to the irregular health problems in Somali coastal communities. They reported that "in Somalia there

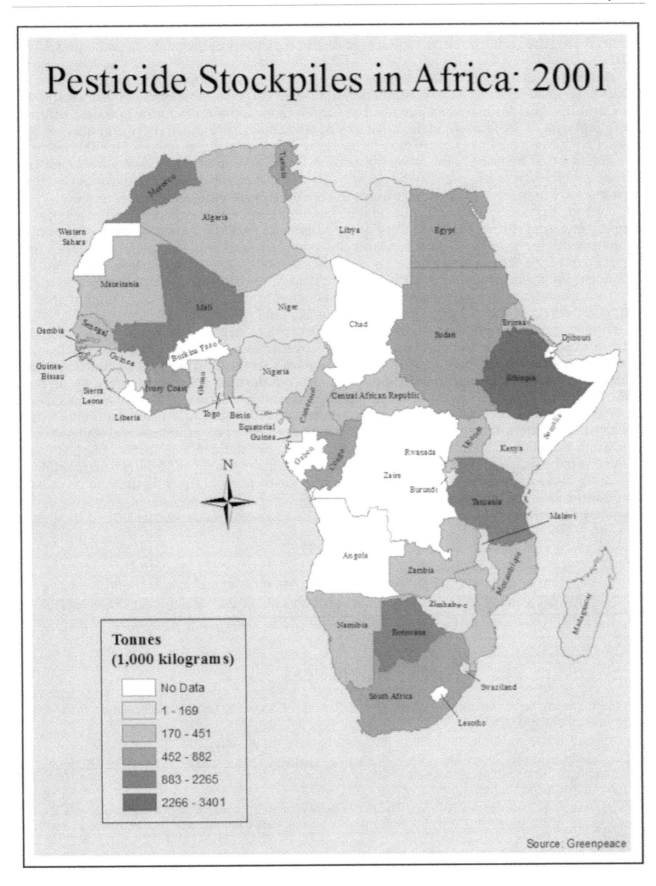

Pesticide Stockpiles in Africa: 2001

Tonnes
(1,000 kilograms)

	No Data
	1 - 169
	170 - 451
	452 - 882
	883 - 2265
	2266 - 3401

Source: Greenpeace

is evidence that hazardous wastes from dump sites have contaminated ground water." Then to make matters worse, the polluted waters were spread due to the effects of the tsunami on boxing day of 2004.

Unknown and unusual skin diseases have affected the Somali people since then and also their livestock. Hospitals and clinics have found it hard to even diagnose some of the infections and diseases, and the situation has been described as 'simply impossible' to examine and deal with the health problems of the local population. The city of Merka has seen a growth in the numbers of people that are suffering from extensive deformities, as well as increasing numbers of malformed newborn children that are being born without limbs or just seem to be underdeveloped. Thyroid, tongue, and colon cancers have also been on the rise within this city, and international aid workers are finding it hard to find treatment and medications to contain this growing health catastrophe.

Over the past seven years, infections and illnesses have sadly been mutating and growing at an alarming rate. And this epidemic seems to be spreading and affecting more and more of the population daily due to the unlucky fact that health aid is expensive and limited, and the people of Somalia just do not have the funds, not to mention the lack of qualified health care professionals and the subsequent long waiting lists to even see a doctor. Also, there has not been accurate research that can give some references to the treatment that the doctors and professionals can assign in order to completely get rid of this growing pandemic in Somalia (and Africa).

Following is a map showing the distribution of pesticide stockpiles in Africa. Developed nations and multinational corporations pay corrupt African governments to dump pesticides and other biohazardous wastes in Africa because many of these chemicals are illegal in developed countries. Oftentimes, the citizens of the countries accepting these hazardous materials are not even aware their country is doing so. The corrupt leaders who take such payments and enter into such agreements have betrayed the public trust. The irony is that if the world discovers an African warlord like Kony is exploiting children, there is an international outcry. But when governments and leaders betray their whole population, and even all the people of Africa, by taking money from developed countries to accept bio-hazardous wastes that are indiscriminate in deforming and killing babies, children, and adults, almost no one says a word. Is this because the corporations paying them to do so have some control over the media and the messaging?

ENDNOTES

1. ("UN envoy decries illegal fishing, waste dumping off Somalia" UN AFP – Jul 25, 2008).
2. "FAO: New treaty will leave fish pirates without safe haven." MercoPress. 2009-09-01.
3. "Johann Hari: You are being lied to about pirates" *The Independent,* Monday, 05 January 2009.

REFERENCES

Commision ready to investigate Eurobian illegal fishing of Somalia. (22.04.09) Retrieved from *http:// euobserver.com/ 885/27983*

"Impacts of IUU Fishing: Economic Losses." http://www.illegal-fishing.info/uploads/Hassan.pdf

Jumah, Adusei & Kunst, Robert M., 2005. "Forecasting Aggregate Demand in West African Economies. The Influence of Immigrant Remittance Flows and of Asymmetric Error Correction," *Economics Series* 168, Institute for Advanced Studies.

M. G. Hassan & A. Mwangura 2007. IUU Fishing and Insecurity Impacts on Somali Fisheries and Marine Resources. A. Standing (eds.) In 'Political Economy of Illegal Fishing in East and Southern Africa'. Institute for Security Studies.

"Pesticides Stockpiles in Africa." (2001). *http://maps.grida.no/go/graphic/pesticides_stockpiles_in_africa*

"Piracy in Somalia." *http://en.wikipedia.org/wiki/Piracy_in_Somalia*

Rena, Ravinder (2006): *TRENDS AND DETERMINANTS OF POVERTY IN THE HORN OF AFRICA—SOME IMPLI-CATIONS*. Published in: Indian Journal of Social Development—An International Journal, Vol. 7, No. 1 (15. June 2007): pp. 65–77.

"Root Causes of Piracy." (2010.) *http://www.mtholyoke.edu/~ahmed24h/pirates/root.html*

"Somali Piracy Threat Map."www.maproomblog.com/2011/01/Somali_piracy_threat_map.phd

"Somalia Ethnic Groups." (2002.) *http://mappery.com/Somalia-Ethnic-Groups-Map*

"UN envoy decries illegal fishing, waste dumping off Somali." www.afp.com AFP, jul 25 2008. Web. *http://afp.google.com/article*

you are being lied to about pirates. (n.d). Retrived from *http://www.huffingtonpost.com/hohannahari/you-are-being-lied-to-abo_155147.html*

http://www.unep.org/

http://somalilandpress.com/somalia-radioactive-waste-surfaces-in-the-coastline-minister-21250

http://www.scribd.com/doc/33208314/the-evidence-of-toxic-and-radioactive-wastes-dumping-in-somalia-and-its-impact-on-the-enjoyment-of-human-rights-a-case-study

SECTION
Five

APPLYING ETHNIC STUDIES IN NEW WAYS: COUNTERCULTURE IDENTITY AND CULTURAL EXCHANGE

What Punk Has to Offer All of Us: An Auto-ethnographic Journey from the Circle Pit to the Classroom

Thomas R. Heffernan

It is upon highly contentious ground that we tread when trying to speak with clarity about punk. I feel that many of my brothers and sisters would cringe at the mere usage of the term to describe who they are and what they are about. I too feel the hair stand up on the back of my neck when someone tries to label and categorize me. So I'm not going to insult you or your intelligence by trying to make some claim that "I have a more clear perspective" on what it is that "punk is" and that other opinions are not actually "punk." Our community is amorphous and refuses at its fundamental core to be defined or understood (Clark 2004; Spheeris 1998). I would even venture that the obfuscation of who and what we are about serves as an important tool in our arsenal in combating those forces who would otherwise exploit us. That being said, I feel that this tool can be a double-edged sword. Often we take to cutting each other down with strict boundary maintenance of "who is an actual member of our community" (i.e., if you don't fit my vision of what punk is, then you aren't one). This is an interesting sentiment considering punk originated as (and still largely claims to be) a community where you are encouraged to "live your life on your own terms" (Rachman 2006); how then do we manage this cognitive dissonance? In all actuality there is far more that ties us together as a community than that which separates us (e.g., anti-sexist, anti-racist, anti-classist, anti-fascist, anti-homophobia, anti-corporate, anti-authoritarian, community-solidarity, and resistance). I speak not for the media-bred caricatures of our community; niche marketing has allowed for any sycophantic youth with money to burn and access to purchasing "punky looking" clothing at Fortune 500 companies like Hot Topic and the ability to pick up the latest "punky" CD at Wal-mart. Our culture is not a commodity that is up for sale. The Avril Lavignes, Good Charlottes, and C.M. Punks of the world are superficial marketing ploys geared towards people who "want to be different, like everyone else." No, I speak of what is going on in the streets, basements, abandoned buildings, and alleyways across the globe. At our core, we understand that the world is a diverse venue in which all players should be respected, honored, and *not exploited*. We do not actively proselytize our messages, but we do demand to be heard. Everyone else seems content with working through the established channels that have given us racism, exploitation, and inequality—even though these processes continue unabated. Our community tends to see the necessity in taking a different and more direct approach to dealing with the exponential growth of oppression. We are that nagging reminder that the path that we are on as a species is the path to slavery, self-destruction, and extinction. We refuse to be placated by the mediocre distractions hoisted upon the masses to purchase their compliance in atrocities at home and abroad. Broadly speaking, punk is a strong voice against oppression, and this places the punk underground in an interesting relationship with the academic discipline of ethnic studies.

Ethnic studies is an ongoing experiment in the quest for equality. Like peeling an onion, ethnic studies educates us on the interconnected relationship between "the other" and ourselves; it is hoped that by examining the lives, histories, and perspectives of people different from ourselves that we will be able to erode the legacy of inequality. By raising our consciousness on our fellow human beings, we tend to see those things that we thought separated us slowly melt into the background. This is a very important step in the process of improving the quality of life for all people and an important first step in improving the quality of life for our living planet. When we start to appreciate our human species for the closely related kin that we are—approximately 98.6 percent of our genetic loci are shared in common with *any* person *anywhere* on the planet (Allen & Darboe, 2010) we see those individuals less as strangers and increasingly as "people like us." It is all good and fine to point this out, however the specter of inequality remains—and until we can fully appreciate our role in our mutual enslavement, little change will result. The process of revelation can be quite slow because it requires much introspection into one's personal attitudes and beliefs. The "unexamined life" that Socrates spoke of is a breeding ground for ignorance, racism, and bigotry. A commitment to developing critical-thinking skills is a necessary first step towards our mutual liberation. Punk has a lot to teach us about the self-evaluation process, as "being punk" is an incredibly introspective experience; this is primarily the case because the community constantly reiterates the necessity of "thinking for oneself" and "being critical of authority." As punk is a dialogue expressing a dynamic community ever in flux, so too is ethnic studies. Ethnic studies always has to look back upon itself, assess, and critique—this is a major strength for the discipline; dynamic systems are far more likely to be sustainable than non-dynamic systems. Both ethnic studies and punk are interested in taking action to create change; this requires education of the issues, community-solidarity, and the ability to work with others as equals.

Auto-ethnography

Ethnographic research is an effective way of attaining a fairly sound understanding of other ethnic populations and is of much personal interest. My initial flirtations with the subject arose while taking a class with Dr. Kebba Darboe where we read the ruminations of Anthropologist Dr. Hortense Powdermaker on her work with the Lesu (a Melanesian society on the island of New Ireland, now a part of Papua New Guinea) and her studies of African Americans in rural America and Hollywood. Shortly thereafter, I read *Lords of Chaos: The Bloody Rise of the Satanic Metal Underground* by Anthropologist Michael Moynihan. It became quite clear to me that the scope of ethnographic field research is a wide and growing field; these works inspired me to do my own ethnographic field research for my Master's thesis. I chose to examine the lives of transient punk rockers in the United States; I traveled over 6,000 miles to document the oral narratives of members of the community via participant observation. It was during the course of this research that I came across a subset of the discipline known as auto-ethnography, which profoundly impacted my study.

I feel that auto-ethnography is a very interesting tool in the writer's arsenal when describing communities. What I most admire about this form of writing on populations is the embrace of self-bias. I agree with Dr. Howard Zinn that bias is inescapable and that even if it could legitimately be risen above, to do so would not be desirable; it is, after all, "impossible to be neutral on a moving train" (Zinn 1997). We find in quantum field theory that the observer (i.e., the scientist) has an impact upon the outcome of their experiments. Subatomic particles exist in a wave of infinite possible locations but only snap into a single location while being observed (Arntz 2004). The scientist's presence effectively biases the experiment; but does that mean that the experiment is invalid? No; one cannot remove their impact from an experiment such as this anymore than we can stop outside forces in the universe from impacting the outcome—we literally are a component of the experiment and this must be accounted for. In this same way, we cannot help but bias any investigation of culture we engage in because our presence alone changes the situation from how it would have unfolded had we not been there.

But is this a true bias? Ethnographers go through much training to lessen their cultural bias when observing their subjects in the field—but no matter how diligent a researcher we are, bias is inescapable because we all have to return from the field, analyze our data, and then interpret it so that knowledge and understanding may be revealed. It is at this point that, no matter how painstakingly in-depth the data collection process was, we must cut, sort, and focus on areas *we think are important and relevant*—bias is inescapable in the interpretation of ethnographic field research. However, auto-ethnography offers a unique way of lessening the impact of bias by examining our own community and our place within it (Chang 2008). Auto-ethnography allows the reader a view into a community from the perspective of members of the community—not those of outsiders who, despite their best efforts, can never fully be a part of what is going on and thusly err in the reporting process. Even those who are able to overcome most of their bias (according to their own purely subjective standards) will not have the knowledge, insight, or access that members of the community have. The real question lies in whom you would have greater trust in conveying accurately the intimate details of a community: a *biased* outsider with limited knowledge and access or a *biased* insider with comparably *more* knowledge and access? I am not the first to write about our community or about the role of social activism in punk, but it is through my story of how punk shaped my life and led me into academia that I hope to convey something that is meaningful to the reader. Interweaved in this narrative is the answer to what punk has to offer to us all.

Path of Resistance

Becoming punk for me was actually a natural extension of my experience growing up in a repressive rural community in South Dakota. When I say that punk rock saved my life, some may take it as a joke—but I'm very serious when I talk of such things. Punk has become a cornerstone for me and has guided my life—I shudder when I think about the other path that I may have gone down. When I look back on my life, I guess I've always been a "punk." I was born in the summer of 1983 during the last great years of the first wave of hardcore punk. While I was being breastfed, bands like Black Flag and the Bad Brains were touring the country. Although my parents were old enough to be in the fray of the first generation of '77 punk, they were much more into what was happening in mainstream arena rock of the time. I remember my father telling me that he had once listened to the Ramones and that he thought that they "sounded like shit." Though my father was far more likely to listen to Boston, he taught me something that would later arise in my years in punk—you need to hold your ground and stand up for what you believe in. I remember my father being outspokenly pro-choice—to do so in the community where we lived was social suicide. Until my father and I had this talk about the abortion issue, I had never thought about it in depth but had just gone along with the crowd. I see that moment as being an interesting turning point for me in how I viewed the world. The opinion of the majority was rapidly losing its hold over me. Around this time, I also started to take notice of how malicious people can be towards each other.

My father developed multiple sclerosis when I was born, and my mother developed gestational diabetes while pregnant with me (which is still present with her to this day). My father has since passed on from complications that arose from the rapid deterioration of his liver in 2004—the end result of a decade of malpractice by his physician. My sister was born with spina bifida in 1986 and has been paralyzed from the waist down her entire life; today she remains one of the smartest and most compassionate friends I've ever known and is currently interning to become a pastor. When you grow up in a small, rural community with a family like this, you can't help but stick out.

During the early 1990s, my parents moved our family to a small town within sixty miles of Aberdeen where they taught science and English at a nearby school district. My mother lost her job after the superintendent told her that, "he didn't think women should be teaching science courses." We tried to sue, but this taught me my first lesson about the justice system and how justice is primarily reserved for those who can afford it. My father lost his job a few years later because the school was unwilling to make reasonable accommodations for his disability. My sister and I were harassed on a daily basis while attending this school—verbally and oftentimes physically. I was called a faggot and a queer from the third grade forward and assaulted by classmates on a regular basis. One night, a group of school kids slashed all of the tires on my parents' vehicles and, although the perpetrators where well known in the community, law enforcement did nothing about it. My family was constantly stared at; people would talk down to my sister as if she had a learning disability, my father would slip and fall on the ice with only his fourteen-year-old son to pick him up while passersby walked quickly into the store. These and other instances really began to make it very clear that we were not welcome there because we were different.

I also learned at an early age that part of my ethnic heritage is Hochunk. However, I am a Métis person and I pass for being white. Any time I'd ever bring up my ethnic heritage when I was growing up I'd get responses like "No way, you're the whitest person I know" or "you're just lying." There is real hostility toward American Indians in South Dakota. Just a few years before I was born, the incident at Oglala and the second Wounded Knee occurred. The American Indian Movement was very active in South Dakota and had earned a nasty reputation amongst the local Whites for disrupting business as usual (i.e., the exploitation, harassment, systematic murder, and neglect of native people). Racial epithets like "prairie nigger" abounded around me, and people would be shocked when I called them out on being a racist; I guess they couldn't see how that would offend me because "I was White too"—even though I'm not *all white, nor* privy to racist remarks about *anyone*. My best friend and former band-mate, Trevor, had a similar situation; he was half Lakota and half French. We once wrote a song together called "*dakuho*" which was about the feeling of disconnect we have with the land and the traditional way of living. *Dakuho* literally means "what happened?" in Lakota.

When I first came to college it was by accident. As I saw it, the university system was a corrupt village pumping the minds of tomorrow's youth with the materialist tools of self-destruction that have plagued our planet and species since the rise of capitalism and industrialization. As I was exiting high school in rural South Dakota, I had decided that I wouldn't be a part of this and would not go to university. However, this all changed in late 2002. I was living in Aberdeen, SD, my surrogate home where I was deeply involved in the local punk scene. My roommates were young, idealistic kids who were willing to quit their job to go to a punk show and, as a matter of fact, we did just that. All three of us walked out at the same time and went to bond and play with our friends on the dance floor and in the streets. I remember that show being important to me and that it felt especially liberating.

A few days later it became apparent that we'd need new employment, and we ended up at McDonald's. Day in and day out as I stood in front of the lathes that they cook *what they call* meat on, my mind would wander to the topic of class struggle and how we all were getting screwed. I worked with single mothers getting paid minimum wage and middle management types that took the shucking of frozen meat pucks far too seriously. I was utterly excited to discover that a Halloween metal-core show was going on in Alexandria, MN, and my friend, Hobo, and I made plans to go together. The show was held in a barn in the middle of nowhere and went from 5:00 in the evening until 5:00 in the morning. We danced, smoked cigarettes, and joked the night away—it was experiencing moments like this that I loved the most with Hobo.

After the show we crawled our way back to Aberdeen, and I came home to find out that my roommates had quit their jobs while I was gone and began their infamous disappearing act. I found myself left with the bill to the apartment and was quickly becoming more screwed by the minute. By December, I made the decision that I'd burn on the rent and move to Mankato. Coincidently, I had looked at MSU at the behest of my parents during the spring of my senior year in high school. I thought the place seemed interesting and, after a little thought, I made plans to head down to Mankato and check out the mad punk scene that I had heard stories about. The plan was to kick it for a few months, take my loan money, and move somewhere else.

When I arrived in Mankato I quickly came to find out that the glory days of Kato punk were all but gone. My arrival was at the low-end slump in the punk community—coinciding with the shutdown of the central venue *Slacker's*. To top it off, the only classes I was interested in taking were filled up. I was alone and frustrated, so I decided that if I couldn't go to many shows or take courses in philosophy that I would just look around for classes that sound interesting. Then I came across ethnic studies. The name intrigued me, and I saw that there were spots open for the introductory course. I had a fair number of classes and every one of them seemed like they wouldn't bore me too much—so things started looking up in Mankato.

It turned out that the first class I was ever to take at university was the ethnic studies course— and it surely was a fateful decision, for it would radically redirect the rest of my life. I remember sitting in the classroom on the first day and the professor (who later would go on to be my academic advisor in both undergraduate and graduate school) had told us all something that sticks with me to this day. Dr. Wayne Allen explained to us that ethnic studies originated as the "voice of the voiceless" in the 1960s as a major component of the Civil Rights era. The voices, stories, identities, and perspectives of the four major ethnic minorities had historically been denied their place in our American history. The legacy of slavery, Japanese internment, the American Indian Reservation/boarding school system, Manifest Destiny, Jim Crowe, women's suffrage, the Braceros, etc., have been framed, understood, and taught from the dominant society's perspective. Our education system is dominated by Eurocentric perspectives that do not provide room for the experiences of people of color to be recognized. Rather, dominant society sweeps these perspectives under the rug. Ethnic studies seeks to remove these stories from the dustbins of history and present them to the world via the avenue of identity politics. Since the 1960s, ethnic studies has become part of college and high school curriculums around the nation and has been instrumental in the ongoing struggle of attaining mutually shared equality. In that first class room experience, Dr. Allen had said that "ethnic studies is fundamentally a critique of Western Civilization," and I knew right then and there that I had struck upon something that demanded my attention.

I immediately started making connections between my beliefs as an anarcho-punk and what ethnic studies was doing. I had a long history of interest in political activism, anti-racism, and an ardent distaste for mainstream consumer capitalism and the plague it spreads in the minds of otherwise competent human beings. The scene I grew up in was conscious of these realities and my circle of friends was doing some pretty amazing things for small town life in rural South Dakota. Our community gave me hope that I thought couldn't be found within the confines of repressive rural South Dakota. Everything in my life up to my first show primed me for embracing a community of people that were outcasts like me. I was now part of a community that didn't tolerate racism, sexism, homophobia, classism, or any type of oppression. Our community in Aberdeen had active chapters of Anti-Racist Action and Parents and Friends of Lesbian and Gays. Out of nothing we pooled together money at the door of the local venue, *Cobain's Arcade* (a former video arcade and adult book store in the late 1970s, turned punk and hardcore venue in the 1990s), to host local bands from around the area as well as national touring groups of fellow DIY-ers. We never had "big" acts come through, but we didn't need them because our heroes musically and philosophically were: the Diseased, Anamnesis, Endahl, Fed by Ravens, October 32nd, With Dead Hands Rising, Transparent Front, Padre Karras, the Dead, Swing by Seven, ill Lust, Passions, Capture the Plague, Discrepancies, Five Point Theory, the Dimbulbs, Dispensing of False Halos, and the Psalters. All of these bands (and many more) had a tremendous impact on the way in which we lived and thought about our lives. At the height of our scene, we had kids coming out to all-ages shows every weekend averaging between 100–300 people crammed into arcades, basements, moose lodges, and coffee shops—not bad for a town of 25,000 people. Bands would bring in zines and books alongside their shirts and CDs and spend hours talking about ideas and tearing it up in the pit. We made our own zines and held weekly poetry nights at the Red Rooster Coffee Shop and weekly gatherings at the Fallout. We held art and music parties and community events like free rummage sales. Many of us hopped trains to find adventure throughout the country only to make periodic stops back in Aberdeen to visit friends and go to the show. We were a tight-knit community and a microcosm of what was going on nationally. Because we were an isolated punk community in the middle of nowhere we (like the first wave punks) had to make do with whatever we had available to us at the time.

I find it to be a real disservice to our community to assume that punks can only come from cities or suburbs. The isolation, systemic racism, and lack of opportunities present in rural South Dakota made for a hot bed of rebellion amongst those kids who never quite fit in. In the early punk scene—all voices were equal and there literally was no "top." Punk was subject to regional variations and tastes and developed into a plethora of expression and form (which is usually overshadowed by the mainstream media depictions of "what a punk looks, acts, and thinks like") (Clark 2004; Mateus 2004). Our early communities were deeply informed by nihilism. Punk burned down all of the old value systems and embraced "the meaningless life," but it is from meaninglessness that "meaning" did arise. Nietzsche's description of nihilism did not necessarily end in what he described as passive nihilism (i.e., where nothing matters so why bother doing anything at all). Active nihilism can be seen as an opportunity to make your life into anything you want it to be (i.e., the old ways are dead to us, now we can accomplish anything) (Perry, Taylor, & Dreyfus 2010). Both of these realities are represented in punk communities. Either you take the path of no meaning or value to life and lead an apolitical existence (*which itself is a choice that can have a value*) or, as was the case in my home community, you create something significant that affects other people's lives. Some may scoff about nihilism's ability to develop meaning in life—but what does it really matter either way? If life has no meaning in the long run and we know that our sun will burn out and that the universe will eventually freeze over (Kaku 2010), then what bearing do the decisions we make in the short spans of our lifetime have on the eventual outcome of our universe? Any decision we make has no consequence; it comes down to personal choice—so why not try to do something you want to do and create meaning in your life? Sitting around and waiting for oblivion is pretty boring; developing your own ideas of how you can make this "meaningless life" meaningful to you at least helps pass the time. The community of punk has largely chosen the latter position; seemingly paradoxically this allowed our community to form emergent identities not limited by dogmatism (everything from the Black Bloc Anarchists to the Krishna-core Vegan Straight-edge movement). It is by this shedding of the values of a broken and destructive society that punks envision a new world (though it is not necessarily important how this world will look, as it is an emergent phenomena that will take form on its own accord). Punks see something that is wrong with society—be it banal suburban existence or mega-corporations dominating the globe at the expense of everyone else. They don't want to be like everyone else because they know the damage that is being done and they don't want to be a part of it. They need to exercise their demons or at least shed the old realities for something that is a little more meaningful to them. Whether they come out and directly say it (and most won't because they generally deny labeling and traditional roles of classification), they are actively creating a growing community that is based in tolerance, respect, advocacy, community involvement, personal growth, and unbridled artistic expression. These are the breeding grounds of effective change. We want to have a world in which all people are honored and respected and free to be who they are. The meshing of ideas present in the discipline of ethnic studies and those which pervade most of punk rock are strongly linked.

Songs to Fan the Flames of Discontent

It is through this path that I've taken in my life that I've come to appreciate the impact that punk can have in the lives of people it touches. My voice is my perspective but it also resonates with the perspectives of many others in our over-arching community. We do not owe anyone any explanations—we are who we are and we are unapologetic. We are amorphous and refuse to be pinned down into any one way of being. We have vastly divergent ideas, but there is, at the same time, much that ties us all together.

Not long ago I came across a video on YouTube that was produced by punkforbrains. I first became interested in punkforbrains' videos when I was searching for media to show my students for a lecture that I had prepared on the prison industrial complex, the drug war, and institutionalized racism. I was seeking out the video of the song "Burn them Prisons" by Leftover Crack that had the lyrics in it. The second verse of the song encapsulated very well a message I was hoping to convey in the discussion about the realities of for-profit prisons, racial profiling, prison lobbyists, and the utilization of the drug war to target communities of color. Punkforbrains did an excellent edit of other Leftover Crack songs, so I began to check out his other videos. One of his videos was entitled "What punk offers to all of us," and it was by far the most intriguing video of his that I've seen. The video examined the universals found in the punk/hardcore scene that permeate our entire community.

I had been thinking about the issue of developing stronger unity in our community for quite some time, and it has become apparent to me after watching the punkforbrains video that we are in agreement with each other on core values far more than we'd like to admit. As I see it, the major goal in punk music is education. "The song" and "its lyrics" are a message one coveys to the audience. Be it singing about living a banal, wasted life in suburbia, corrupt politicians, heroin addiction, nosebleeds, or stealing people's mail—the common thread is revelation of that which had previously been hidden—usually something shocking or grotesque. Punk music puts you out of your comfort zone when you listen to it—coincidently this is the *only way* that anyone *ever* learns *anything*. If you only choose to learn about things you already know of and are comfortable with thinking about, your perception and understanding of reality will not expand and will ultimately remain quite small. To do so would be to lead the "unexamined life" that Socrates foreboded us of. It is by stepping into the unknown that we gain insight into the world around us. Punk has some important lessons to teach us, and many of these lessons are embedded within the music itself. A friend of mine in Aberdeen once said, "Going to punk shows is a lot like going to church." After we thoroughly gauffed at the initial absurdity of the idea, he went onto explain that, "We come here and we listen and learn from the singer on stage and from each other—then we take what we've learned and live that life out here on the streets and in our community."

Lessons to Be Learned

Punk teaches us some very important lessons about the obscured legacy of manipulation and White privilege that has blinded the nation to what gets carried out in their name. We understand that the system was never broken, but that it was designed by powerful elites for their benefit at the expense of the rest of us (Zinn 1997). We have been offered meager accommodations designed to abate and placate us in the form of: housing (*indebtedness for life either to a landlord or to a mortgage*), food (*toxic chemical slop grown and slaughtered on the backs of family farmers around the globe*), clothing (*which is almost exclusively made by child labor and sold as empty status symbols to "middle-class" western markets*), entertainment (*electronic trinkets, "professional" league sports, and sitcoms designed to sell you diversion from the reality of inequality*), voting (*the illusion of choice in our own destiny*), and organized religion (*as the promise of a better life once you're dead and can't complain about everything taken from you*).

We understand that this nation was built on the backs of slave labor and the genocide of indigenous peoples from coast to coast. We understand that the development of the concept of race as part of the American social hierarchy has been used to divide people who would otherwise see their mutual disadvantage in society and rise up together. We understand that the ethnic other has been blamed for all of the ills of the people ranging from drug use and communism, to illegal immigration and moral decline. This fear has allowed us to do horrible things to our fellow human beings while the elite fan the flames. We are core members of direct action resistance against the commodification and exploitation of the globe. Many of us believe that we must take action on an individual level to combat these forces because we cannot rely on the master to disassemble the master's house. The system that started inequality relies upon inequality in order to function.

As I was entering into graduate school as a teaching assistant, it was a natural thing for me to talk about punk in the classroom. I had come full circle in my life, like my parents before me—I now was a teacher. I ultimately decided to stay with going to school because it became apparent to me that I had much to share with people about the world around us. I saw that I had an opportunity to put myself in a position where I could reach the minds of the youth that I once feared would be surely corrupted by the university system and bred to become the next generation of mega-consumers putting a stranglehold on the planet. If I could reach them with the dual insights of punk and ethnic studies, hopefully I could cause them to think more about their role in the world in which we live and maybe even get a few of those students to change the way they think and act. It has been a longstanding tradition in our community to take whatever opportunities that you can get to help get the word out. Some of us do this with dumpster-dived cardboard and stolen Sharpie's; some get on stage and belt it from the top of their lungs at the crowd; some print political zines and leave them in office buildings and truck stops; some satirically tag billboards and drab city walls; some of us sneak into tea-party rallies and give blazing speeches about illegal *European-Immigrants* stealing land and jobs from the *true Americans* (the indigenous tribes of Turtle Island) (Neiwert 2009); and some of us find our way into academia to help educate those who are unable to see their role in our mutual enslavement. If we hope to combat those forces that hold all people down we must develop critical thinking skills that will allow us to analyze and understand the issues macroscopically. The current system of inequality cannot stand once the truth is exposed; humanity is resilient and we can make lasting, sustainable change to our world if we only are brazen enough to keep asking the question.

REFERENCES

Allen, W., & Darboe, K. (2010). *Introduction to Ethnic Studies: A New Approach.* Dubuque, IA: Kendall Hunt Publishing Company.

Arntz, W. (Director). (2004). *What the #$*! Do We (K)now!?* [Motion Picture].

Benally, J., Benally, K., & Benally, C. (Composers). (2007). Peak's Song. [Blackfire, Performer] On *[Silence] is a Weapon* [CD]. E. Stasium.

Chang, H. (2008). *Autoethnography as Method.* Walnut Creek, CA: Left Coast Press, Inc.

Clark, D. (2004). The Death and Life of Punk, the Last Subculture. D. Muggleton, & R. Weinzierl (Eds.), In *Post-Subcultures Reader* (pp. 223–236). Berg Publishers.

Graffin, G., & Olson, S. (2010). *Anarchy Evolution: Faith, Science, and Bad Religion in a World Without God.* New York City: Harper-Collins Publishers.

Hannah, C. (Composer). (1996). A peoples History of the World. [Propagandhi, Performer] On *Less Talk, More Rock* [CD]. San Francisco, CA: R. Green.

Hannah, C. (Composer). (1996). I was a Pre-teen McCarthyist. [Propagandhi, Performer] On *Less Talk, More Rock* [CD]. San Francisco, CA: R. Greene.

Kaku, M. (2010). *Escape to a Parallel Universe.* Retrieved November 12, 2011, from *www.bigthink.com: http://bigthink.com/ideas/18973.*

Leblanc, L. (1999). *Pretty in Punk: Girls Gender Resistance in a Boys' Subculture.* Piscataway, NJ: Rutgers University Press.

Lyxzen, D. (Composer). (1997). Racial Liberation. [Refused, Performer] On *The Demo Compilation* [CD]. Burnheart Records.

Moynihan, M. & D. Søderlind. (1998). *Lords of Chaos: The Bloody Rise of the Satanic Metal Underground.* Port Townsend, WA: Feral House.

Neiwert, D. (2009, November 16). *Teabaggers punk'd by anti-racists who get them to cheer rant against European-American immigrants.* Retrieved November 12, 2011, from *www.crooksandliars.com: http://crooksandliars.com/david-neiwert/teabaggers-punkd-anti-racists-who-ge.*

Perry, J., Taylor, K., & Dreyfus, H. (2010, February 4). *Nihilism and Meaning.* Retrieved November 11, 2011, from *www.youtube.com: http://www.youtube.com/watch?v=TzfZKFDNMBA.*

punkforbrains. (2008, November 14). *What punk offers to us all.* Retrieved November 12, 2011, from *www.youtube.com: http://www.youtube.com/watch?v=ma7JmDkalv8.*

Rachman, P. (Director). (2006). *American Hardcore* [Motion Picture].

Sherwood, M. (Composer). (2001). Refusal. [Strike Anywhere, Performer] On *Change is a sound* [CD]. Richmond, VA: Jade Tree Records.

Spheeris, P. (Director). (1998). *The Decline of Western Civilization: Part III* [Motion Picture].

Stza (Composer). (2004). Burn them Prisons. [Leftover Crack, Performer] On *FUck World Trade* [CD]. New York, NY: S. Albini.

Zinn, H. (1997). *A Peoples History of the United States.* New York: Harper Perennial.

Video Gamers and Gaming: Virtual Counterculture that Cuts across All Ethnic and Racial Differences

Joe Riska

Thinking outside the box is the heart and soul of ethnic studies. Instead of adhering to old notions of what a person is supposed to study or whose history to accept, the discipline encourages thinking outside of the standard parameters of academia and questioning some of the basic values of our culture and society. With that in mind:

We need to start talking about video games.

I don't just refer to discussing the plots of games that we are currently playing with our friends or relating the time where you finally beat Bowser (née King Koopa when first introduced) in Super Mario Bros. when you were nine, saved Princess Peach (née Princess Toadstool when first introduced), then found out that the game started over again and all the Goombas had been turned into Buzzy Beetles, and the game "just got, like, so much harder." (By the way, there are no spoiler alerts for twenty-five-year old games.) I mean that those of us who like to think of ourselves as intellectuals and cultural critics need to start looking at video games and start talking about them in a more serious and analytical light.

We spend hundreds of hours writing about film, music, works of literature, and even television, critiquing and looking for deeper meaning in our entertainment. In fact, we have entire university departments dedicated to this very concept. In recent decades, a new medium for expression, creativity, and unprecedented interactivity has appeared and the academic community has largely ignored this growing influence on our collective culture. This should not continue any longer.

According to the Entertainment Software Association, the group chosen to represent the video-gaming industry in matters regarding legal issues and government agencies, 72 percent of American households play computer and videogames, the average player is thirty-seven and has been playing for twelve years and 29 percent of all people playing video games are over the age of fifty. This is no longer just kids' stuff.

There are plenty of articles out there about games and their supposed connection to increased violent tendencies after exposure to violent games and the possible link between playing video games and obesity or whatever societal ill you want to pin on this electronic boogeyman. A person seemingly can't trip over a newspaper or news-related magazine (the ones that still exist anyway) without finding some sort of "new study" making those claims. There are so many of those types of studies that it's not worth it to even reference them when they can be obtained from a couple of clicks on Google Scholar and most of them tend to harp on the same one note while not really understanding the subject of video games in the first place. Of course, every once in a while there is a fun or odd study that comes out, and easily the most interesting piece about the "scary" links between playing games and health, though, is one from Jordan Poss (with T. Marshall, F. Qian, K. Weber-Gasparoni, and C. Skotowski) at the University of Iowa, who had a presentation at the 2010 American Association for Dental Research meeting in Washington, D.C., entitled "Video Gaming Teenagers: an Examination of Diet and Caries." This presentation used data from a sample population of forty-eight children between the ages of twelve and sixteen and displayed that those children who ate unhealthier snacks or drank soda while playing games tended to spend more time playing games than those children who don't snack (1.5 ± 0.6 vs 0.7 ± 1.0 hours; $p = 0.019$). His study also touched on other various factors involving time watching television, level of activity, structure of mealtimes, etc., and compared all of that data with the dental records for each participant in the study. The findings indicated potentially cariogenic habits with screen activities *(http://iadr.con-fex.com/iadr/2010dc/webprogram/Paper128821.html)*. To put it another way: games may cause tooth decay.

I know that for me, personally, my teeth were actually quite stellar—if not just a little crooked—when I was young and played games all the time. In fact, my teeth were amazing until I no longer had insurance. I wonder if there's some sort of correlation there? Nah. That's just silly thinking. Forget I wrote that.

Instead of looking at links between video games and what they may or may not cause, we need to start looking at the games themselves. Video games are no longer the child's toy that they once were: they are immensely popular, completely ubiquitous, and they can be easily as engaging and worthy of our time and effort to study them as film, theatre, or television. Of course, we have to remember that games are different from those other media because of a massive difference, which is, of course, interactivity. Unlike other forms of entertainment, the audience is not supposed to empathize with the character we see on the screen, the audience becomes that character.

Before we get to that final point, though, I want to emphasize exactly how big this phenomenon is and how it came to be that way.

Videogames are a Huge, Massive—Brobdingnagian Even—Market

Whether we like to admit it or not, our lives have come to be dominated by electronic gadgets and virtual media. We spend nearly all of our waking hours on our computers or phones hooked up to the single greatest repository of human knowledge that has ever existed, the Internet, and yet with the power to learn about anything that our minds could possibly conceive—we get bored. Yes, even when presented with the opportunity to learn anything imaginable, contact anyone on the planet, and tap into the wealth of creativity all at the push of a button, what do we do? Well, if download statistics are any indication, we throw birds at pigs because we're bored.

If you are unaware, I am referencing one of the most popular videogames in the history of the world, *Angry Birds*. In this game, it is the player's objective to launch various types of birds from a slingshot located at the left-hand side of the screen into structures built of glass, wood, and stone where evil green pigs live and snort with derision. Each bird has a different game mechanic (e.g., the yellow bird speeds up with a press of a button and is effective at destroying wood, the black bird speeds up with the press of a button and explodes on impact with the tower and is effective against stone, and the blue bird splits into three different birds and is good at destroying glass), the rules of the game are easy to learn, the gameplay is based on simple physics, and each level has a different design and increasing challenge as it goes on. As if to completely eschew the advancement of the importance of storyline in modern gaming, the basic story of *Angry Birds* is that the evil pigs stole the birds' eggs and now the titular birds are—get this—angry. And that's it. That's the premise, and getting revenge is the motivating factor for the characters in the game.

So just how popular is this physics puzzle with simple gameplay mechanics and an odd story? As of November 2, 2011, *Angry Birds* had been downloaded 500 million times in less than two years from its launch as an Apple iPhone app on December 11, 2009 (*http://www.reuters.com/article/ 2011/11/02/us-rovio-idUSTRE7A137Q20111102*). The newest addition to *Angry Birds, Angry Birds Space*—don't ask how birds work in space—was released on March 22, 2012, and according to Angry Birds' Twitter Feed, @AngryBirds, the new offering had received 20 million downloads by March 30, 2012 (*http://twitter.com/#!/AngryBirds/status/185874296642617347*).

The ineffectiveness of what appears to be a kamikaze mission, sacrificing hundreds and thousands of adult birds in the process of getting back a disproportionately small number of eggs is not touched upon, but is a rather odd thing to think about in the grand scheme of things. We'll come back to this seemingly random observation in a short time, so keep it in the back of your mind.

Angry Birds is just one game (with several expansions) though and, oftentimes, it's free. In fact, a person could download it free on Google Chrome right now and play it on the browser at work and the boss will be none the wiser—as long as this completely hypothetical person is fast with the Alt+Tab or Ctrl+PgUp/PgDn command and keeps the computer speakers on mute, that is. Perhaps it's not the best form to pick out a game that can be free. How about some games that cost about $60 retail on release day? Surely that would be a better example of how many people might be interested in playing video games.

On November 8, 2011, Activision released the game *Call of Duty: Modern Warfare 3*. In a press release (*http://investor.activision.com/releasedetail.cfm?ReleaseID=624766*) dated November 17, 2011, Activision announced that *Call of Duty: Modern Warfare 3* had "shattered theatrical box office, book and video game sales records for five-day worldwide sell-through in dollars." Just how much money did this game make in five days' worth of retail sales? Seven hundred, seventy-five *million* dollars. This surpassed the previous five-day sales record, which in comparison was a paltry $650 million. What had that record before? *Call of Duty: Black Ops,* which was released the previous November. That's right. In two consecutive years, with two consecutive games, Activision broke media records for amounts of money received within less than a week's time. In fact, this one gaming franchise— *Call of Duty*—has made over $6 billion in retail sales of new games.

This is just based on one franchise. There are dozens more titles that may not do *Call of Duty*-level sales, but are no slouches either. According to vgchartz.com (Video Game Charts), one of the leading industry research firms that collects publically available game sales data and presents it all in one easy-to-access space, there were eighty-seven games worldwide that sold at least one million copies in 2011 (*http://www.vgchartz.com/yearly/2011/Global/*). Thirty-seven of those eighty-seven games sold one million copies in the U.S. in 2011 alone (*http://www.vgchartz.com/yearly/ 2011/USA/*). Games released on separate platforms count as different games on this chart (e.g., worldwide Portal 2 sold 1,368,403 copies on the Xbox 360 and 1,128,037 copies on the Play Station 3 and, despite being the same game, it was counted twice on this chart). The same happens with several other games, including but not limited to: *Dead Space 2, Call of Duty: Modern Warfare 3, Battlefield 3, Elder Scrolls V: Skyrim, Just Dance 3, Assassin's Creed: Revelations, Batman: Arkham City,* and many others).

This sales data is without even considering the vast secondary market of used games. Due to the fact that game publishers like Activision do not see a dime from those sales, much like the market for used CDs, DVDs, cars, musical instruments, etc., it is nearly impossible to determine how many people have actually purchased any one game, let alone how many have played a game by renting, borrowing, or pirating a videogame. All that can be discerned is that the largest purveyor of used games, GameStop, posted a worldwide total gross of $9.5 billion in sales for 2011 (*http://news.gamestop.com/ press-release/business/gamestop-reports-sales-and-earnings-fiscal-2011*). Although GameStop does sell new games, which is reflected in the gross sales number, a multi-billion dollar per year used game industry is nothing to scoff at. In addition, according to the NPD Group, the official tracker of the video game industry's sales data, video game sales in 2011 were between $16.3 and $16.6 billion in the U.S. alone (*https://www.npd.com/wps/portal/npd/us/news/ pressreleases/pr_120116*).

Video games are huge, but numbers alone don't tell the whole story.

Video Games are Everywhere, Man

First, a very brief, abridged, and mostly home console-specific version of modern gaming history:

In 1981, Space Invaders allegedly caused a shortage of 100 yen coins in Japan.

On March 27, 1982, *Pac-Man Fever* by Buckner & Garcia made it to #9 on the Billboard Hot 100 Charts. The song made it to the Hot 100 Chart for nineteen weeks despite the notable handicap of being objectively terrible because Pac-Man was huge. (*http://www.billboard.com/song/buckner-garcia/pac-man-fever/2600558#/song/buckner-garcia/pac-man-fever/2600558*). For comparison, a few weeks later, the classic Kool & the Gang song *Get Down on It* topped out at number 10 on the Hot 100 Chart and lasted for seventeen weeks (*http://www.billboard.com/song/buckner-garcia/pac-man-fever/2600558#/song/kool-the-gang/get-down-on-it/2008677*).

From 1983 until 1985, the video game industry crashed. While impossible to know all the reasons behind the crash, it is likely that companies overestimated the appeal of the games that could be produced with the technology at the time—washed out Atari graphics and rudimentary gameplay weren't for everyone—and latecomers to the videogame industry during its boom tended to put out inferior products on the store shelves (which has since become known as shovelware), leading to a loss of consumer confidence. This is where the mandatory E.T. the Extraterrestrial video game reference goes in: In 1982, Atari won the rights to produce a videogame based on Steven Spielberg's film *E.T. the Extraterrestrial.* Wanting to get the game out in time for the Christmas season and capitalize on the film's popularity, the game ended up being a rushed mess—often considered to be one of the worst videogames of all time—and millions of copies ended up being returned, unsold, and eventually buried in the desert in New Mexico (Hubner, John; William F. Kistner Jr. 1983). "What went wrong at Atari?" *InfoWorld* 5 (49): 145–155. *http://books.google.com/books?id=6C8EAAAAMBAJ&pg=PA146&dq=%22Atari+games,+VCSs+and+home+computers%22#v=onepage&q=%22Atari%20games%2C%20VCSs%20and%20home%20computers%22&f=false).*

Then, in 1985, the Japanese company Nintendo released the Nintendo Entertainment System (NES) in America and, within a year (and with help from an 8-bit Italian plumber stereotype and his brother), came a resurgence of interest in video games (*http://www.wired.com/thisdayintech/2010/10/1018nintendo-nes-launches/*). Popular game series such as *Super Mario Bros., Metroid,* and the *Legend of Zelda* started on the NES and continue to this day on the Nintendo Wii. Nintendo was huge. There were several cartoons and live action series (*Captain N—the Game Master, Super Mario Bros. Super Show, Legend of Zelda*), a breakfast cereal (Nintendo Cereal System—the Legend of Zelda side tasted the best), a movie starring Bob Hoskins, Dennis Hopper, John Leguizamo that completely missed the point (Super Mario Bros.), clothes for kids, and toys. So many toys.

In the '90s, gaming continued to grow. The stalwart NES was replaced by the Super Nintendo Entertainment System (SNES) and later Nintendo 64 (N64). The SNES was joined by the Sega Genesis initiating the 16-bit era and the "console wars" where each company tried to outdo each other, Sega going so far as to make their slogan for use in both television and print ads "Genesis does what Nintendon't" (*http://www.youtube.com/watch?v=yIAA66rZTLI&hd=1*). The SNES, being the machine with slightly superior sound and graphic abilities ended up selling more units—61.91 million worldwide (*http://www.vgchartz.com/analysis/platform_totals/*).

The next generation kicked into high gear with the release of the Sony Playstation and the N64. With this new technology, home video game consoles were able to render 3D polygonal graphics and no longer relied on game sprites for main visuals. The Playstation, being disc instead of cartridge based also had the ability to play CD-quality audio, marking a great leap forward in game sound design and helping to usher in an era of recorded voices for characters. Unfortunately, many games of this era look and sound extremely dated due to great leaps in computer technology since the 1990s. Also, as a general rule, just because game companies could record voices at this time did not mean that they should have done so. The voice "acting" in the first *Resident Evil* game provides a good example of the stilted delivery endemic to early video game voice acting.

It wasn't until the 2000s and the release of the Sony Playstation 2 (PS2) and the Microsoft Xbox (Xbox) that gaming started to really explode in popularity. The PS2 ended up selling 153.68 million units worldwide (*http://www.vgchartz.com/analysis/platform_totals/*). With the new hardware offered by the PS2 and Xbox, games started to get closer and closer to creating lifelike graphics.

Then, in 2007, gaming exploded. The Nintendo Wii introduced millions and millions of new people to video games with its intuitive system of motion-control gaming. While the Wii's hardware was underpowered and offered graphics similar to what could be found on the Xbox or PS2, the newest iteration of hardware from Sony and Microsoft, the Playstation 3 (PS3) and Xbox 360 offered even better graphics, bringing graphical representations of people and things ever-closer to the uncanny valley (the theory that at some point as robots or computer representations of humans get closer and closer to actually looking like humans, there will be a time that the representation of humanity will become off-putting because it won't look human or inhuman enough to properly relate to it) (Pollick, F. E. (forthcoming). In search of the uncanny valley. In Grammer, K. & Juette, A. (Eds.), Analog communication: Evolution, brain mechanisms, dynamics, simulation. The Vienna Series in Theoretical Biology. Cambridge, Mass.: The MIT Press.). *http://www.psy.gla.ac.uk/~frank/ Documents/InSearchUncannyValley.pdf*).

Now that games can exist on cell phones such as the iPhone (e.g., *Angry Birds, Cut the Rope,* and *Fruit Ninja*) and embedded in social media sites like Facebook (e.g., *Words with Friends, Gardens of Time,* most anything with the word –ville at the end of it and published by Zynga), as a society we have chosen to play. Games are around us everywhere and an entire generation has grown up playing video games; the importance of looking at them critically should be quite evident.

Finding Video Games' Masterworks

First off, I absolutely have to address the "are games art?" question. Answer: yes. This is especially accurate if operating from the postmodern definition of art as a work that is consciously aware that it is also a product then videogames may be the ultimate postmodern medium in which an artist may work. There are many games out there that exist solely as entertainment and product to be enjoyed, but that doesn't mean that a person should discount those out there that are designed to make a person feel something and tell an evocative story.

Film, television, books, music, art, and theatre all have their own canon of greatness. There are few who would deny the brilliance of *Citizen Kane, Breaking Bad, The Brothers Karamazov, Les Miserables, Thriller,* or *Starry Night* regardless of personal preference. There are always going to be contrarians out there, but these are truly great works of art in each of their own unique ways. Take a step back from these singular works of greatness, and you can begin to see how each one floats above a sea of mediocrity and detritus. For every great film director (Kurosawa, Kubrick, Miike) there are several Michael Bays or Uwe Bolls. For every great television series (*The Wire, The Sopranos, Breaking Bad*) there is a *Two and a Half Men* and twenty or so starring a Kardashian. Tom Waits and Nick Cave stay semi-obscure and Nickelback are the best-selling and most award-winning "rock" artists for the first decade of the twenty-first century. Even for each great work of literature designed to move the human spirit and uplift the soul—books that have the power to transform a person forever and teach the reader something about the greater human condition—there exists a *Twilight*. Hold on a second, let's make that worse: for every *Twilight*, there's a pile of *Twilight* fan-fiction and about 100 subpar imitators that actually got published. Let that sink in.

What I'm getting at here is that the potential for an entire medium cannot be judged by the mediocrity around it.

So what could count as worthwhile cases to study when it comes to games and what will ultimately be the most important way to judge a game's worth as far as artistic merit goes? Will it be gameplay, interactivity, story, or will it have to be taken on a case-by-case basis? Does a great storyline trump subpar gameplay? Is a nonsensical storyline a detriment when paired with stellar gameplay [think about the *Angry Birds'* kamikaze mission]? How should difficulty factor into game design?

Is a game worthy of more introspection just because it's fun? Is a well-made game necessarily a better game than one that may have design flaws? Are open world designs automatically superior to linear worlds? Why are the heroes of games almost always white males or cartoon animals? How do games treat their minority characters? Are characters even important at all in the long run when they act as the proxy agent of the player?

I don't have the answers to these questions, but they are something that should be thought about when playing a game.

With those questions in mind, here is a list of games that should be played:

Final Fantasy VI—The menu and turned based combat system is a relic of when early role-playing games drew most of their inspiration from pen and paper RPGs like Dungeons and Dragons, but the story involving one of the greatest video game villains and the superlative cast of characters may be enough to conquer some of its poor design elements.

Super Mario Bros.—

"One day the kingdom of the mushroom people was invaded by the Koopa, a tribe of turtles famous for their black magic. The quiet, peace-loving Mushroom People were turned into mere stones, bricks and even field horse-hair plants, and the Mushroom Kingdom fell into ruin.

The only one who can undo the magic spell on the Mushroom People and return them to their normal selves is the Princess Toadstool, the daughter of the Mushroom King. Unfortunately, she is currently in the hands of the great Koopa turtle king.

Mario, the hero of the story (probably) hears about the Mushroom People's plight and sets out on a quest to free the Mushroom Princess from the evil Koopa and restore the fallen kingdom of the Mushroom People.

You are Mario! It's up to you to save the Mushroom People from the black magic of the Koopa!" (Nintendo. Super Mario Bros. Instruction Booklet. 1985. *http://www.replacementdocs .com/download.php?view.258*)

That's the plot to Super Mario Bros.

Mushrooms are consumed to get larger, flowers give Mario the power of throwing fireballs, Mario can break bricks with his fist by jumping underneath them and along the way crawl down a sewer pipe or two. As nonsensical as this game seems on paper, the mechanics of this game are so smooth and so fair that this one game basically invented a new genre of game known as the platformer.

Dark Souls / Demon's Souls—The player controls a character of his own making through a bleak and dismal world of extreme difficulty. Every single inch of progress is hard-fought and the terrain over which the player travels is fraught with peril, but the controls are spot on and the game is never unfair. Making it through this game is considered to be an exercise in both masochism and skill. To make it through to the other side is an accomplishment, but why would a game be designed in such a way when many games these days can be finished without ever seeing a "game over" screen?

Uncharted 2—Playing through this game is like controlling Indiana Jones. It's a perfectly polished popcorn experience. It's unbelievably fun and the action set-pieces are fantastic, akin to a summer blockbuster. Does that mean that this game will be destined for greatness or merely something that captures the zeitgeist?

Shadow of the Colossus—A boy carries a dead girl into a temple on horseback. He was chased by a cadre of men along the way, but through dogged determination he makes it inside. Laying the body of the girl on an altar and praying, he hears a voice who tells him that he can bring the girl back to life but only at a great cost. There are sixteen colossi, guardians of the land, who must be destroyed to return the girl to live. Alone on his horse, he travels through the desolate countryside to meet the first colossus, a hulking beast several times larger than the boy that does not attack unprovoked. Is the boy doing the right thing?

Heavy Rain—The player doesn't so much play the game as the game plays the player. Reacting to various prompts on the screen, the player watches the main characters react to what's happening to them all in hopes of solving a mystery and saving a child.

Deadly Premonition—This game objectively sucks. The controls are terrible, the voice acting is bizarre, the writing is off, the combat is repetitive, the driving is unbearable, and the music cues are out of place. This game *should* exist as an example of exactly what not to do when creating a game. All that aside, this is one of the best and most interesting games that a person will ever play. If *Twin Peaks* was a videogame, it would be *Deadly Premonition.* How could something that seems to get everything wrong end up being so right?

Mass Effect 2 (or all three of them if you want the full experience)—Games often get flak for not starring minorities or treating the minority characters as anything but token representatives—if not overt stereotypes. Some games try to buck that trend; this is one of them. You have the option to play as a male or female, engage in sexual relationships with other characters of either gender, make legitimate choices that alter the course of your game, including ones that the player may not like.

There are so many more games out there worthy of our time to look at and understand and perhaps if these games got the proper recognition and analysis they deserved besides the cursory reviews they get on websites and magazines, it would not only legitimize a hobby enjoyed by the vast majority of Americans, but force game developers and publishers to look beyond the bottom line and treat what they are making as something creative and possibly special—if that is indeed the idea. It is possible for a game to elicit feelings of triumph, exhaustion, fear, sadness, and hope. It is up to the so-called experts to weigh in and give credence to the content within games and not just vilify games for their mere existence as a possible distraction for children.

Applying Ethnic Studies while Teaching and Traveling Abroad: A Memoir

Charles Elton

Sitting on the couch one afternoon, I picked up the phone to call a professor about a class for which I was thinking about registering. I was in a state of limbo in regards to my tentative schedule and needed information about this ethnic studies class that seemed as far away from me as the moon. For the last three years I had been planning on majoring in Human Resource Management and had been taking classes from the Department of Business with a plan to graduate in another two years. Since I was behind in the four-year plan, I had been casually looking around at other majors that might get me out a bit sooner. When I passed by the brochures for a new Ethnic Studies major one afternoon, I was sure I had found what I was looking for. The program had been divided into different focuses like human services, government services, and exactly what I had been looking for: business and corporate concentration. The program included business classes that I had already taken and would get me that bachelor's degree in only one more year! I wouldn't lose any credits or even have to take any more business classes at all. So I began paging through the descriptions of the ethnic studies classes that would not only occupy my next school year, but change my life as well.

Staring out the window while the phone was ringing, I hoped someone would say "hello" and be able to offer me an answer about this class. The registration book said it was a "Special Topics" class, and the secretary of the department told me that the professor would determine its topic. This really sparked my curiosity and suddenly I heard that "Hello?" I quickly introduced myself as a converted business major and inquired about the course content and what we would be learning. What happened next, I will never forget. I intently listened as this booming voice described the social, cultural, and historical forces that have shaped the face of our world today. He digressed into how it relates to the governments that dominate our political platforms today. Nonetheless, I registered for this course and opened my eyes to a whole new world, one much larger than before.

After completing my undergraduate degree, I joined what would become the first graduating class of the only Ethnic Studies Master's Degree in the Upper Midwest. Taking many courses where I was learning about the multitude of other cultures on our planet, I was growing uneasy living here and not experiencing them myself. I knew I had to save some money for the long adventure and experience as much as I could handle. I had been with my girlfriend for over five years, and I was delighted that she was as interested in doing this as I was. After two years of saving, we finally had enough cash and began planning our adventure. My goal was to fly to the other side of the world to teach English, or at least learn how.

Some may think it odd to go over there to train for teaching English, but the demand for teachers is high in Asia and there are many TESOL certifications to choose from. I found TEFL International to be one of the leaders of this industry, with schools worldwide. We signed up for their location in Ban Phe, Thailand, because it was their main school and you learned from the person who wrote their curriculum. It seemed that this small town might offer me a glimpse into Thai culture that a school in a tourist town would not.

First, though, we had to get there, and our first step was securing a visa. I would be there longer than the thirty-day tourist visa they administer at the International Airport's Immigration office, and I had to apply with the Thai consulate for a sixty-day Visa. After securing this vital piece of red tape, we were on our way to the other side of the world.

Our arrival in Bangkok was met with monsoon rain and a confusing number of taxis all charging different rates. We eventually ended up at the official taxi booth that had a set rate and we were on our way to the Guesthouse whereat I had reserved our lodgings. We spent the next few days taking *tuk-tuks*—little three-wheeled taxicabs—around Bangkok to see the many temples and attractions that make this sprawling city the metropolitan jewel of Southeast Asia. After Bangkok, we were ready to hit the beaches of the town we would call home for the next month. The pictures on the school's website previewed it to be some sort of lost paradise, but what we found was far from that. Rather, it was an uneventful everyday small town in Thailand with heavily polluted beaches because of the barge traffic going through the area. In retrospect, I feel it was probably best that we lived in this town for a month because we never would have experienced it otherwise.

Once we arrived down in Ban Phe, we knew we wanted to make the experience the most it could be and felt like we should rent a place in town for the month instead of staying in the school's dormitory. It turned out that there was a Music Festival taking place on the weekend of our arrival and it was right across the street from the nearest bungalow for rent. I inquired about a room and realized right then and there that I was the only *farang* (foreigner) around. I did not speak Thai, and they did not speak English. My Thai phrasebook was of no help at this time as I was frantically thumbing through its pages.

Finally, another employee escorted up a young man who apparently spoke English. It turned out that he spoke enough of my language for me to get the point across that I wanted to rent a bungalow for the month. They showed us to our lodging, and I was pleasantly surprised. Tucked away in some dense jungle bush was our own bungalow, which housed a bed, ceiling fan, and a bathroom. What more could you want? We soon realized we needed to get some earplugs the next morning on account of the rooster crowing and cackling outside the bungalow. Other than that, though, I just wanted to find a scooter for rent so we could get back and forth. Naively, I chose the first place I saw, which also happened to be across the street from the school. I paid about 35 percent more than I should have, but it only worked out to be around forty extra dollars. I was amazed at how cheap everything appeared to be. I would insert my ATM card and withdraw $300, but I was given 10,000 Baht. It was as if I were playing with Monopoly money and it seemed to spend as easily.

The first lesson I learned was to expect that things would be a bit backwards. Instead of giving me my money and then my ATM card, it happens the other way around over there. After years of walking away from an ATM after taking back my card and then getting my money, I got my money and then walked away leaving my card in the machine. Luckily, though, the card was sucked back in and shredded. This though, was after ten minutes of asking every employee around if they knew how to contact that particular ATM's bank; none of them seemed to catch my drift.

Starting our TESOL course the next Monday, our curriculum consisted of 120 hours of classroom instruction on the principles, behaviors, and methodologies associated with language learning and acquisition. A large part of our classroom training consisted of us rehearsing our roles as teacher in preparation for the real-world practicum. The first week was spent entirely in our classroom learning the approaches, methods, and techniques of language acquisition. Our specific methodology at TEFL International was unique to their curriculum and was designed by Dave Hopkins, the instructor teaching us during our course. Language is likely to be acquired more easily when presented in a communication situation familiar to the learner, so many of our examples in class revolved around when the student would actually be using their English skills (Hopkins, 2nd ed.). We call this "context setting" and use four to eight lines of dialogue being listened to, spoken, and written on the board as cues for practice and memorization. After drawing a picture summarizing the context of the lesson plan, the teacher begins by verbalizing the dialogue in front of their class. The lines are then rehearsed for the students out loud and they practice them with the instructor and fellow peers. The students are then shown how to write the words on the board one at a time.

Another activity involves listening to an audio recording and attempting to fill in blanked words on a worksheet. We also learned how to use games like tic-tac-toe to help facilitate language acquisition by injecting a little fun into the lesson plan. The TEFL International methodology designed by Dave Hopkins incorporates a listening activity and a communicative activity (or group work) into every lesson plan. Group work allows the students to practice amongst their peers, allowing the teacher the opportunity to float around the room and help more students at one time. I felt this freed up the demands on the teacher by allowing the students to assist each other in the learning process. It also allowed the teacher to expose them to the different ways to express the English language and its alphabet. Pictures from a book and ones you draw yourself are the most helpful visual aids you can use and were an integral part of every lesson plan.

Eventually it was time for some real-life teaching, and we went to Bansamnaktong School in Rayong Province. Here we worked one-on-one with a student for a couple days so we would get a feel for communicating with a young person that knows very little English. My student was named Wii, a young girl from a nearby village. I was told that my student would speak enough English for us to communicate and we were to work on conversational skills. Upon meeting her, though, I realized that she only knew single words of English and the lesson plan I had prepared would be of no use to us. At first, I sat there stunned and wasn't sure how to proceed since I had prepared a lesson for an intermediate-level speaker. I wanted to develop a rapport with her so I simply began pointing at pictures of everyday items and practicing their names. As time went on, we began to draw pictures of what we were trying to communicate with each other. Information started to come out about our families, likes and dislikes, and even pop culture as she described herself a fan of the American band Linkin Park. The next day we practiced vocabulary expansion and tried a listening activity where we recorded ourselves going through our lesson plan, playing it back for us to critique.

The next week was spent in another school near Ban Phe that had classes at every grade level. These were open-air classrooms where we would conduct one-hour classes incorporating the different dialogues and activities we had been learning about, oftentimes with stray dogs lounging on the floor. Getting to put this methodology into real-life practice allowed the steps we were learning to employ. Soon enough it was becoming second nature to effortlessly move through our lesson plans and progress through each step. All of us had the chance to teach classes to beginning English speakers, intermediate levels, and seniors in high school that already had a very strong command of the language.

We even had the opportunity to instruct classes at a Buddhist Monastery to a room full of monks. Erin, my wife, encountered an interesting hurdle in teaching the monks, where she could not touch them or even hand them a piece of paper. Instead, she had to place the object she needed to give them on the floor and they would in turn pick it up. It really made us realize the myriad of cultural considerations we would encounter wherever we might teach.

Our instructors at TEFL International were very adamant about us keeping a professional relationship with our students at all times and not to even give out our e-mail address. There had been one instance where a teacher like us had given a female student his e-mail address and her father ended up threatening that man's life. It is a whole other way of life over there, and people's reactions are often much different than what you'd expect. Another thing to take into consideration is the sexual exploitation of women there and the multitude of men that visit this part of the world with that on their mind. Schools are now scrutinizing prospective teachers' backgrounds in their native countries and abroad before hiring them into teaching positions. Considering the nature of the student-teacher relationship, you can imagine the problems that might occur. Not surprisingly, there are also increasing numbers of ESL teachers in Asia that are doing their part in weeding out those whose first priority may not be education.

After a month of the structure the teacher-training program gave my life, I was very excited to move on. With that excitement, though, was the uneasy feeling of the unknown. Prior to this, we had planned on staying in Thailand for three months since it seemed like there was plenty to do and see. It was also the safest country, per se, and that appealed to us on the surface. Now, though, after a month in Thailand, we were beginning to wonder what else was out there. We were talking about going into Cambodia to see what it was like. Why did I want to go there? When I considered where I was on the planet and why I'd come, it seemed only logical to take on the next frontier. And, hey, we would get to take a boat down to Southern Cambodia.

The border crossing ended up being one of the most memorable experiences of the trip. It was not that it ended up being good or bad; it was just how it happened. Upon arriving at the border, about ten young boys ran up to our car cupping their hands around their eyes to see if there may be some *farangs* inside. There seems to be good money in carrying luggage over the border. There is actually a whole racket in escorting tourists over the border, luggage and all. It starts when you get out of your vehicle on the Thai side and you are surrounded by boys trying to lift your backpack and carry it for you. They will carry your belongings to another guy who takes over for you on the Cambodia side and introduces you to a few more young men who are willing to fill out your immigration and visa paperwork for you. All this hospitality does cost a few dollars, though. It is an established enterprise here that seems to net enough money for the boys involved to keep it an ongoing concern.

Border crossers are then shuffled through the official Cambodian immigration office where you purchase the thirty-day visa for $35. The government website says it is only $20 and do not give them more than that, but my attempts proved futile and they keep insisting it was $35 and the website is wrong. I paid the $35 and was now legally able to enter into the Kingdom of Cambodia. The boys loaded our backpacks into the car and we had a smooth car ride across the countryside, surreal almost. I kept thinking, wow, so this is Cambodia, it doesn't look so scary.

After a twenty-minute cruise and a short jaunt across Cambodia's largest bridge, we arrived on the island of Koh Kong to catch the boat down south. Ironically enough, our driver also worked for the guesthouse we pulled up to, and he insisted that this is the best place in town; a steal at only $10 a night. It didn't look bad, we were tired, and so we tried to give him the money. He then tells us that he also sells tickets for the boat trip we are taking the next morning and comes up with as grand total for the ticket and the room. He then lets us know that if we need anything, and he meant anything with a wink, he will help us out. After checking into the room, Erin gets ready to shower and undresses. It's around this time that I see a kid peeking into our room visually molesting my girlfriend. I try to sneak out the door to surprise him, but as soon as I am out the room I see him running into the dark hallway of this old French colonial mansion. To stay here was at our discretion, but to leave now after checking in would have been equally uncomfortable.

Our first night in Cambodia was restless but the freshly baked baguettes in the morning made up for our lack of sleep. After hopping a motorbike taxi to the ferry port from the guesthouse, we boarded the high-speed boat to Sihanoukville. We headed down to the lower deck and took the furthest seats in back. Ironically enough, the only other White people around sat in the seats opposite us. Ben was a bartender from San Francisco and Anna was a student from South London. I was very comforted to have familiar faces in such an unfamiliar situation. We exchanged conversation as a means to not only build friendship but to somehow show off each other's travel itinerary thus far.

We made small talk for a while until a small Cambodian man sat down in the seat right next to me. He offered me a piece of gum and spoke English very well. I immediately remembered a warning in my guidebook about strangers offering you candy spiked with something to put you to sleep. Apparently many a groggy traveler has awakened to find themselves devoid of valuables. I disregarded this thought anyways and obliged his offer. Conversing with him was exciting as he was the first Cambodian I had randomly met. He was very interested in why I came to his country and I simply told him that it was to experience this; that I was curious about the way other people live and I was there to travel and see for myself.

After disembarking the vessel, Ben and Anna seemed interested in looking for a place to stay together, so we found a taxi and negotiated a price. The driver started by offering us a ride down to the beach area for $8, but we hold steady at $4 until we settle at $5. Not bad for four people and a fifteen-minute ride. The reason you can get by here so cheaply is that human labor costs next to nothing. The gasoline costs the same, but the money the driver is making is nothing compared to the wages earned in the U.S. Since haggling down prices is the way it is done here, it is common-place to negotiate. I also encountered people trying too hard to get the price they think the locals are paying and going a bit overboard for an amount roughly equal to a quarter. Many backpackers try to get by on $20 a day, an amount that equals about half a month's wage for many full-time work-ers with a family to feed. I felt that you were taking away more than you were actually giving when some tried so hard to negotiate the lowest possible price.

We found a nice room for ten bucks that was also only a hundred yards from the beach and a nice little restaurant. Inside the eatery we admire the crashing waves in front of us and felt a sense of relief as we were finally where we wanted to be, wherever that may be. Looking up at the bar, I was surprised to see some White guy mixing drinks so I went up to introduce myself. Andy was a British fellow that said he would never go back to the U.K. He was plenty happy here making $2 a day in wages because he made enough in the commission off selling tickets for boat rides and the like. The owner let him sleep upstairs from the bar and he got to eat and drink for free; it did seem like he was doing alright.

We ended up spending a week there exploring the town and neighboring islands, since boat rides were only $10 for a full day trip with lunch, snacks, and snorkeling. They even spear the fish from the boat for lunch and serve it filleted with a Coca Cola. The most memorable part about our stay in Sihanoukville was the huge market they have downtown. I think the best way to see and meet the people is by interacting in the local economy, and that seems to center around the local mar-ket. Aside from the usual trinkets and sunglasses for sale was any type of food that is eaten in the area. Tanks of fish lined the rows alongside piles of raw meat, and a lady with a magic wand that shooed away flies. After this was the poultry area, piled high with half dead chickens and ducks awaiting sale. There was not a lot of electric refrigeration that I saw in Southeast Asia; typically they used ice blocks in a chest to keep beverages and food cool. That day taught us to seek out the mar-ket in each new town as they are fabulous and they are the best chance to sample delicious new street food.

Bidding Ben and Anna farewell, we moved a few hours up Cambodia's only paved highway to a small town named Kampot. From there, we moved on north toward Phnom Penh. We were rewarded with one of the best bus rides of our trip. It was six hours of traveling over dirt roads through many villages, pulling over for bathroom breaks along the way. The bus stops were a great snapshot into the lives of the local people since we usually stopped in a central location with small shops and businesses. Once again, we were the only foreigners on the bus and found ourselves sit-ting next to piles of produce and other supplies. Some lady got on and laid a bag of something warm on Erin's feet, while another lady came over to remove the satchel and apologize. We never found out what was in that bag and the memory became another mental side note in the multitude of mys-teries during our adventure. Our bus ride also had magnificent views of the vast expanses of rice pad-dies, with the occasional set of limestone karst formations standing tall on the horizon.

Soon enough, our surroundings became more industrial, and I knew we were getting close to the Cambodia's capital city, Phnom Penh. Taking a tuk-tuk from the bus station, we chose a small guesthouse near the Nam Song River. The next afternoon I was walking near the Royal Palace when a van pulled up alongside me and asked me if I needed a ride. I replied no, and then noticed that there were about eight people too many inside the van and another thirteen sitting up on the roof, holding onto a makeshift guardrail. I stared in amusement as the cordial driver sped away into the busy afternoon traffic.

The Royal Palace and Museum offered an informative exhibition of Cambodian culture and history. There was even a benefit taking place in the courtyard, and I was able to observe what appeared to be very important people go about their social networking.

Back in the room, Erin and I were discussing what we wanted to see and do in this sprawling city. The tuk-tuk driver out front recommended the shooting range and we half-heartedly agreed to try it out. We were happy riding in a tuk-tuk out to the military base because the ride was long and offered the best chance to see the city. If you had told me ten years ago I would be wandering the streets of Cambodia without a worry on my mind, I never would have been able to believe that was possible. We did not feel threatened in the least while we were in this country, even here at a Cambodian military base where they offer us a menu of guns to shoot. The man offering this menu is leaning against a glass case containing land mines and what looks to be a rocket propelled grenade. I ask about this and the man excitedly replies that I can fire this bazooka at a cow for the right price. However tempting that may have been in days past, the appeal was not there for me now and I politely declined. On the ride home, the driver asked us if he could make a stop to pick up his wife who was waiting after class. We agreed and enjoyed a tour through countless neighborhoods and alleyways until we ended up outside the school in a sea of fresh young faces, happy to be finished with another long day. Some things are familiar no matter where you are in the world.

We agreed on a cooking class for the next day, but I woke up with an upset stomach and Erin went off to learn the art of Cambodian cuisine on her own. I walked around town practicing En-glish with various people and tried to take it all in. I was also mentally preparing myself for our excursion out to the Killing Fields and Tuol Sleng torture facility, better known as S-21.

Seeing the rows of prison cells and torture rooms first hand sends a shiver up your spine, especially after you have seen a wall of pictures that catalogue those who bore witness to its heinous past. "Thousands of pictures of Khmer Rouge victims hang on the museum walls: men, women and children who were duly photographed, then tortured and killed. S-21 was known simply as 'konlaenh choul min dael chenh'—'the place where people go in but never come out.' Nearly 20,000 people are known to have entered Tuol Sleng; of these only six are known to have survived" *http://www.pbase.com/maciekda/tuolslengmuseum.*

Over at the "Killing Fields," each viewer peers up at the tower of skulls that serve as a memorial to those murdered under Pol Pot. There are also trails leading visitors throughout the fields where you pass the exhumed mass graves that look like little more than holes in the ground. I realized that it wasn't just thousands, but millions that suffered under this cruel regime. Back in town, though, you'd never know of such a history. I encountered only friendly faces and a genuine desire to make my stay in their country the best it could be.

The next morning we boarded a bus for a seven-hour ride through central Cambodia that will take us up to the temples of Angkor. Some of the richest aspects of Cambodian culture are found in the art and architecture of the Angkor area temples. We find a nice guesthouse to stay at in the nearby town of Siem Reap. This place also has a driver to take us around in a tuk-tuk to see the vast expanse of temples and villages that make up the attraction. I was amazed at how big this place was; it would take about three full days just to see the main temples. We spent these days walking countless miles exploring temple after temple, oftentimes by ourselves with no one else around. There was nothing more amazing than coming up on a Buddhist monk in some forgotten room that smelled of incense and kneeling down to pray together.

Driving around town with our driver, we happened to go past a clinic that had a bright red sign out front declaring "Severe Epidemia of Hemorrhagic Dengue Fever, Please Give Blood." Erin was very intent on donating and since I had to go arrange our flight to Laos, I told her I didn't have the time and she went on by herself. Her story astonished me as I listened to her describe the hallways filled with mothers holding crying babies and the dark room that housed the chair she would sit in for the withdrawal. Before she knew it, there was a needle being shoved into her arm and her blood was draining like a bathtub. Where had the needle come from? Had it been used on someone else before?

My attempt at scoring these airline tickets was proving to be a bit more difficult than I had anticipated. I figured I should start by going to the local airport to see if I could buy the tickets there. My moto-taxi driver brought me to the old airport first, a place that resembled what I thought a ghost town might look like. He then brought me over to the new airport where I walked around in circles for a while until I met a Scottish lad named Paul, who happened to be looking to take the same flight. After jumping through the same hoops together, we finally ended up back towards town in a little office that housed Lao Airlines. We found out that the flight was the next morning and headed back to our rooms with the agreement to meet the man with the tickets at the airport before the flight. Erin and I found Paul and his wife, Fiona, at the airport the next morning where we met the man for the tickets and then almost missed our flight. We must have chosen the slow line through immigration because we ended up hearing our names being called over the loudspeaker. We eventually made it through the passport check and noticed a group of airport workers holding Erin's bag and waving us over and ushering us out the door to board the plane. We were escorted across the tarmac towards a plane with both propellers spinning and a nice little stairway leading up to the door, apparently we were late and had missed the official preflight boarding.

Up in the air, I found the food was better than I had anticipated and they even gave us free Beer Lao, the national brew of Laos. We had a stopover in the small town of Pakse on our way up to Vientiane. The views from the airplane afforded us the most spectacular views of this landlocked country. Vientiane is the capital city of Laos and, after arriving, we realized it was not the bustling metropolis that I had found in the capitals of Thailand and Cambodia. It is a laid back city located on a bend in the Mekong River surrounded by fertile alluvial plains (Cummings & Burke 2005). The French seized Vientiane in 1883, with the rest of the kingdom becoming a French protectorate in 1904 (Funk & Wagnalls 1955). You see this most visibly in the architecture that compromises most of the buildings here, and also in Luang Prabang. Leaving the city and venturing out into the rural landscape on our bus ride up to Vang Vieng, I began to see beautiful rolling mountains covered in dense rainforest and a layer of fog. Laos is extremely undeveloped with few roads and offers a truly unaltered beauty (Leibo 2007). We passed through many villages and saw it was the corn harvest and people were bagging it up in burlap sacks for sale by the road. Our bus stopped at a stand that has a most peculiar kind of fruit for sale. I have never seen them before and our driver showed us how to peel it properly to expose the tasty goodness inside. Since this was our lunch stop, Erin grabbed a couple freshly steamed ears of corn and I went searching for bread. Laos was a French protectorate in days past so there were fresh baguettes and delicious cheeses available. We stopped once more on our journey and the driver told us that good fish was available only at this market and she must stock up. It was a typical Lao village of stilted thatch homes and a market offering a long row of fish for sale and various fruits and vegetables.

Once in Vang Vieng, we found a spectacular room with a balcony overlooking the Nam Song River and the area's renowned limestone karst formations shrouded in mist. We spent the next day touring the area on a motorbike, where we visited villages and caves and went swimming in a blue lagoon. Walking back across the bridge from the lagoon we saw a few young boys jumping off a bridge into the river, it looked like fun so we decide to join them. Our time in Vang Vieng was the most relaxing thus far, and we found it difficult to leave. Besides touring villages, we also took a seventeen-mile kayak trip down the Nam Song River. Since there are many people taking advantage of river trips here, the locals have built ramshackle huts that serve as bars along the riverbanks. Along with the bars, they've also built thirty-foot high swings up in the trees to swing down from. We were there during monsoon season and the river was flowing wildly enough to make the thirty-foot drop seem like a bad idea, but everyone else was taking their turn so we made the climb and took the plunge.

Heading north again a few days later, we had a six-hour bus ride through the most winding roads I have ever witnessed. The landscape was stunning and my eyes were fixed on the landscape around us. We passed a military checkpoint where an armed soldier surveyed the riders on the bus and allowed us to continue. There were attacks on buses traveling this stretch of road in 2003 that killed 22 people (U.S. Dept of State 2007), something I'd forgotten all about. When I first read this warning on a travel website, it seemed far away and I thought I would avoid this area all together. But as it popped into my mind while we were right there in a bus, it seemed very probable considering the dense cover and rolling terrain. That is what these State Department warnings do, though; they frighten people into staying away, and I wanted to see for myself. The picture that they paint for you on their website ended up being much different from the Laos I experienced. They focus on perceived negatives associated with Laos' Communist Government and the presence of bird flu. There is also half a million tons of unexploded ordinance lying around the land from the Vietnam War (or the American War as they call it) that kill more than a hundred people every year. I think the reason these warnings seem so scary is that we do not have to worry about dangers of this nature back home. There are no government agents spying on tourists, and you don't have land mines, or bird flu, or military checkpoints to arrange your day around.

Making it to Luang Prabang around suppertime, we find a room to rent that is little bigger than a closet, but with a communal balcony overlooking the Mekong River. Luang Prabang is regarded as Laos' cultural center and is arguably the most picturesque town in the entire country. There is a nice mix of traditional Lao architecture mingled with the large buildings from the French colonial period. I noticed a very distinct contrast between the Laos you see in Vientiane and Luang Prabang and the country you see everywhere else. As I said before, Laos is very traditional and undeveloped. Most towns and villages consist of traditional Lao homes made of thatch and very few buildings, if any at all. A walk down the street in an average village would be on a dirt road lined with homes, a few shops or eateries, and rice paddies extending into the horizon. Luang Prabang, though, has paved streets lined with buildings of French architecture housing fine restaurants and hotels. One popular attraction is to watch the procession of monks making their way through town when the sun rises; here you find people lining the streets to offer them alms, a gift of money or food.

We had taken a kayak trip down the Nam Song River while staying in Vang Vieng and had such an amazing paddle that we decided to do a similar trip up here. This trip offered another new experience in that it included an hour-and-a-half elephant ride through the jungle. After meeting their three-year-old baby elephant, we took a ferry across the river to the adult elephants and began our jungle tour. The men ushered us into a basket made for two people that rested on the elephant's back, while a girl from Belgium sat on the neck. I had assumed we would have a guide driving the elephant but that was not the case. Two guides walked alongside the six elephants carrying our group of fifteen people down the forest trail between trees, even descending a steep hill. We then trudged through a small stream for a while and laughed to ourselves as the lady on the elephant next to us screamed with fright as her husband heckled her with his video camera. After the ride, we boarded our kayaks and headed out for the four-hour river tour. About half-way through the float we happened upon a small village on the banks of the Nam Song, where we saw a lady wailing loudly with outstretched arms toward the sky. Our guide motioned for us to beach our vessels onshore and we pulled up alongside her. I didn't need to speak Lao to understand that she was grieving for a lost loved one. Our guide began to explain to us that two of her sons had recently died in the rapid we'd just completed after their raft sank. Erin and I sat on the riverbank in silence, contemplating our own feelings, while he consoled this grieving mother. This experience was to be the most profound of our entire trip.

The next morning we caught a tuk-tuk over to the little airport where we would catch our flight to Hanoi. After such a tranquil experience in Laos, I was not prepared for the hustle and bustle of Vietnam's largest city. After arriving at our guesthouse, I was informed that I would need to pay in Vietnamese *dong* (the local currency) and had to find an ATM. I headed a few blocks east to the closest dong dispenser and, as I was completing the transaction, I watched the row of vendors selling Pho on the sidewalk. Pho is the national dish of Vietnam and is a light soup with chewy rice noodles, sweet spices, and scintillating herbs that flavor a truly heady broth (Nguyen 2004). The lady nearest to me suddenly reached into a bag under the table, pulled out a duck, cuts off its head, and threw it into the boiling pot. This was not a big deal, but the mental image of this was seared into my brain as one of the most vivid memories I have of Hanoi.

Later on that evening, Erin wanted to have a soak in our bathtub since we were staying at a fairly nice hotel this time. I wanted to see more of the city so I hired a moto-taxi to drive me around. He understood enough to know that I wanted to see the "real city" and to my surprise that is what he showed me. We left the Old Quarter of Hanoi and he took me over to the neighborhood where he lived. We rode the motorbike through alleys dark and narrow until I was sure we were somewhere that no White man had walked before. Soon enough we were at his home. He invited me in and I sat there for almost a half-hour watching TV and exchanging smiles with his family. None of them spoke any English, and I only knew the Vietnamese basics like hello, goodbye, thank you, and bathroom. The brother kept offering me cigarettes and the kids were rolling balls across the floor for me to roll back towards them. I don't know how I ended up where I was, somewhere in Hanoi that night, but I know I will never forget hanging out with that family.

Our next stop was Ninh Binh, a town about four hours away by bus. We were told that the bus left at 7:00 p.m., and we had to get across town to the pickup area. Upon arriving, we noticed that this place was overflowing with people who all hoped to get on the same bus. All of a sudden the bus was full and takes off; a lady came to tell us that another bus will be here in awhile. I went across the street to what appears to be a restaurant and buy a couple beers for the wait. Inside, I visited the most disgusting bathroom I experienced in Southeast Asia and, upon walking out, I had a group of young girls surround me and start talking loudly. I don't know what this was all about, but one of them handed me a pad of paper and a pen. I quickly sign my name and leave without a moment's hesitation. This had happened before in Thailand, where girls thought I was Harry Potter.

The next bus got there a little too soon for us, as they only sold thirty-two ounce refillable beer bottles, and we hadn't necessarily been that thirsty. We quickly returned the bottles across the street and we were helped on through a crowd of people trying to push their way on board. I figured we were helped on because we most likely paid ten times more than the others (still a bargain at $9), and they wanted to keep the foreigners happy. For some reason, the driver stopped after only an hour and a half and we were stuck at this roadside market for ten minutes. This is the place where I made my most erroneous language barrier SNAFU yet, and walked right into the ladies bathroom. This may not have been such a problem, had we not been in the middle of nowhere in Vietnam where the bathroom is a channel formed into the concrete across the floor. Here, woman sit with a leg on each side of the trough, and I came strolling in like I own the place one night and ended up catching a woman in a compromised position. It was quite embarrassing for both of us.

When we finally reached our destination city, it was about midnight and there was not a lot still open. The bus drop was a random street with no stores nearby, but we saw a very stately looking hotel down the block and went to rent a room there. We headed up to the room and soon realized we had nothing to eat and there weren't any stores open. I went down to the front desk and asked if they have any bread for sale; surely this huge inn had a well-stocked kitchen. The thing is, though, we were in Vietnam and there wasn't a lot of toast or sandwiches being eaten. The clerk had me hop on his motorbike and we spent the next fifteen minutes driving around town looking for bread, stopping at the few shops that were still open. Finally, we happened upon a dimly lit corner market and I scored a bag of crackers; now satisfied with how close to bread I actually got, we headed back towards the hotel. Five hours later we were awakened by a loud speaker, which I came to learn was the "Voice of Vietnam," a radio broadcast that plays every morning at sunup for a few hours.

After sleeping a bit longer by way of the earplugs we packed, we were awakened by a phone call asking us if we were ready for our breakfast yet. Upon reaching the lobby, we were escorted to a private room where we enjoyed our morning baguette with jam, butter, and a cup of Nescafe. Fully charged for the day, we went about to find a motorbike to rent for our trip over to Tam Coc, a geologic attraction revered for its limestone karst formations surrounded by endless rice paddies. The attraction was a rowboat ride along a river that meanders between karsts and through a number of caves and tunnels.

After a couple nights in this town, we were a bit pressed for time to make it out to Cat Ba Island. We were told that the bus left for Haiphong at 9:00 a.m., so we arrived at 8:00 a.m. to be on the safe side. It turns out that the bus doesn't leave until 1:00 p.m. and we ended up spending the morning at an Internet café catching up on correspondences.

The bus ride to Haiphong was interesting in that the girl next to us was vomiting the entire time. Upon filling the barf bag, she simply threw it out the window as if it is an inconvenience to her; I figured what the heck, it's better than in her pocket. Next, we arrived to who-knows-where in Haiphong and we were forced to take a taxi to our connecting bus station. Exiting the taxi with our backpacks, I noticed a bunch of people heading our way. They seemed to want to help us conduct our business in acquiring the boat tickets, but I had no idea what they are saying. Up at the ticket window, I inquired about a boat ticket to Cat Ba Island and ended up with a bus ticket back to Hanoi. I don't know how this happened, but I think that it had something to do with the guy helping me secure my ticket and him thinking I need to get to Hanoi. Once we sorted this out and I was refunded, I saw our previous taxi driver still waiting outside for another fare. I waved to him for another ride and told Erin we need to go to another station. The guys out front of the station were like a bunch of hawks waiting for prey and they saw that they could assist by carrying her bag, but the guy takes off towards the wrong taxi and we though he was running off with all her stuff. Erin ran after him and swings her daypack into his face, stunning him into releasing her main pack. Who knows what the deal was with all that commotion, but I sure was happy to be into that same old taxicab that had brought us here. Our driver was a real straight shooter and brought us to one of the better places in town.

They arranged our tickets to Cat Ba Island for us and we boarded a hydrofoil boat for the journey. It started out great but soon hit rough seas and we were riding huge waves up and crashing back down with an immense force that is making many around us lose their lunch. Once in the protected waters of Ha Long Bay, we enjoyed the rest of the two-hour trip. The island itself was like something out of Jurassic Park, with rolling mountains covered in dense foliage, and it was actually a protected National Park in Vietnam. I asked the kid working the desk at our Hotel if he knew where to rent a motorbike and we ended up negotiating a deal for his own bike at a better price. Renting your own mobility is by far the best way to do what you want, when you want. Riding to the far end of the island, we stopped at the end of road to admire the karsts that surround us, the stone formations surrounded by the crashing waves of the South China Sea.

We noticed that the women wear coverings over their hands and faces, much like we had seen on many women in Southeast Asia. But here, they were sitting under umbrellas as well. Our question was answered on our bus trip back to Hanoi when I asked a Vietnamese man next to us why the women cover their skin. He explained to me how people believe that lighter skin is more beautiful than darker skin and they are trying to prevent any tanning. I could have assumed as much, but it really made me think about the people back home thinking that darker skin is more beautiful and spending hours out of their week in a tanning bed. I guess that is a part of human nature, where the grass is always greener on the other side, and I contemplate this on the entire bus and airplane ride back to Hanoi, and ultimately Bangkok a few thousand miles away.

After our time doing the tourist thing on Koh Tao, we got back to the mainland and explored the port town. We had six hours to kill, and I brought us down to the river where there was a pathway along the water. Walking and talking here we saw a lot of locals going about their day and a bit surprised to find a couple of farangs, foreigners, walking the path. An old lady came up to us and said something, while later on some young dude was smoking and acting cool in front of Erin to impress her I'm sure. It may not seem like much, but these insignificant events ended up being the memories that stuck.

After this, we stayed in Bangkok for a few nights while I had some tailored clothes made. Tailored suits, shirts, and pants here cost a fraction of what they do in the western world because the price of human labor is so low. Like the gasoline in the taxicab, the price of material will be rather constant while the variables are the people's wages. On our last night in Asia, I had a bowl of Tom Khaa soup and found it to be one of the most magnificent flavors my palate has experienced. Considering I had been in Southeast Asia for the past ninety days, I felt it was pitiful that I was finally enjoying these flavors on my last night here. But, then again, there were plenty of things that I hadn't indulged in while I was over there and I should be happy that I hadn't missed the soup completely.

Being that this adventure was my first experience outside of the United States, I think that I got a pretty good dose of reality when it comes to life on the other side of the planet. But now as I sit here typing away on this keyboard at my parents' house in southern Minnesota, all I can think of is what I would do if I were to go back. This adventure started out with us teaching English to ethnic others and ended with us learning about human diversity firsthand from those same people. I guess teaching and learning diversity are both but different sides of the same coin, bound together by one's life experiences. And one thing my education has taught me is that the more diverse our life experiences, the better off we all are when it comes to communicating with and understanding the ethnic other.

About the Contributors

Wayne E. Allen, Associate Professor, Department of Ethnic Studies, Minnesota State University-Mankato, 2000–present; earned Ph.D. Cultural Anthropology, University of California-Santa Barbara

James Burnett, Visiting Assistant Professor, Department of Sociology, Social Work, and Criminal Justice, Idaho State University; earned MS in Rehabilitation Counseling and Ethnic Studies, Minnesota State University-Mankato; Ph.D. in Sociology, South Dakota State University

Miho Chisaki, graduate student majoring in Ethnic Studies at Minnesota State University-Mankato, 2011–present

Dalton Crayton, Assistant Professor and Predoctoral Fellow, 2011–present, Department of Ethnic Studies; earned Masters in Urban and Regional Studies and Ethnic Studies, Minnesota State University-Mankato,

Kebba Darboe, Associate Professor and Chair, Department of Ethnic Studies, Minnesota State University-Mankato, 2004–present; earned Ph. D. in Sociology, South Dakota State University

Michael T. Fagin, Professor, Department of Ethnic Studies, Minnesota State University-Mankato, 1970–present; earned Ph.D. in Educational Psychology, University of Minnesota

Tonya Fagin (Phillips), First Director of the College Access Program, Minnesota State University-Mankato, 2006–2010; earned MS in Cross-Disciplinary Studies, Corrections, and Ethnic Studies, Minnesota State University-Mankato

Francisco J. Gonzalez, Attorney at Law, MN Dept. of Labor and Industry, Adjunct Faculty, Department of Ethnic Studies, Minnesota State University-Mankato, 2000–present; earned JD, Hamline University School of Law

Nayoung Heo, graduate student majoring in Ethnic Studies at Minnesota State University-Mankato, 2011–present

Abdirahman Ibrahim, undergraduate student majoring in International Relations at Minnesota State University-Mankato, 2010–present

Avra Johnson, Associate Professor, Department of Government, Minnesota State University-Mankato, 2003–present; earned Ph. D. in Public Policy, Indiana University

Sandra King, Assistant Professor, Urban & Regional Studies Institute, Minnesota State University-Mankato, 2004–present; earned Ed.D. in Leadership, Saint Mary's University of Minnesota

Sebastian "Bronco" C. LeBeau II, Archaeologist (Fire Program), Environment, Safety and Cultural Resources, Great Plains Regional Office, Bureau of Indian Affairs MC-208, Aberdeen, SD; earned Ph.D. in Cultural Anthropology, University of Minnesota

Jose Javier Lopez, Professor, Geography, Minnesota State University-Mankato, 1998–present; earned Ph.D. in Geography, Indiana State University

Agnes A. Odinga, Assistant Professor, Department of History, Minnesota State University-Mankato, 2007–present; earned Ph. D. in History, University of Minnesota

Olufunsho Mary Oguntoyinbo, undergraduate student majoring in Political Science at Minnesota State University-Mankato, 2011–present

Martel Pipkins, graduate student, Sociology and Corrections, Minnesota State University-Mankato, 2011–present; graduate of University of Wisconsin-Parkside

Maria Qanyare, undergraduate student majoring in Ethnic Studies at Minnesota State University-Mankato, 2009–present

Raj Sethuraju, Assistant Professor, Department of Sociology and Corrections, Minnesota State University-Mankato, 2011–present; earned Ph.D. in Sociology, Texas Woman's University

Ahmed Shiiraar, undergraduate student and majoring in Environmental Sciences at Minnesota State University-Mankato, 2012–present

Adam Svendsen, undergraduate student majoring in Geography at Minnesota State University-Mankato, 2008–present

Sherrise Truesdale-Moore, Associate Professor, Department of Sociology and Corrections, Minnesota State University Mankato, 2004–present; earned Ph.D. in Sociology, Howard University

D. J. Williams, Assistant Professor, Department of Sociology, Social Work, and Criminal Justice at Idaho State University; earned M.S.W., M.S. in Social Work and Exercise and Sport Science from the University of Utah; Ph.D. in Leisure Sciences, University of Alberta, Canada